As Ever Yours

The love story of
Carrie Huldah Drew
&
William Edwin Rappleye

POST CARD

The Signal Lanterns of Paul Revere, displayed on the steeple of this Church, April 18th 1775, warned the country of the march of the British troops to Lexington and Concord.

Miss Carrie H. Drew
137 pearl street
Burlington
Vermont

JEANIE R. DAVIS

I hope you enjoy this story that is so close to my heart.

Jeanie J Davis

As Ever Yours

By Jeanie R. Davis

Based on the true love story of
Carrie Huldah Drew & William Edwin Rappleye

Cover and interior design, layout and formatting by David Arnett
dba PunkinRoller Publishing Services (www.PunkinRoller.com).

Contributing editors include Anna Arnett, Avonell Rappleye,
Cindy Williams, Joyce Horstmann and Madelyn Williams.

Printed in the United States of America

ISBN Number: 978-0692419984

Library of Congress Control Number: 2015906953

v 15.08.03

Dedicated to William and Carrie
And their posterity

A chance meeting, a forlorn but beautiful damsel in distress together with some knight-in-*honor* instincts combine to give birth to new hope, fruition and joy, mingled with sorrow, as Jeanie Davis spins her fact-based tale of family ancestry.

With the deftness of a schoolgirl skipping rope, Jeanie moves us back and forth from one side of the continent to the other; from settled, urbane New England to the raw, primitive Wyoming frontier.

Jeanie's major story line deals with the life and love of William Rappleye, a Mormon missionary from pioneer Wyoming, and Carrie Drew, whose family owns a boarding house in Burlington, the largest city in Vermont. The gospel of Jesus Christ is the cementing factor, which she describes in action, with precepts coming as they illuminate the stalwart character of her individual ancestors.

Missionaries must obviously limit contact with single girls to mere handshakes, so neither Elder Rappleye nor Miss Drew are able to express the growing feelings they harbor for each other — nor to anyone else.

The overriding theme embraces faith, trust, fidelity, courage, tenacity, and all-encompassing love. The correspondence between them, from the early to last letter, each ending with *As Ever Yours*, inspired the title and encapsulates their eternal pursuit.

— Anna Laurene Arnett
author, editor, friend

To the reader,

The events in this story are true and the names of the people are real. I only added a fictional character here and there to fill gaps in the storyline. Some alterations in the timeline and other embellishments were also needed to enhance the flow — nothing major, mind you. This story is told from several different points of view, as they were all too important to keep quiet and were clamoring to be heard. I hope you enjoy getting to know these remarkable people.

Thank you for reading *As Ever Yours*.

- Jeanie

Table of Contents

Barre, Vermont
June 1885

"And by the power vested in me, I now pronounce you husband and wife." The minister smiled and extended his hand to the beaming couple.

Aaron Drew wasn't certain his feet touched the ground. He had waited what seemed like forever for this day. He would never forget meeting Carrie Foster — the most beautiful woman he had ever laid eyes on — exactly two years prior.

The whistle on the steam engine blew at the Rutland Railroad as the brakes squealed to a halt, but it wasn't the train Aaron was waiting for. This was a passenger train. He was waiting for a freight train, hopefully loaded with goods for the mercantile — *Drew's Mercantile*. The store his father had passed on to him and the store he planned to pass on to his son — if such a blessing were to ever be bestowed upon him.

He watched as waiting loved ones greeted passengers. One woman in particular caught Aaron's eye. She had a small, towheaded boy clutching her hand as she craned her neck this way and that until eventually finding whom she was looking for — a much larger version of the lad — disembarking the train. The woman pushed through the crowd to greet him and melted into the man's embrace, tears glistened in her eyes. The young boy, a grin on his face, had his arms extended, waiting patiently for his turn.

Oh, to have someone there at the end of a long day — or trip, as it were. Aaron watched the couple disappear into the crowd, feeling a bit guilty, as if he'd witnessed a private moment. At that instant, his thirty-seven years felt old. Perhaps he was destined to be a bachelor the rest of his life.

As the platform cleared, one passenger still struggled with her trunk. Aaron looked around, wondering if no one were coming to collect the young lady.

"May I help you with that, Miss?" Aaron pulled the heavy trunk from the platform.

"Thank you. I can manage from here." The dark-haired beauty spoke politely, yet with an air of finality.

Aaron was mesmerized by the clear blue of her eyes as well as the tendrils of hair that were beginning to escape her neatly pinned coif and framed her face.

Aaron scanned the thinning crowd, looking for someone — anyone — who might be there to collect the young lady.

She breathed a heavy sigh as she sat on her trunk. Aaron thought she looked weary. Reaching for her traveling bag, she retrieved a scrap of paper with writing scrawled across it.

At that moment, another whistle blew, catching Aaron's attention. This was his train. He sprang to action, located the car containing his goods and began unloading crate after crate onto the platform, then into his waiting wagon.

Once his wagon was loaded and he was preparing to leave, Aaron glanced over to where he left the young lady from the passenger train. She was still there, head down and shoulders slumped. "Should I approach her again?" he muttered. "Her tone of voice made it clear she didn't want my help, but I can't leave her there alone."

His conscience won out and he approached her. "Miss ...?"

The young lady raised her head and looked at Aaron, her eyebrows furrowed. Aaron guessed she was feeling uncertain. After all, she was no doubt taught to never speak to a perfect stranger, especially a man. "Uh ... Foster, my name is Miss Foster." Her voice trembled.

"Miss Foster, is someone coming for you? I would be happy to take you wherever it is you're going."

Miss Foster reddened as if she realized her circumstances not only appeared, but were, pathetic. With moist eyes, she stared at Aaron. He could nearly hear her silent debate. At last she held up the paper. "This is the address of my aunt and uncle. They were to meet me here, but I suppose they forgot." Tugging at the watch pinned to her blouse, she continued, "I've been here past an hour, maybe they were just delayed." A tear finally lost its fight against gravity and made a path down her rosy cheek.

Aaron took the paper from Miss Foster's delicate hand and read the instructions. Delivering her to her uncle's residence would take him to the opposite side of town, but he couldn't leave this young lady sitting alone at the depot. "I would be happy to take you there; it's no problem at all."

"Oh no ... I shouldn't. I mean you're not a relative and there's no chaperone, and..." her voice trailed off.

"Well, I don't feel I should just leave you here alone, Miss Foster, and I really do need to get my goods to the mercantile. It's up to you, but I'm happy to give you a ride."

Worrying her bottom lip, Miss Foster looked down at the trunk she was sitting on as if she were wondering how hard it would be to pull it down the road. Then, resignation written all over her face, she looked up at Aaron and nodded. "I suppose I'm not left with much of a choice. Everything I own is in this trunk. I could not even lift it, let alone lug it through an unfamiliar town."

Adding her trunk to his already nearly full wagon, Aaron helped Miss Foster up. "It will be a bit of a squeeze, but it's better than sitting in the wagon with the goods."

"I thank you for your kindness, Mr.—," Miss Foster's smile froze. Aaron chuckled, realizing he hadn't properly introduced himself.

"Drew. Aaron Drew," he said as he squeezed in beside her. He took the reins, gave them a yank and they were off.

Aaron felt determined to put this, obviously distressed and deserted, young lady at ease. "So, are you here in Barre for a visit, or have you come to stay?"

"Evidently I'm here to stay." There was a bitter edge to her voice.

"May I ask where you came here from, Miss Foster?"

"I came from Middlesex." Aaron watched her carefully as memories of her home town appeared to bubble to the surface until she could not contain her emotions any longer. The tears flowed freely now.

"I'm so sorry, Miss Foster. It seems I asked the wrong question." Aaron pulled out a handkerchief and gave it to her, wishing he could wipe her tears away himself.

He patiently waited until Miss Foster was able to keep her emotions in check. Then her words came tumbling out.

"My mother died two weeks past. My father ... has always been distant to me and, although I'm twenty years of age — quite old enough to not require a guardian, he decided I should live with his sister and her husband here in Barre."

Aaron was sincerely sorry to hear Miss Foster had lost her mother at such a young age. Several years had passed since his own mother died, but his father had only been gone for a couple of months. Especially close to his father, having worked side by side with him since he was a youngster, Aaron could not imagine a father being so heartless as to send his daughter away, especially in her time of grief. "I am truly sorry, Miss Foster. Do you get on well with your aunt and uncle?"

"I have never met my aunt and uncle." She nearly spat the words out. "I do not think they are any happier about my arrival than I am. You can tell by their warm reception."

"I'm sure there was just a misunderstanding."

Miss Foster merely looked away.

Aaron lightened the conversation by telling her about his mercantile and Barre in general. "I think you shall come to like it here, Miss Foster. I can't imagine living anywhere else."

She managed a weak smile.

It was enough to warm Aaron's heart. "I know we have just met, but if it is okay with your aunt and uncle, may I call on you, Miss Foster?"

Her eyes grew wide, clearly surprised by Aaron's boldness. She seemed to mull it over for a moment before she nodded her head in the affirmative. "And since we have dispensed with proprietary formalities," Miss Foster motioned to the wagon, insinuating the obvious inappropriate situation she was in, "you may as well call me Carrie."

"Carrie." He smiled. "That's a very pretty name. It suits you."

Aaron pulled the wagon to a stop in front of Miss Foster's new residence. The door flew open and a middle-aged woman burst out, pulling at her apron with one hand and smoothing her bush of hair, as if she could somehow tame it, with the other. "Are you Carrie? We weren't expecting you until tomorrow."

Aaron had the trunk out of the wagon and to the front door when he heard the woman tell Carrie how happy she was to have her in their home. His heart warmed, relieved Carrie would be well received after all.

Aaron did call on Carrie quite frequently. He knew she was only twenty years of age, quite a few years his junior, but he was fast falling in love with her. On the other hand, Aaron felt Carrie might be hesitant about their relationship.

After two full years of wooing, Aaron finally convinced Carrie that she might be someone worth loving. Once able to return Aaron's affection, she agreed to become his wife, making it the happiest day of his life.

So in a quaint, little white chapel on a warm summer day in June, Aaron and Carrie took their vows and their family began.

Children couldn't come too soon for Aaron. He hailed from a big family of eleven children — ten of them boys. Both he and Carrie happily anticipated having many children of their own. Unfortunately, as the years rolled by without any little ones on the horizon, they realized that the blessing of having a family could perhaps be withheld from them. Aaron was disappointed, but still very happy to have Carrie by his side. He adored her.

Carrie spent much of her time at the mercantile, working with Aaron. He knew now that she had grown to love and cherish him as much as he did her. He was concerned for her, however, as the prospect of having no children was undoubtedly difficult. After all, a girl was groomed her entire life to be a mother. Without children, Carrie told Aaron, she felt incomplete.

On a cold February morning in 1891, Carrie awoke to horrible nausea and vomiting. "I'm certain it is just something I ate for dinner," she assured a very anxious Aaron.

"I can get Doc Jones, Carrie. Tommy can watch the store."

"No ... no, Aaron, you go off to work now. I'll be fine in no time." She attempted a weak smile.

With a little more persuading on Carrie's part, Aaron reluctantly kissed her on the cheek and headed to work. It was a short walk. His father had built a home just behind the mercantile for his family to reside. After both parents had passed on, Aaron stayed in the family home.

One of his favorite things about owning a mercantile was getting to know many different people. Aaron thrived in this environment and was thrilled to see Carrie take her place at his side and fall in love with the residents of Barre, as well. They loved her back. He saw it in every interaction. And what wasn't to love? He smiled to himself. When any of the store's regular customers became ill, Carrie was the first one there with a pot of soup and a loaf of homemade bread. She would also volunteer to mind children for parents needing to run errands.

"Is Miss Carrie here today, Mr. Drew?" A young girl, who seemed especially fond of Carrie, tugged on Aaron's sleeve.

"I'm sorry, Millie, but Miss Carrie is a bit ill today. I'm sure she will be back before you know it."

Unfortunately, he was wrong. Carrie didn't feel any better the next day, or the next. Aaron and his customers grew concerned for her, so the food and visits began. Mabel Johnson, their nearest neighbor was among the first to visit Carrie.

Mabel was a plump, kindhearted woman with a brood of children. She and her husband, Samuel, lived just a short distance away from the Drew's home.

Mr. Johnson was a banker with very little knack in the way of farming. While most homes in the area boasted a midsize to large farm in back, theirs had only a couple of cows and some chickens. The home was bigger than most, however, because of the number of progeny they were rearing. Three or four of those children could always be found playing in the front yard.

Mabel peered into Carrie's eyes, felt her head and asked a multitude of questions. Aaron quietly opened the bedroom door and announced that he was off to get Doc Jones; Mabel caught him by the arm. "Aaron, I don't believe your wife is in need of a doctor quite yet."

"Mabel, she's been sick for days. She may not want one, but she's getting a doctor," Aaron said, his voice firm.

"Aaron, Carrie isn't sick, Carrie is with child." A smile began on Mabel's dimpled face.

"She's what?"

"You heard me. You are going to be a father."

"How ... how can you be sure, Mabel?"

"After eight children, do you not think I know the symptoms of morning sickness?" Mabel chuckled.

Aaron wrapped his strong arms around Mabel and kissed her on the cheek, then turned his attention to his wife. After overhearing the news, tears glistened in Carrie's eyes. She was finally going to be a mother.

Mabel peered into Carrie's eyes, felt her head and asked a multitude

The sickness went on for another two months, then eased off. Carrie made it clear that she didn't mind the nausea if it meant there was a baby on the way ... her baby. Finally their little family would feel complete.

"If it is a boy, we shall name him after you, Aaron."

"And if it's a girl?" Aaron's eyebrows arched as his eyes twinkled.

"Then you can name her." She smiled up at her husband. "A boy will carry on the family name and be an heir to the mercantile, but I have always wanted a daughter of my own."

"I shall have to think about it then. Picking a name is a serious job." He winked at Carrie and pulled her into a quick hug.

"Did you feel that?" Carrie's voice rose. "The baby kicked!" She pulled Aaron's hand around and placed it on her stomach. "There it is again."

Aaron's smile grew wide as he felt his baby son or daughter come to life. After a few kicks, Aaron gazed up from her stomach to look at his sweet wife and said, "I hope that if it is a girl, she will look just like you." He tilted her head up and gave her a kiss.

Carrie continued to work with Aaron at the mercantile; however, Aaron was very careful about letting her overdo and was ever solicitous to her needs.

"You're spoiling me, Aaron. Many women have had babies before me without a hovering husband and they did just fine."

"And many women aren't you, my Carrie." He truly enjoyed treating her as royalty. After all, he felt like a king with her on his arm. "Enjoy it while it lasts, my dear. Before you know it, you will be washing out diapers and wiping noses. For now, let *me* dote on *you*."

Carrie just smiled up at him, love reflecting in her eyes. "Very well, then."

Mesa City, Arizona
May 1891

David Franklin Marcellus Rappleye, better known as Frank, held his young son tenderly on his knee. Four-year-old William loved to hear his father tell stories about his grandfather, Tunis Rappleye.

"My father, Grandpa Tunis, was converted and baptized a member of the Church of Jesus Christ of Latter-day Saints in 1832, just two years after the Prophet Joseph Smith restored the gospel to the earth. Tunis was a devout believer and a hard worker."

William had heard the story so many times, Frank was certain he knew it by heart, but William never seemed to tire of it.

"After the martyrdom of Joseph Smith, Brigham Young was called and appointed to be the new Prophet of the Church, which came to be known as ...?"

"The Mormon Church!" William smiled proudly.

"That's right, Son. Tunis was a great help to Brigham Young as the saints were persecuted, driven from their homes and eventually forced to find and settle a land where they would no longer be subject to the ignorance and cruelty of others. Tunis traveled with Brigham Young, and a few chosen men, in a vanguard company to locate this place of refuge."

Frank could go on and on, but he skipped parts, sensing young William's anxiousness for his favorite story.

"*Gampa* spent seven years going back and forth from Salt Lake to *Nebaska*?" William said in his four-year-old voice. "Why, Papa?"

17

"Because, Willy, he knew the Saints needed his help crossing the plains, and because the Prophet asked him to."

"And when the *Pophet* asks you to do someping, it's like God asking you, right Papa?"

"That's right, William, and one day, Son, if you are faithful, you will be called on by the Prophet to serve, too."

"Will I have to ride a horse for seven years?"

"No, Son, you will be called to go out into the world to serve a mission and spread the gospel to those whose hearts have been prepared by the Lord to listen to His word. We all get called upon to serve in different ways."

Frank couldn't help but smile as William put his chubby, little hands on his father's whiskery cheeks and peered into his eyes.

"Where will I go, Papa?"

"Wherever the Lord sees fit to send you, William. And you will make a fine missionary."

"Can you come with me, Papa?" William's face creased and his lower lip jutted out in a pout.

Frank chuckled to see the concerned look on his small son's face. "No, Willy, my boy, you will be old enough to go without me. But you will never be alone."

"Who will be with me?"

"Why, of course, the Lord will be with you always."

William sat up straight, squared his shoulders and smiled. "Because, with the Lord I can move mountains, like you always say. Right, Pa?"

"That's right, Son." Frank gave William a kiss on the top of his head and set him off his lap. "But just now, you and I should peek at what your mama is cooking up in the kitchen." He winked and held out his hand.

William took hold of his father's large hand and skipped alongside him to where the warm aroma of a sumptuous supper was cooking.

Baby Roy, now eight months old, had become proficient at crawling and followed his mother's skirt as she scurried about the kitchen.

"Frank," Laura said, looking relieved to see her husband, "can you please pick Roy up before I accidentally squash him flat as a pancake?"

The thought of his baby brother looking like a pancake must have been entertaining. William began to giggle.

"And you, young man," as Laura's forefinger nearly touched William's nose, "will you please fetch your sisters to help get supper on the table?"

"Yes, Mama." William scampered off to find Nellie and Clara.

"That one is a fine boy." Frank stepped behind his wife, wrapped his arms around her and gave her a squeeze. "There is already a fire burning within him. He will make a fine man one day — a man who is willing to serve the Lord without question."

Laura smiled. "Just like his father." She planted a kiss on Frank's cheek.

Barre, Vermont
1891

Spring and summer came and went. The months passed slowly for Aaron and Carrie as their anticipation increased. Doctor Jones made regular visits to check on Carrie. Everything looked good. His best estimation had the baby making his or her arrival sometime in November.

"Autumn has arrived early this year," said Aaron. "It's just September and look at the color of those leaves." He pointed up to the huge maple trees lining the street. Aaron and Carried admired the vivid colors as they walked the few yards to the mercantile. "This surely means we will have an early winter." Aaron kicked at a few fallen leaves in his path.

He looked at his wife, who had slowed down and was crouching over. "What is it, Carrie? Are you well?"

"I don't know, Aaron; I have never had this kind of pain before."

Aaron promptly turned his wife around and pointed her toward the house. "Let's get you home and I will send Tommy to get Doc Jones."

Tommy was Mabel and Samuel Johnson's eldest son. He had worked for Aaron since he was twelve years old. Now, at eighteen, it felt like he was part of the Drew family.

After a careful examination, Doc looked grim. "It seems your baby would like to enter the world a bit earlier than scheduled, Mrs. Drew."

Aaron's face screwed up in panic. "Will it live, Doc? It is two months too soon. Babies can't live arriving so early."

"I'm afraid you are right, Mr. Drew, but Carrie's water sac has burst leaving the baby no choice but to make his or her way out into the world."

Aaron knelt beside his wife. Tears were sliding down her cheeks.

The doctor went on, "I will do what I can, but the rest is up to God."

Three hours passed and Carrie was in full labor now.

"Mr. Drew, could you get Mabel Johnson to come assist me? I have delivered many babies alone, but it is easier with a second pair of hands."

"I can help you, Doc," said Aaron, hesitant to leave his wife's side.

"Mr. Drew ... Aaron, you are already as pale as a ghost and the worst is yet to come. Ordinarily, men stay outside while their wives give birth. Please fetch Mabel. She has given birth eight times and will know how best to assist me. I won't forbid you to come back in to be with Carrie, but I highly recommend that you don't."

Aaron was feeling put out with Doctor Jones, but had to admit that a bit of fresh air cleared his head.

He jumped on the nearest horse and rode like the wind to the Johnson's home. "Ho there, Adam," hollered Aaron to a young boy sitting on a wooden swing, which hung from a limb of a large maple tree.

Adam startled and looked up to see Aaron. "Hello, Mr. Drew, how do—"

Aaron cut him off short, "Adam, I need your mother, can you please get her quickly?" Adam scurried off.

"What is it, Aaron?" Mabel rushed out the door.

"There's no time, Mabel, can you come with me? Carrie is in labor. Doc needs your help." He pulled Mabel up onto his horse.

Once they reached the house, they heard Carrie's moans. Aaron was off the horse and through the door in seconds. Mabel was right behind him. The scene before them was ghastly. There was blood everywhere, but no baby yet. "Doc?" he asked in a small voice.

Doc's face was ashen. "It's not good, Aaron. You should wait outside."

"I can't do that, Doc." He rushed to take Carrie's hand. "What's happening?"

Her eyes were closed and her hands were clammy. With every contraction, Carrie let out a low moan and more blood poured out.

"She is hemorrhaging." Doc's face was pinched with worry.

Carrie moaned again. Each moan became a bit weaker until they stopped. Aaron had been massaging her hand and speaking softly to her when he realized her hand was limp.

With a last gush of blood a tiny baby appeared. Doc cut the cord and handed the fetus to Mabel without even taking the time to check the gender. He immediately turned his attention back to Carrie. Feeling for a pulse, he looked at Aaron and realized what Aaron already knew. Carrie was gone.

Aaron laid his head atop his wife's chest and cried deep, wracking sobs. It felt as if time stood still in some nightmare for Aaron, as he tried in vain to hear his wife's heart beat again. Then ... there was the tiniest of cries somewhere in the room.

"Aaron, you have a daughter," Mabel whispered.

With all the commotion, Aaron nearly forgot Mabel was there. He looked up to see her tear-stained face, clutching a tiny bundle.

Taking the infant in his large hands, the doctor just shook his head. "This baby weighs no more than two pounds, Aaron. She will never survive. I will just put a towel over her nose, then you can bury her with her mother."

Aaron didn't even try to contain his anger at that point. "You'll do no such thing! As long as my daughter is breathing, I will do all within my power to keep her alive."

"And I will help you, Aaron," Mabel chimed in.

The doctor shrugged his shoulders and said, "I can guarantee she will die before the month ends."

There was no backing down. Aaron watched over his new baby girl protectively while the doctor and Mabel cleaned up. She was bundled up in a dishcloth and fit within the palms of his hands.

Once the doctor was gone, Mabel set to work in the kitchen. "Bring her in here, Aaron. We must keep her warm, as if she's still in her mother's womb. If we keep a low fire to warm the range just enough, but not too hot, it will give us our best shot at keeping her alive."

Aaron was astonished at the notion of putting his frail baby girl in the range, but trusted Mabel's wisdom.

For the next few weeks he did everything Mabel instructed, and with additional help from a wet nurse, supplemented with goat's milk, somehow the baby kept breathing.

"What are you going to name her, Aaron?" Mabel asked after the first two weeks of struggling to help him keep his child alive.

He had only recently given it much thought, not daring to hope the baby would live. But live she had. "I believe I will call her Carrie Huldah — Carrie, after her mother who gave her very life for her, and Huldah, after Carrie's mother, whom she loved so dearly." He said it almost as a whisper, as tears welled up in his eyes at the memory of his sweet wife.

"I think it's beautiful," was Mabel's equally reverent reply.

Aaron and Carrie's baby not only grew, but she flourished and Aaron adored her. He would, perhaps, never get over losing the love of his life, but having this small part of her with him eased the heartache.

Once baby Carrie was declared a healthy, bouncing baby by all who saw her, many relatives and friends offered to relieve Aaron of the burden of raising her as a single father.

Aaron's sister, Sarah, residing with her husband nearby, was among the first to offer and then several friends who frequented the mercantile. Aaron's reply was always the same, "Why would I not want to raise my own daughter?" He would graciously thank them for their kind gesture, but politely refuse.

Mabel Johnson was an indispensable help to Aaron, as well as a friend. She often took care of Carrie while Aaron worked at the mercantile. She always treated her as one of her own. But, many a day Aaron would take Carrie with him to work. It was not uncommon to enter the mercantile to find little blue-eyed Carrie, her head of unruly, brown ringlets dancing about her shoulders, perched upon one of the grain barrels greeting customers. She became a neighborhood favorite.

Cowley, Wyoming
1900 — 1903

William Rappleye, now a young man, didn't complain when his parents, Frank and Laura Rappleye, made the decision to relocate to Cowley, Wyoming. The Arizona heat was stifling. The reason for the relocation, according to his father, was for him and his sons to work on a canal project taking place in that part of the country. There was also plenty of untamed land for the Rappleye men to farm, once the canal project was completed.

The drastic change in altitude and temperature did nothing to dampen the Rappleye's enthusiasm for the gospel — especially William's. He had grown into a hardworking man. He was not only a great help with the work at home, he was also obedient to God's commandments and willing to serve in whatever capacity to which he was called. William, always looking for ways to build his missionary fund, took many odd jobs as well as worked on the railroad, which was finally discovering the West. He was determined to be one of the valiant men called upon to spread the good news of the restored gospel.

Snow fell hard and deep in Wyoming. One needed to be prepared to hole up and stay indoors for a few days, if need be. When the roads were clear enough to get horses and a wagon to town, the Rappleyes would make the trek to stock up on food and other necessities.

It was one such December day when sixteen-year-old William and his father, Frank, prepared their wagon to do just that. It wasn't snowing — it was too cold to snow. Yet, there was nothing but white as far as William could see. He pulled his scarf a little tighter around his neck, grateful for a mother who worked wonders with a ball of yarn and a knitting needle.

As they passed Widow Callahan's humble home, William yanked on his father's arm. "Pa, do we have time to help Widow Callahan? It looks like she's about to run out of firewood, and with all those children—"

Before he finished his sentence, Frank turned the wagon around and headed for home. Father and son spent the rest of the afternoon chopping wood and loading it onto the wagon for the Widow Callahan. "I'm glad you noticed Widow Callahan's woodpile, William. Or should I say lack thereof." Frank smiled at William. "Mrs. Callahan has had a difficult time caring for those five, small children since her husband died in September. I only wish we'd realized her need for wood sooner."

They once again set out on the snowy path — this time with the wagon loaded with firewood.

"Mrs. Callahan is a gallant woman and is doing the best she knows how, but this harsh Wyoming winter climate is difficult, to say the least."

"Yes, Pa, I don't know how she manages without a man about the house."

Once Frank and William reached the Callahan residence, they immediately began unloading and stacking wood in the widow's puny pile.

Mrs. Callahan must have heard the men. She looked out the window and caught William's eye. Tears began to stream down her cheeks. She called out to them to come into the house when they finished.

Upon entering the home, William found several little faces huddled together in an attempt to keep warm. Mrs. Callahan gave the men an icy handshake and thanked them profusely ... the tears still moist on her face. "I would offer you a warm drink, but ..."

William knew exactly why she couldn't offer them a warm drink. The house was freezing and some of the children had no shoes. It was obvious there was not money for such things. They hadn't stopped to help a minute too soon.

"We don't really have time for that," Frank jumped in. "We must be off to pick up some supplies for the farm."

"We have been down to our last few logs for a while now," Mrs. Callahan choked out between sobs. "I was saving them for Christmas, but now we will be able to light a fire tonight. God bless you both."

William felt a lump forming in his throat. The Rappleyes weren't rich by any stretch of the imagination, but they always had wood for a fire and clothes on their backs. William tried to remember if his family ever had to miss a meal because of lack of funds. No, he couldn't think of a single time. He felt truly humbled.

After they took their leave, William asked his father, "Pa, isn't there more we can do for the Callahans? They need so much."

"There's always more we can do, and now that we know of their condition, we will do it."

When the men made it back to their own warm home, the hearty aroma of stew and homemade bread baking for supper wafted through the air. William felt a mixture of happiness and guilt. "Ma, do you think there's enough stew for us to take a pot over to the Widow Callahan's place?"

"Well, you know I always make enough stew to feed a small village, so I'm certain we can part with a pot-full."

Giving him a pat on the back, Frank blinked away rising emotion. His nod to William said so much without a word being uttered.

With the help of his mother, William set to work looking through his brothers' and sisters' old clothing and shoes to see if there were any they could spare. When he was finished, William and Frank were able to fill three wooden crates with food and clothing for the Callahans.

It was late now, but the Rappleyes once again loaded the wagon with the goods and drove their team back down the snowy mile to the Callahan's place.

"Can we just leave everything on the front porch, Pa? I don't want Widow Callahan to be embarrassed. Besides, I also don't want her to know it was us." William's voice was muffled, his face wrapped tightly in his scarf.

His father just nodded.

William took it upon himself to keep an eye on the Callahan's stack of firewood for the rest of the winter and he delivered several food items as well. It felt good to serve.

Barre, Vermont
1894

The bees were up early, making their rounds collecting pollen from new blooms this warm, spring morning. Three-year-old Carrie pulled her dress on backwards and put her shoes on the wrong feet. Rushing into the kitchen where her father was eating his breakfast, she tugged on his sleeve. "Papa, I'm ready. Can I go with you to the store today?"

Aaron chuckled and lifted his sweet daughter onto his lap. For some reason Aaron had an uneasy feeling about taking his Carrie to the store on this particular day. He had learned to listen to his heart.

"Didn't Aunt Mabel promise to bake cookies with you today?"

"Yes, but I wanna go with you, Papa."

"We don't want to disappoint Mabel, do we now?"

Carrie looked thoughtful for a moment. "I guess not, Papa." Her bottom lip jutted out with a look of dejection on her cherubic face.

Aaron had a hard time telling Carrie no. She was the light of his life and he adored her, but for some reason, he felt Carrie needed to stay at the Johnson's today.

He helped her turn her dress around and put her shoes on the correct feet and then he brushed her hair. "Mabel will have to braid your hair, sweet girl. One day maybe I will learn, but right now it's time for us to go." He lifted his daughter into his strong arms, put his hat on and headed out the door.

Once Carrie was safely deposited at the Johnson's home, Aaron walked directly to his mercantile, the feeling of unease still niggling in the back of his mind.

Nothing was out of place, but there was an instinct of foreboding that overcame Aaron. A couple of men he had never met before came into the mercantile. After scanning the store, they made a very small purchase and took their leave. "That's odd," Aaron mumbled, "I'm pretty sure I know every resident in Barre."

Tommy Johnson's brows furrowed. "Mr. Drew, who were those two men that just left our place?"

"I've never seen them before, Tommy, but by the way they were looking over the merchandise, I doubt they were up to any good."

"I'll just follow them for a bit and see where they're off to, okay?"

Aaron nodded, and Tommy was off.

He returned twenty minutes later, panting. "I followed them to the diner a couple of blocks down, but it looked like they were just there to eat, so I left. I hope they are just passing through."

After flipping over the closed sign on the door, Aaron told Tommy to go home with the message that he would come for Carrie later, as he needed to tend to the bookkeeping.

Tommy stood, silently fidgeting with his pockets, obviously worried there was more to Aaron's hesitation to leave. Reluctantly, he left Mr. Drew to the books.

Evening turned into night; Aaron still felt like something was amiss. He decided to walk home to find a bite to eat, then return, should he still have this feeling of doom. Once home, the only thing Aaron could think about was the mercantile. He retrieved some leftover meat from the previous evening's meal from the icebox, devoured it in a few bites and called it good.

As Aaron approached the shop, a sinking feeling overcame him. There was a wagon pulled to the side of the store filled with goods. His goods. How could this happen? I was gone less than an hour's time. And why didn't I bring my pistol? Because there is never a need for a pistol in Barre, Vermont, that's why.

Through the broken door, he could see someone inside — at least one person, probably two. His first instinct was to charge into the store and demand the intruders leave at once, but on further contemplation, he decided it might be a wiser course to walk back home and retrieve his pistol. The latter would cost him precious time and the thieves could easily escape before he returned.

In that moment of indecision, one of the men caught sight of Aaron and called out to the other. They both instantly tried to flee, but Aaron planted his body in front of the store's entrance in an attempt to stop the intruders. Unfortunately, he was outnumbered and was fast becoming the victim of not only a robbery, but also a severe beating. The first man to the door punched Aaron in the stomach, doubling him over in pain. The second man took advantage of his weakened condition and pushed him to the ground where the two of them violently kicked Aaron in the head, chest and back. Aaron wanted to fight back. In his mind he did fight back. But in reality, his broken bones and leaden arms were motionless. At last he plunged into a dark abyss.

Tommy returned to the mercantile to see why Aaron hadn't picked up little Carrie. As he approached the front door, he froze. A stream of blood made a path between his boots. His legs felt like lead as he pushed through the door to find Aaron lying on the ground unconscious. Terrified, Tommy managed to shake himself out of the shock at seeing Aaron's bleeding, lifeless body and began yelling for help. He managed to find both a doctor and the constable.

When the doctor arrived, he worked quickly to stop Aaron from bleeding to death. A massive amount of red liquid stained the wooden floor in the store's entryway, mostly coming from blows to Aaron's head; his scalp nearly torn off from the force of the thieves' boots. With yards of gauzy material, the doctor tightly wrapped Aaron from his chin to the top of his head to hold everything together.

Once his head was attended to, the doctor, with the help of an ashen-faced Tommy, carefully carried Aaron to his home and tended to his broken bones.

Tommy sat with the constable at Aaron's kitchen table, clearly shaken up. "I should have never left him." He buried his head in his hands. His voice struggled past a lump in his throat. "Mr. Drew could tell something was up when the two out-of-towners came into the store. I should have never left him alone."

The constable, after reassuring Tommy that he wasn't to blame for the break-in, took down a description of the two men. It was a little too late for the thieves to be collared, however, as they had surely fled the city some time ago. But the neighboring towns would be alerted.

Tommy's eyes followed the constable's as he observed the doctor walking toward them. "Will he be all right, Doc?" He sobbed aloud, no longer trying to contain his emotions.

The doctor's countenance was not much better. "The question you *should* be asking, Tommy, is 'will he live?'"

Tommy blanched at the harsh honesty of the doctor's statement.

"I suspect that if Mr. Drew makes it through the night, chances are he will live. However, I cannot guarantee that there won't be permanent damage. He sustained some serious injuries, especially to his head. But Tommy, your quick thinking when you found Mr. Drew just might have saved his life." The doctor nodded his appreciation to the boy, who still sat dumbfounded. "Don't worry, my boy, I will stay with him through the night."

Aaron lived, but once conscious and mobile again, felt violated. Not only had the thieves emptied his shelves of their goods, they had done a fair amount of damage in the process — both to him and his store. Running the mercantile had never been abundantly profitable in the small town of Barre, but now... "Now I shall *never* recover the loss!" His eyes took in the broken glass and refuse littering the ground.

Aaron's injuries were severe enough, especially his lacerated head, that it became evident he would not be able to run the store for a very long time — if ever. Aaron attempted to coach Tommy to fill orders, but lacking the experience and know-how necessary to keep it afloat, Aaron realized his mercantile would not survive. Eventually, the

Drews' Mercantile lost customers to neighboring shops and was forced to close its doors for good.

Tears welled up in Aaron's eyes as recollections of working — first, side by side with his father, then with his late wife at the mercantile — flooded his memory. It was almost too much for Aaron to bear. He needed a change of scenery.

Without anything but ghosts keeping Aaron in Barre anymore, he researched the possibilities and decided to relocate himself and his little daughter to the Burlington area. He found a wonderful, large plot of land with plenty of green grass, a creek with wild berries growing along the side of it, and best of all, there was a farmhouse in the middle of the land — the perfect place to raise his daughter and do some farming. It was difficult to move away from so many people he loved, but it also felt like an escape from memories that haunted him. It was a fresh start.

It was here Aaron attended church and met Emily Alapa. Aaron felt as though he could never love anyone the way he loved Carrie Foster, but it wasn't fair to his daughter to grow up without a mother, especially in a place so strange to her. He observed the way Emily treated Carrie — the same way she would treat a child of her own — with love and tenderness. That won Aaron's heart. Before long, he proposed to her and subsequently they married.

Aaron and his new wife, Emily, reared Carrie as an only child. Aaron realized that this was, at times, difficult for Carrie, being quite an outgoing girl. She often expressed her desire to have siblings to play with. Unfortunately, another baby was a wish Aaron could not fulfill.

A few years after the Drews' marriage, Emily received the sad news of her sister's death, leaving a four-year-old daughter, Clara, motherless.

"Clara's father is doing his best to rear her, Aaron," Emily explained, "but it's hard for him, especially when Clara loves spending her days here with Carrie. I hope you don't mind the amount of time she spends with us."

Aaron didn't mind at all. Having little Clara around satisfied two needs: Carrie's wish for a sibling and his wife's longing for another child.

Young Clara, Aaron noticed, became very comfortable at the Drews' home and, over time, made it clear that she preferred to reside there over her own, lonely house. Her visits became longer and longer until, rather than argue with the child, Clara's father consented to allow her to stay with the Drews indefinitely. Aaron didn't argue. He happily welcomed Clara to their little family.

Now Aaron and Emily were raising two girls and Carrie had a little sister, which suited everyone just fine. The two girls would explore the meadows around the farmhouse, wade in the creek and eat wild berries. Carrie was a few years older, but they became inseparable.

Tired from a long day of work, Aaron reached to open the screen door of the farmhouse. He stopped when he heard voices, then crying coming from just inside. Pausing to hear the conversation, Aaron hesitated to enter. He could see into the kitchen as the drama unfolded.

"Mama, Mama, look at this package the postman gave me." Nine-year-old Carrie stared in confusion at the writing on the brown paper.

"Who is it for?" Emily asked, reaching for the package.

Carrie's hands began trembling and her face drained its color.

Still clutching the package, Carrie read the label. "It says this, *'To my dead sister's little girl'*. What does that mean, Mama? You are very much alive."

Emily gasped and sudden tears sprang to her eyes. "Carrie, there is something you need to know, but I would like your father to tell you."

Being a tender three years of age when Aaron and Emily wed, Aaron observed how well Emily took to being Carrie's mother. Carrie never questioned who gave her birth. On several occasions Emily pleaded with Aaron to never tell Carrie about his first wife, her birth mother. This gnawed at Aaron for many reasons, the first being the love he had for Carrie Foster. Surely her memory should be honored, not forgotten. He also thought Carrie deserved to know the truth. But, respecting Emily's wishes, he remained quiet about the matter.

When he worked up the nerve to enter the house, he found his wife crying and his daughter looking dazed and puzzled. Emily pulled Aaron aside and explained what happened. "Aaron, I never wished her to know." She sniffled as tears made their way down her cheeks.

"I know, Emily," Aaron pulled his handkerchief out and began mopping her face. "But you knew this might happen at some point. Too many people are familiar with Carrie's mother, and it looks as though Carrie's Uncle Arthur wishes to know his niece. Let me speak with her." He gave Emily a gentle, reassuring squeeze.

When it was time for bed, Aaron went into Carrie's room to tuck her in and sing her a song — a ritual he'd done since her birth. "Carrie, I know you are confused about the package your Uncle Arthur sent to you. Please let me explain." It was difficult for Aaron to talk about Carrie's mother without becoming emotional, as images of her life were still hard to separate from images of her death. He missed her dearly. He tried to spare his young daughter the details that still haunted him about her passing and, instead, focused on the miracle of Carrie's birth and the fact that she defied the odds by living.

"And do you know, when you were but six years of age, old Doc Jones was here in Burlington and spotted the two of us on the street and asked, 'This isn't the baby, is it?' and I looked him square in the eye and said, 'Yes, it is. She looks pretty good for a month old, don't you think?' I'm pretty sure old Doc Jones was quite ashamed after that — as he should have been. You're a miracle, Carrie." Aaron tenderly kissed his daughter's cheek.

"Papa, will you tell me what my mama was like?"

"Of course I will, my love. She was beautiful, just like you are. She had rich brown hair, beautiful fair skin and sparkling blue eyes that twinkled when she smiled. She was loving, kind and gentle and always smelled of lilacs. And, Carrie, when I look into your eyes, I see her." That part made Aaron tear up a bit, but it also brought a huge smile to his sweet daughter's face.

Carrie was her mother's daughter in every way, from her brown hair and sparkling blue eyes, to her kind and gracious disposition. She made friends everywhere she went.

The next morning, Aaron and Emily sat at the breakfast table speaking in low tones. A tear slipped down Emily's cheek. When Carrie entered the room, Aaron kept kind eyes on her, and then motioned his head toward Emily, who stared intently at her eggs.

"Mama," Carrie said just above a whisper. Emily raised watery eyes to meet Carrie's. "Mama... it's just ... how can I miss someone I've never known? I love you as if you gave me birth." She rounded the table to give her mother a hug.

Aaron looked on with pride. Happy the truth was revealed, and happy his daughter was strong enough to bear it.

Aaron always made sure Carrie attended school — a Catholic school at first, until his brother, Rueben, persuaded Aaron to enroll her in a school with less indoctrination.

Aaron was one of ten brothers, but of her uncles, Carrie declared Rueben her favorite.

One day when Carrie came home from school, Uncle Rueben was there for a visit. Aaron noticed how excited Carrie became when his brother was present.

"Papa" young Carrie whispered in Aaron's ear, "can I show Uncle Reuben what I've learned in school?"

"Sure you can." Aaron smiled down at Carrie.

Pulling out her Rosary beads, Carrie proudly recited each component of prayer.

Reuben's mouth turned down into a straight line. He was clearly unimpressed and, in fact, looked perturbed.

"Aaron, *you* are *not* Catholic! So why is it that your daughter is?"

Aaron had, of course, noticed his daughter's new fascination with Catholicism, but up to this point hadn't worried about it. He didn't think she was converted. Maybe she was. Aaron began to twist his wide mustache.

Watching Carrie's face form a frown, he knew she was crestfallen at Reuben's declaration. She'd been so excited to awe Uncle Rueben with her newly learned knowledge, but instead had disappointed him.

The very next day, Aaron pulled Carrie out of the Catholic school and enrolled her in a different, more secular, school.

No matter where it occurred, Aaron insisted that she receive an education. Besides being important for her future, Aaron knew Carrie hungered for knowledge and was a quick study. In addition to her regular schoolwork, she learned to speak French, play the piano and sing. Carrie stayed happily busy.

Cowley, Wyoming
Spring 1911

"It's here, Pa, it's here," an excited William hollered across the large expanse of Wyoming farmland.

His father, Frank, looked up to see what the commotion was and spotted William waving a large envelope in the air. Recognition seemed to dawn on him as he dropped his shovel and hurried across the field.

His wife, Laura, came out the back door at the same time. "What is it, Son?" she panted, wiping bits of the dough she had been kneading onto her apron. Then she spied the envelope and smiled at what she surely knew it contained.

All of the available Rappleyes gathered together in the front room to hear the exciting news. "Well, Son, are you going to read it out loud, or just keep us in suspense?" his father blurted out, impatient for the news.

"It says, 'Brother William E. Rappleye, you are hereby called to serve the Lord by laboring in the Eastern States Mission of the United States of America. You will report to the LDS Mission headquarters in Salt Lake City, Utah on June 1st, 1911'. And it is signed by the Prophet, Joseph F. Smith." William looked up to see his family's smiling faces. His mother had tears streaming down her cheeks.

"That's very soon. There is much to be done before you go so far away." His mother's forehead creased in worry and concentration, as if she were counting the days until his departure.

"Ma, it's not so far away. Many men are being sent overseas. This is just across the country."

"That's true, Son," his father spoke up. He looked more concerned than the rest of them.

"What is it, Frank?" Laura turned her attention to her husband.

"Well, to be honest, I would almost rather have William sent to another country. As it stands, he is being sent to some of the very areas the Prophet Joseph Smith was driven out of. There has still got to be a lot of misunderstanding and hostility toward the Saints in those parts."

William listened to his parents' doubts and concerns and then held up a hand to quiet them. "Well, if that's where the Lord wants me to go, then that is where I shall go. Don't worry, Pa, I'm twenty-four years of age — hardly a kid any more. I can handle a bit of ignorance and animosity."

"We shall pray for you every day, my dear boy," his mother sniffed, still weeping into her handkerchief.

William wrapped his arms around her and kissed her cheek. "Then I am certain I will be protected."

William had grown into a strong, hardworking man. His family let him know he would be sorely missed, but after saving his money for the better part of his life, nothing could keep him from serving a mission.

June 18, 1911 was a day to remember for William Rappleye — now Elder Rappleye. It was on this day, after traveling by train for seventeen days from Cowley, Wyoming (with a few days stop in Salt Lake City, Utah to be set apart as a missionary, and also at the mission headquarters in New York City) that William arrived in Burlington, Vermont to begin his missionary service.

All of William's twenty-four years, thus far, had been spent in the far western regions of the United States, first Mesa City, Arizona and most recently, Cowley, Wyoming. It was quite a change to be deposited almost as far northeast as one could go and still be in the country, as well as lonely to be so far away from family and friends.

William made his way from the Burlington train station to the Vermont Conference headquarters by following directions given to him before he left. There he was greeted by Brother Austin, president of the Vermont Conference, and another man.

"Welcome to Burlington, Elder Rappleye." President Austin extended his hand to William.

Elder Rappleye shook it vigorously.

"This is your companion, David Hanks." President Austin motioned to the other missionary. They also shook hands. "You two will be leaving for the country tomorrow morning, so clean up, rest a bit and get your grips ready."

William wasn't quite sure what that meant, so he turned to Elder Hanks with a questioning look.

"It is the custom for missionaries in this area, during the summer months, to embark on 'country trips' or 'country work', as we commonly refer to it. We leave mission headquarters and walk, and walk, and walk some more, knocking on doors as we go. We pass out tracts to anyone we meet who will take them, sell "little books" with information about the church for a dime and also copies of the Book of Mormon. I hope you brought sturdy shoes, Elder," David Hanks said with a grin.

The President jumped in, "You may leave your trunk here. Only take your necessities, as you will want to travel light and will be carrying literature."

"Do we return to headquarters each evening for our meals and bed?" William's brows were drawn together ... perplexed.

President Austin and Elder Hanks looked at each other, as if waiting to see who would break the news. Elder Hanks shifted his weight from one leg to the other before looking back at William. "Uh ... no, Elder Rappleye, we don't return until the weather turns cold. We will ask the people we visit for our meals and a bed. It isn't uncommon for missionaries to sleep on a haystack, or even under the stars. Oh, and bring a parasol, as it rains a lot in this part of the country."

If either President Austin or Elder Hanks thought this bit of information would dishearten Elder Rappleye, they were wrong. William squared his shoulders and said, "I guess, then, I had better begin preparations for our journey."

The elders arose early the next morning, bags loaded with just a few necessities and loads of information about the Restored Gospel to be shared with the good folks of Vermont.

Elder Hanks looked out the window. "It appears our first day will be spent under cloudy skies. Hopefully, the heavens will refrain from dumping too much moisture on us."

President Austin accompanied the men to the edge of town, where he took their pictures, then sent them on their way.

"Did he take our pictures in the event we don't return and they have to send a search party after us?" William asked, only partly in jest.

Elder Hanks just chuckled in response.

After a few hours of walking and knocking on doors, mostly to be turned away, the elders were lucky enough to find a kind lady willing to chat. Her name was Mrs. Rollins. She not only listened to what the elders had to say, she also fed them dinner — noonday meal. They left some information, thanked Mrs. Rollins, and went on their way rejoicing.

The two continued tracting until six o'clock, when once again it was time to begin their search for supper and a bed for the night.

After enquiring at eleven houses, only to find them full, or housing sick residents, Elder Hanks said, "Let's go into the woods and say a prayer. The Lord will guide us to the right place."

By now the thunderstorms had begun in earnest and the clouds were dumping their contents with a fury. A parasol could only do so much to keep the men dry.

A very wet Elder Rappleye agreed, so they retreated to a nearby woods and knelt in prayer.

Buoyed up by the spirit, they began again in their quest to find a bed. They had given up on supper, it being nine-thirty by now. After the fourteenth "No," Elder Rappleye was sure that his first night in the country would be spent under a tree in the rain, but a very faithful Elder Hanks said, "I feel like we need to try just one more house." Fifteen was the charm. They were finally taken in and each given a warm bed out of the rain.

And so it went day after day for Elder William Rappleye and Elder David Hanks. After walking and proselytizing ten to fifteen miles in one direction, they would turn and go a new direction. William soon found that it took great faith and a sturdy pair of shoes to serve the Lord as a missionary.

Several days later, Elder Rappleye and Elder Hanks headed to a town called Jerico. Upon entering the village, they met a gentleman who began hollering at William, calling him names and hurling accusations at him. William just stood motionless in disbelief wondering what was happening.

The man finally concluded his tirade by saying, "You ought to be in jail and all the rest of the Mormons with you."

After tolerating the Scotch blessing he had just received, William could stand it no longer and proceeded to tell the foul-mouthed man all he knew about Mormonism. Hardly stopping for a breath and unable to restrain himself, William was getting pretty loud when, looking around, he heard his companion softly singing *School Thy Feelings*.

Elder Rappleye, embarrassed at first, chuckled and took the hint. He bid the man good day and pressed on.

"I guess I can't shove gospel principles down the throat of someone who isn't willing to open his mouth to receive them," William said.

"You did manage to keep him quiet for at least ten minutes. That was impressive," said Elder Hanks. "I was just concerned about the attention we were gaining from the passersby."

After the hard day's work, they tried to get supper. About ten o'clock they succeeded. However, the bed failed them.

"What do we do now, Elder Hanks?" William asked, pretty confident he already knew the answer.

Elder Hanks pointed down the road to a weathered outbuilding.

"So, it appears we will be staying in Hotel De Barn tonight?" William chuckled.

"It will be cold," said Elder Hanks, "but at least we'll keep dry."

Burlington, Vermont
1904 — 1911

Automobiles were rare in 1904, but were beginning to appear on the roads in Burlington, Vermont more and more often. Carrie found them both intriguing and intimidating.

Carrie and Clara were outside visiting a neighbor when an especially nice motorcar slowed to a halt next to them. There were three people in the roofless car, a driver and, judging by their attire, an obviously wealthy couple. Carrie was puzzled as to why such a trio would be driving through her humble neighborhood, and even moreso why they would stop in front of her house.

"Are you Carrie Drew?" The well-dressed man motioned to Carrie.

Carrie was leery to talk to the man, but he seemed to know her, so she answered in the affirmative.

"I thought so. I would know you anywhere. You are a mirror image of my sister — your mother."

Arthur Foster and his wife, Josephine, resided in Hartford, Connecticut. He was a very successful businessman, owning a string of men's clothing stores. Up until now, Carrie only knew him from the few letters and packages he'd sent over the years.

"You must be my Uncle Arthur." Carrie's face went from cautious to gleeful at the realization.

"That, I am. And this is your Aunt Josephine." Arthur patted his wife on the shoulder.

"I'm happy to know you, Carrie." Josephine extended a gloved hand. "Arthur speaks of you often. So much so, in fact, that we decided it's high time we met face to face."

Carrie suddenly grew shy, but before she completely forgot her manners, she invited the couple into her home.

After their initial meeting, Arthur, clearly enchanted with Carrie, made the trip often.

Carrie grew to love Uncle Arthur and thought Aunt Josephine was the prettiest lady she had ever met. She was also in awe of his motorcar. Nobody Carrie knew owned a motorcar — especially a Packard. She felt like a princess when he drove her through town.

Arthur took on the role of doting uncle quite well. Whenever they were together, he would slip her a few ten-dollar bills. It was like giving Carrie a small fortune.

"Uncle Arthur, you don't have to give me money every time you come. You are much too generous," was always her reaction.

"Let him spoil you, Carrie," her Aunt Josephine would say with a wink. "He can afford it."

Carrie always graciously thanked Arthur for his generosity, but would secretly give the money to her mother and father, who Carrie thought needed it more than she. Carrie liked new things and would love to wear the latest fashions, but their modest income from the farm did not allow for much that was unnecessary.

Carrie and her family spent many happy years at the farmhouse on Susie Wilson Road. Unfortunately, as time went by, their perfect neighborhood became a bit ragged.

They lived near Fort Ethan Allen, where some of the soldiers transferred to the area were rather rough, having little to no scruples. Many of the Drews' neighbors began to evacuate the area and rent or sell their homes to the incoming soldiers. This was hard on the Drews, as they had finally found a home they loved and did not want to leave. They resisted until one event changed their minds.

Carrie had grown into an attractive, independent teenager. She awaited the streetcar to take her into town one spring afternoon, when a soldier she knew to be one of the Drews' neighbors, Mr. Jackson, came running up to her. "Miss Drew, Miss Drew," hollered the man, a strained look on his face. "You have to come to my place. My wife is very sick and I need your help. Come now, Miss Drew."

Carrie, being quite charitable, but also inheriting her father's good instincts, closely observed the panicked man and answered, "I will send a doctor as soon as I reach town."

"That will be too late, Miss Drew. I need you now." He tugged at her arm, urging her to follow him.

"No, Mr. Jackson, I will send a doctor. Now, please, take your hand off of me." Carrie yanked her arm away and began to walk quickly to the next corner to catch the streetcar.

She got there just in time. The streetcar came to a halt as she approached. Out of breath, she climbed in. Her encounter with Mr. Jackson made her feel uneasy for some reason. *I should have helped him,* an internal debate began, *but something about him frightened me.* After composing herself and settling in for the ride to town, Carrie glanced around at the other passengers riding the streetcar. Her heart gave a lurch when she saw Mrs. Jackson and her daughter sitting right across from her.

Carrie didn't say anything to the woman, but offered a silent prayer of thanks for the prompting she received to tell Mr. Jackson *no.* His intentions were obviously not honorable.

That evening, around the supper table, Carrie told her parents about the strange encounter with Mr. Jackson. The look on Aaron's face said it all. "I believe this neighborhood is becoming too dangerous for us to raise a family in. I will start looking for another home tomorrow." And he did.

A few days later there were shouts in the road, which brought everyone outside. "What is it, Mother?" Carrie asked.

"I don't know, but it looks as though Mr. Jackson is being arrested."

It didn't take long for the news to reach the Drews' home. Mr. Jackson was hauled out of his house ranting and raving as he was arrested for assaulting a young woman. Carrie's eyes welled up in tears, both for the young woman, and also for being blessed to have heard the prompting which warned her away from Mr. Jackson, thus escaping the assault herself.

The Drews purchased a home closer to the heart of Burlington on Pearl Street. It was large enough to take on boarders, thus providing an income as well. Carrie and Clara missed the large expanse of farmland, but felt safer at their new address.

Carrie didn't take long to adjust to Burlington, becoming fast friends with Eva Savoy, a fun, outgoing girl Carrie's age.

Vermont
June 1911

Country work was difficult. Sometimes punishingly so. William was a hard worker, but this was a different sort of hard. It was a lonely, rejecting and frustrating sort of hard. William often thought about home and what he would be doing if he were there. Then he'd snap out of it and force his mind back to the reason he left Wyoming – to serve the Lord. Letters never came to missionaries out on a country trip. How could they? The men were in a different location each day. William still took the opportunity to write to his family, and right now he was having a difficult time finding the words.

"Tracting isn't always a negative experience. We oftentimes meet kind people who are ready and willing to hear our message." William put his pen down while thinking of the best way to reassure his mother. He knew she worried about him, and although some of her worries were well-founded, he didn't want her to dwell on the negative. He settled on telling her about the day to day activities of an average missionary.

"When we aren't tracting, or searching for a meal and a bed, we are looking for ways to serve. We bale hay, cut grass, hoe potato patches and whatever else needs doing. On Sundays, however, we rest and worship. Sometimes we hold our own service and other times we find a local church to attend. We don't worry much about what religion it is, as long as they worship God. Now and then we happen in on a minister warning their parishioners about the Mormons, but this frequently backfires, and we find some of our best investigators as a result of the curiosity the very minister stirred up. The Lord works in mysterious ways."

It was good to write home. It forced William to recognize the Lord's hand in his daily activities. He truly did feel blessed and watched over. He knew his family prayed for him — he felt its power and the comfort of the Holy Ghost daily.

For the most part, time went by quickly in the country. Before long, the weather began to turn, sending William and his companion, Elder Hanks, back to Burlington.

William didn't know what to expect in Burlington. Life seemed like it would be much easier with a meal and a bed to return to each evening. He was happy to find that he was correct. However, while it was easier in some ways, the missionaries still kept very busy. They held cottage meetings or street meetings to teach their doctrine, administered to the sick and needy, and continued to serve in any capacity they were called. William became well acquainted with the people he and the other missionaries assisted and worshipped with. In a way, they became a second family.

A favorite pastime of the missionaries was to spend an evening singing with some of the Burlington saints or investigators. They sang together often and became quite adept at harmonizing. William sang especially well and was frequently called on to sing solos. Some of his favorites were *O, my Father* and *Brightly Beams our Father's Mercy*. On more than one occasion, his audience was brought to tears as he sang.

At the end of November, all of the area missionaries met together in South Royalton, near Joseph Smith's birthplace. Conferences generally consisted of a few days of meetings, singing and the ever important reassignments for the winter months. Three were assigned to Montreal, Canada; two to Barre, Vermont; two to St. Albains, Vermont; two stayed on the farm at headquarters to help cut out some logs for building. William was assigned to Burlington with a new President — President Larsen.

Thanksgiving arrived. William ached to be with his family in Wyoming. He could smell the turkey roasting as family members sang songs around a crackling fire. The homesick feeling he'd kept buried for several months began to surface. William did his best to tamp it back down. He knew he wasn't alone, however. Most of the elders, several of whom had families at home, acted melancholy and uncharacteristically quiet.

Surprisingly, Thanksgiving turned out to be a wonderful day for William. He took some time that evening to write a letter to his parents, describing his experiences in South Royalton, Vermont, and, of course, Thanksgiving dinner.

After giving them details of the conference and his new assignment, William wrote, "Thanksgiving came and we all felt like giving thanks to God for having the opportunity of eating Thanksgiving dinner in such a sacred place — the place where the Prophet Joseph Smith was born. After spending the busiest part of the glorious day roaming and playing ball, the large table was set and ready to be surrounded. When we all arrived, there were twenty all told seated up to the table at once with two large turkeys dressed and cooked with the daintiest taste. The table, with all the other necessary articles in the line of food and ornaments, looked just beautiful. After the blessing was asked by President Larsen, we all began to eat and it wasn't long till we were filled to our satisfaction."

He ended the letter by letting his parents, especially his mother, know that he was happy doing the Lord's work, and to please continue praying for his success. He never mentioned how the holidays had made him homesick. He rarely wrote anything in his letters home that would cause his mother to worry. Therefore, several details were often excluded. He knew his mother well.

William was growing to love the work, love the elders who were called to serve with him and he especially loved the people whose lives he was able to touch by serving in Vermont.

Burlington, Vermont
1911

When she came of age, Carrie, being both beautiful and friendly, did not have a shortage of admirers. She knew this was a concern to her overprotective father, but was quick to reassure him that he had raised her to be discerning. Still, she knew he was critical of every man that called on her.

Her suitors included one Doctor Earl Hunt, who had a fine reputation, but was several years Carrie's senior. After calling on her a few times, he decided she was the one he wished to marry. As was the custom, he took the request first to Aaron.

When Carrie learned of this, she couldn't help but be apprehensive. At age twenty, she was old enough to be married, but felt she hadn't yet courted any men she loved — including Earl Hunt.

Aaron reassured her. "Carrie, I simply told Earl that, while he's a good man, it's a question only you can answer. After all, you are still so young and lacking in experience."

Carrie breathed a sigh of relief.

Aaron went on, "I will give him my blessing, but only if it is what you want. I also told him not to rush things."

She thanked her father for his gentle response.

Carrie very much believed in marrying for love. She knew there were many who married for other reasons, but she didn't wish to be one of them. No, she thought, I will know love when I feel it.

Doctor Hunt, however, didn't waste any time, nor did he heed Aaron's advice about rushing into a proposal to Carrie. She was prepared. When the proposal came, she explained that while she was still so young, she would like to have plenty of time to make a decision as important as this one.

Reluctantly, Dr. Hunt acquiesced and told her to take her time.

⁓

There was a commotion in the boarding house as a stack of carefully arranged books tumbled to the ground. Carrie had put them on a table near the front door so their guests could have something to read, if desired. She rushed over to pick them up. "It must be the Romprey kids again," she muttered under her breath.

As she rounded the corner, Carrie was surprised to find a gentleman with a guilty face trying to restack the books.

"I'm so sorry, Miss, I didn't mean to knock down your display," the man said.

"Please don't give it a second thought." Carrie knelt down and reached for a book. "These things happen, and I can clean it up." She began to arrange the books on the table once more. "I suppose I shouldn't have put them so near the door. It was an accident bound to happen," she laughed.

The man seemed to relax at that comment. "My name is Josiah Taylor. I am new in town. And you are ...?"

"Oh, yes, I am Miss Drew." A blush began as she realized how handsome the man was. He had black hair and intense brown eyes.

"Well, Miss Drew, it is very nice to meet you," he said with a slight bow.

"And you, Mr. Taylor. What brings you to Burlington?"

"I was teaching math in Montpelier, which is where I hail from, when my uncle enticed me with an obscene amount of money to relocate here to help him manage his affairs." He exaggerated the word obscene making Carrie laugh.

"Am I, then, to understand that you came here against your will, or at least against your better judgment?" she teased.

Mr. Taylor laughed now, too. "Perhaps, but I have to admit that you are helping me acclimate quite quickly." He grinned.

Carrie could feel her face warming.

"I need a room, just until I get settled in a house of my own."

Carrie set him up with their last remaining room, as there were only six to rent. "Please let me know if there is anything I can help you find, Mr. Taylor. I'm never too far away," she said, turning in the direction of an incoming customer.

Several men who wanted to court her called on Carrie, but none were as handsome as Mr. Taylor, and most were at least ten years her senior. "I must tell Eva about Mr. Taylor," she said to herself after both customers vacated the area.

Eva Savoy was Carrie's best friend from the time her family moved to Burlington. Of course Carrie had Clara, but their age difference of eight years made talking about courting awkward. With Eva, however, there were no secrets. They enjoyed spending much of their spare time with each other, and they especially liked talking about men. So when Carrie left the boarding house that evening, she marched straight over to Eva's house to tell her the good news.

After knocking on the door, Eva opened it to find her dear friend wearing a huge grin. "Come in, and do tell me what that smile is for." Eva pulled Carrie through the door.

"Eva, there's a new man in town. And he is so handsome."

Looking around to see if anyone heard them, Eva motioned for Carrie to follow her to her bedroom where they could speak privately. Sitting side by side on a small settee, Eva was eager to hear more. "I want details, Carrie; tell me everything."

There really wasn't much to tell, but Carrie managed to make her short encounter sound like a grand event. "Oh, Eva, I do hope to see him again soon."

Eva was all lit up with excitement, as well. Having someone, anyone, especially a handsome man, move into their little neck of the woods was a novelty.

"Where will he live? Who is his uncle?" The questions were coming faster than Carrie could answer, and besides that, she had not asked him.

"I don't know, Eva. We barely made it through introductions before I needed to assist one of our guests. If his uncle is someone from around here, we are sure to know him."

Eva looked disappointed in her friend's ability to ferret out information.

"I'm sorry, Eva. I'm sure to see him again and I'll ask more questions then.

"I guess we can only hope Mr. Taylor has a leaky roof and mice in his new house so that he is forced to stay at your boarding house a good long time." At that, both girls dissolved into laughter.

Mr. Taylor only stayed at the boarding house two days, much to Carrie's dismay. During those two days, however, he spent a fair amount of time talking with and getting to know Carrie, which she couldn't complain about.

Carrie managed to find out the necessary information to report back to Eva. Josiah Taylor's uncle was Earnest Taylor, a big landowner in the area, with a reputation to match. I should have thought of that, Carrie realized. I hope he isn't like his uncle, she mused, remembering some of the stories she had heard about his uncle's unfavorable dealings with the local businessmen. She decided that a man as kind as Josiah had been to her would surely be nothing like his uncle.

"I am afraid I won't be seeing much of you after tonight," Mr. Taylor said on his second night at the boarding house. Dinner was cleaned up and Carrie had taken a seat across from him in the parlor. "It seems my house is ready and I need to make a trip to Montpelier to gather my belongings to relocate."

Carrie suppressed a frown, disappointed to have Josiah leaving so soon, but she determined not to show it. "I'm sure you will be happy to move into a house of your own."

"Perhaps, but I cannot lie, I have thoroughly enjoyed my stay here in your home, Carrie. Would you care to take a walk with me? It is unusually warm for this time of year — perfect for a stroll." He gave her his heart-stopping smile.

Carrie's heart thudded. "That would be nice, but do you mind if I call on my friend, Eva, to join us?" Even though Carrie, at twenty years of age, didn't necessarily want a chaperone, she felt uncomfortable without one. Besides, she knew her father would absolutely insist upon it.

Josiah frowned, clearly disappointed, but then agreed. "I shall return in one half hour then?"

Carrie nodded her agreement, then found her father to let him know of her plans.

"Have I met this Josiah Taylor, Carrie?" He put down the book he was reading and removed his glasses.

"I'm sure you have, Father. He has been staying here for these past two days."

Aaron paused as if he were trying to conjure up a face to match the name. Shaking his head as he realized he couldn't. "Before you go out wandering the streets with this stranger, please bring him in to meet your mother and me. Then be sure Eva stays with you the entire time."

Relieved, Carrie kissed Aaron's cheek. "I will, Father."

Josiah Taylor came back thirty minutes later, as promised. Eva stood with Carrie, acting almost giddy to meet him.

"Mr. Taylor," Carrie said, "this is my friend, Eva. Eva, this is Josiah Taylor."

"Pleased to meet you, Mr. Taylor. Carrie has spoken to me about you."

Carrie gave Eva a warning look.

Eva continued, "But not much," she tried to recover.

Josiah chuckled, "Pleased to meet you too, Miss Eva ...?"

"Savoy." Eva extended her hand to Josiah.

"I see Burlington is bursting with pretty girls." He winked. "Please call me Josiah. Mr. Taylor is so formal."

"Now, if you don't mind stepping back into our living quarters, my father and mother would also like to meet you, Josiah." Carrie motioned for him to follow.

After the introductions were made, Carrie, Eva and Josiah left for their walk.

Conversation on the walk was light and they were back shortly after an hour's time.

"I guess I'd best be packing my bags. Thank you for your time tonight, ladies. It was delightful." Josiah gave a slight bow, then turned to leave the room.

Once he was out of earshot, Eva was ready to talk. "Oh, Carrie, he's so dapper; and oh, those brown eyes." She peered up to the sky as if she were in dreamland. "Surely he'll come back and call on you, once he is settled."

"I hope so, Eva, but he has never said anything that would lead me to believe he sees me in his future," Carrie said, feeling a surge of disappointment.

———

A week later, Mr. Taylor was back. Carrie brightened as she saw him coming up the walk to Mrs. Drew's Rooming House, as it had come to be known among the locals, although to many it was still the Drews' boarding house.

"Mr. Taylor ... Josiah," she grinned, "welcome back. I trust your move went well?"

"It did indeed, Carrie."

They talked about his move, the weather and a few other inconsequential things. Then, he was on his way.

When the Drews sat down for supper that evening, Mrs. Drew asked about Josiah. "I noticed you speaking with Mr. Taylor this afternoon, Carrie. Did he come to call on you?"

Carrie narrowed her eyes and wrung her hands, then finally answered, "Mother, I'm not certain why he came. I feel comfortable when we are together, but he has never called on me. Don't you find that a bit curious?"

Carrie's mother patted her hand and answered, "Maybe he just needs more time, Carrie."

"There is something I don't trust about that boy," chimed in her father. "I'm not sure what, but I just get a strange feeling when he's about."

"Aaron, you get a strange feeling when any man is interested in your little girl." Emily smiled up at her husband. "Don't worry, Carrie. If he's the right man, you'll know it."

Grateful she could speak openly to her parents, Carrie just nodded. She hoped her mother was right, but still felt doubt crowding its way into her soul.

Burlington, Vermont
December 1911

Christmas was approaching, bringing on a fresh bout of homesickness for William, but his buoyant attitude kept him busy serving others instead of dwelling on his loved ones in Wyoming. Thankfully, his family hadn't forgotten about their missionary. He received a few packages all bundled up in brown paper and twine.

Following a cottage meeting on December 24th, William and his companion set out to buy the fixings for a right, good holiday feast.

Gathered around the table on Christmas day, William said to the group of eight missionaries, "It's not my mama's cooking, but it will do."

"Hear, hear," replied one of the men, lifting his glass of milk in a toast to the holiday.

William and the other seven elders polished off their Christmas meal then stuffed themselves with the sweets they had purchased — a rare treat for the men. In the end, William admitted, the rich food and sugary sweets made for a nice Christmas, but a dumpish stomach afterward. He and the other missionaries were content to allow for a little bit of sluggishness as they rested for the remainder of the day.

Two days later, President Larsen stormed into the small mission office holding a newspaper. "I can't believe some people's ignorance." He slammed the paper on the desk.

The headline read:
"Begin Campaign Against Mormons"
The elders gathered round the desk to read it. "They think the Mormons are trying to entice girls to go to Utah to marry our men?" Elder Brown was incredulous.

"And they're holding a mass meeting to begin a campaign against us?" Now it was Elder Rappleye's turn to absorb the news. As he read on, he couldn't help but chuckle a little to hear how twisted a reporter made them appear. It was one thing to have doors slammed in their faces and hear aspersions whispered in their direction, but to read it in big bold letters, as if it were gospel truth, right there in the Burlington Free Press, was just plain wrong.

"And how many years has the practice of polygamy been banned, both from the state of Utah and from the church?" Elder Brown went on. "It's time people quit associating us with that practice."

"Elder Brown," began President Larsen, "you know and I know that there were reasons for polygamy back in the mid-1800s — just as there were in Biblical times — and we all know those reasons no longer exist. But I fear that for generations to come, Satan will do his best to keep arguments about that and other untruths circulating among those who choose to believe them."

"So what should we do? Nothing?"

"How about we write a rebuttal — you know, explain the misstatements in this article, then march ourselves down to the Burlington Free Press to see if they are broad minded enough to give us equal space?" Elder Rappleye suggested.

"I think that is an excellent idea, Elder Rappleye. I will set to work on writing something right away. In the meantime, you two go on over to the Burlington Press to see about securing a spot for our refutation." President Larsen opened his desk drawer and retrieved a pad of paper.

It was blustery outside. The previous day had dumped mounds of freezing snow upon the Vermont landscape and conditions hadn't improved much today. However, Elder Rappleye and Elder Brown, determined to right a wrong, wasted no time making their way to the Burlington Press. There they met with the manager, Mr. Howe, who was surprisingly fair-minded and agreed to allow them a place in the paper to refute any misstatements made in that day's article about the Mormons. Relieved, they returned to mission headquarters, which was really just a basement apartment in a boarding house, to report back to President Larsen.

After congratulating the elders on their success, President Larsen showed the two what he had written in their defense thus far. Both agreed that he was doing a fine job.

"I know you two just returned and it is mighty cold out, but after you get a bit warmed up, I need you to walk over to Mrs. Drew's boarding house to see about securing a room for a new elder arriving next week — Elder McFarlane."

The elders nodded their willingness to run another errand in the freezing weather, but first they huddled up to the radiator to thaw a bit before they left their warm apartment.

Thirty minutes later, the elders pulled on their hats, boots and gloves, and trudged back out into the wet, frigid air.

"I don't think I could ever get used to Vermont winters," Elder Brown grumbled as he kicked a clump of snow sitting squarely in his path as if it had fallen there just to vex him.

"It's cold, there is no doubt, but I don't think it's quite as cold as Cowley, Wyoming," replied Elder Rappleye. Winter begins early and ends late there.

Talking about Cowley made William a bit homesick, but it was also nice to have someone who felt the same way to talk to. As they walked, they shared stories about their hometowns. The elders' apartment was only a few blocks from the Drew's boarding house, so it wasn't a long walk.

"Have you ever been to the Drews' home?"

"Just a couple of times with President Larsen, but I've only met Mrs. Drew."

They shook off the snow, removed their gloves and knocked on the door.

Burlington, Vermont
December 1911

Carrie Drew picked up a nasty cold over the Christmas holiday, and had been laying low for the past few days, hoping to feel better. She was quite a bit improved today, but thought one more day of rest wouldn't hurt.

Just as she snuggled into her bed with a good book, Eva burst through the door. "Carrie, you've got to come downstairs and see who's in your boarding house!" Spotting and retrieving a robe, she hurried over to Carrie and tapped her foot, waiting for Carrie to respond.

"Eva, what are you doing? I can't go downstairs like this! I'm not properly dressed, and my hair — it isn't pinned up." She motioned to her long brown hair spilling over her shoulders.

"But you have to. Anyway, we can just stay in the parlor where none of the guests ever go. I just want you to see who is there."

"Who ... who is there that you are so excited for me to see, Eva?"

"Mormons!" Eva said with a smug grin.

Carrie just stood there with a bewildered look on her face. She didn't know a thing about Mormons except for the rumors she had heard that they all had many wives and possibly a few horns, which she knew was ludicrous. But Eva seemed to think they were a spectacle worth looking at, so Carrie reluctantly pulled her robe over her nightgown, slid her petite feet into her warm slippers and allowed Eva to pull her down the stairs and into the parlor.

"Why are they here?" Carrie whispered as they made their descent.

"I think they need a room. I didn't get a good look at them because I was behind them as they entered your home and heard them say they were Mormon missionaries. That's when I knew I had to find you. I've never seen a Mormon before. Let's just peek through the door and see what they look like. Uh ..." Eva finally slowed down and took a breath. "Why were you in bed, Carrie?" Her eyes moved to a clock hanging on the wall. "It's the middle of the afternoon." Carrie was certainly not lazy and, as a rule, was up early preparing for guests at the boarding house.

"I've been feeling poorly with a cold. I think I'm over the worst of it, but I certainly don't want to be seen in my nightgown and robe."

"Oh, don't worry. Aside from your family, you know nobody ever uses the parlor."

As they peered through the parlor and into the part of the house where guests normally conducted their business, Eva gave a great sigh. "They're beautiful – especially the one with the dark hair. He's so handsome."

Carried rolled her eyes at her friend's dramatics. "Eva, they're here to save souls, not find wives."

"But still–"

Before Eva could finish her sentence, the missionaries were pushing through the parlor doors and being shown to the sofa. "And can I get you two something warm to drink ... coffee, tea?" asked Mrs. Drew.

The girls stood frozen. There was no escape, so they just tried to blend. Carrie managed to back up to the piano and sit on the stool that sat before it. Eva continued to just stand there and gawk.

"Oh, girls, I didn't realize you were in here. Are you feeling better then, Carrie?" Mrs. Drew crossed the room and laid a hand on Carrie's forehead.

Carrie just nodded.

"These men are Mormon missionaries. It's so cold outside; I asked them in so that they can warm up a bit."

Eva must have realized that she was standing awkwardly in the middle of the room, as she quickly found a chair to sit on.

Mrs. Drew turned her attention back to the missionaries.

"Oh, no thank you, Mrs. Drew. But we appreciate the offer," said Elder Rappleye in reply to her offer of a hot drink. "And you ladies are ...?"

Carrie blushed profusely, being in her nightgown with disheveled hair. Eva, however, beamed and spoke up first. "I'm Eva, Carrie's friend."

"So you must be Carrie, then," Elder Rappleye said, his eyes twinkling as he looked at her with intrigue.

Carrie's heart began beating at double time. Eva was right; he was very handsome indeed. She managed to remind herself of her own counsel and snapped out of the trance she seemed to be in. "Yes, I'm Carrie Drew. I apologize for my appearance. I have been under the weather all week."

"I'm sorry to hear that, Miss Drew. We don't mean to intrude. We should probably be leaving," Elder Rappleye said, standing to leave.

"Oh, no, it's really okay. I'm much better now. Just a bit embarrassed is all," Carrie said with a shy grin.

"Do you play the piano, Miss Drew?" Elder Rappleye motioned to the instrument behind her.

"She plays very well," Eva piped up.

"We often need someone to accompany us on the piano at our cottage meetings. Would you be willing to help us out sometime, perhaps on Saturday, if you're feeling up to it?"

Surprised at Elder Rappleye's bold request, Carrie gave her mother a nervous glance, as if to see if it would be okay. Mrs. Drew nodded her approval. "I guess I could do that. Do you have the music you would like me to play? I'd really like to practice before the meeting."

Elder Brown pulled a hymnal out of his large overcoat pocket. "I have it right here, Miss Drew. We missionaries enjoy singing quite a bit." He crossed the room to hand the book to Carrie.

She put it on the piano, opened it to the first hymn, and began to play. It was as if the elders couldn't restrain themselves. Before they knew it, they were all gathered around the piano, including Eva and Mrs. Drew, singing the hymns together.

When they finished several songs, Elder Rappleye commented that they should really get back to their apartment. "Thank you, Mrs. Drew, for your hospitality, and Miss Drew for accompanying us on the piano. It was delightful." He shook her hand, looking deep into her blue eyes. "We will see you on Saturday, then?"

"Yes, I'll be there." Carrie ducked her head to hide a smile.

"I'll be there, too," chimed in Eva. Elder Rappleye and Elder Brown each shook her hand, as well, and bade them all goodbye.

When they were out of the door and walking down the road, Eva gave the same sigh she had earlier. "Like I said before, they're beautiful — especially Elder Rappleye."

Carrie and Mrs. Drew just laughed. "And I'm sure I made a lasting impression being caught in my nightclothes," Carrie groaned. "At least I can possibly make up for it on Saturday."

She sat back down at the piano to practice the hymns, all the while thinking how nice the room felt when the Mormon missionaries were there singing.

Burlington, Vermont
January 1912

"Elder Rappleye, I do believe you are walking with an extra spring in your step," Elder Brown observed. "Could it be that one or both of those pretty girls at the boarding house caught your attention?"

William had very few secrets from Elder Brown. Living with someone twenty-four hours a day for seven days a week prevents such a thing, but he wasn't about to divulge the instant attraction he had toward Carrie — especially when it felt so completely inappropriate while he was serving the Lord on a mission. "They were pretty," he said, "but that's not what I'm here for, Elder Brown."

"Still, you'd have to be blind not to see how beautiful they were, especially Miss Drew. And her voice — she sings like an angel. I'm just glad you were on your toes about it."

"And how's that, Elder Brown?"

"Inviting Miss Drew to accompany us on the piano at the cottage meeting this Saturday. That was a brilliant move."

"Elder Brown, we actually *need* someone to accompany us on the piano this Saturday. There was no ulterior motive there," William replied, feeling a bit annoyed by his companion — albeit understanding of his emotions. "Perhaps that was not a wise move on my part, seeing how you are so smitten with her."

"No, no, Elder Rappleye, like you said, we need an accompanist."

William smiled to himself and hoped Elder Brown would drop the subject already.

He did.

"I thought you boys got lost somewhere," President Larsen said as the pair walked through their apartment door.

The elders gave each other a guilty look, and then Elder Brown spoke up, "No, not lost. We just took the opportunity to get to know the Drews a little bit better is all. And Elder Rappleye here was able to secure an accompanist for Saturday's cottage meeting."

"That's great news. And speaking of news, I finished the article stating our beliefs for the Burlington Press. It's too late today, but perhaps you two can deliver it to Mr. Howe first thing tomorrow."

The two agreed and asked to read what President Larsen had written.

"This is excellent, President Larsen. You have a way with words," said Elder Rappleye.

"Thank you, Elder. I've always enjoyed writing and I must admit it felt good to get a few things off my chest after reading that newspaper article this morning."

Saturday arrived and the men were ready for their cottage meeting. It was a very cold evening, but the fire in the warm home of Albert Jacobsen, one of the handful of members of the Mormon congregation, kept everyone toasty. The elders never knew what to expect at these meetings. Sometimes they would get just a few curious attendees; other times the place would be packed. Tonight, he feared the cold weather and icy walks would keep people away. He was happily surprised. The Jacobsen home began to fill to capacity.

Keeping an eye on the door, William couldn't help but watch for Carrie. He was a bit worried that she might forget, or just decide she didn't really care to rub shoulders with Mormons; it wouldn't be the first time. Not having an accompanist wasn't the issue; they had many a meeting without one — although it would be really nice to keep everyone on the same pitch. Rather, William had been able to think of little else since meeting Carrie Drew. She had blushed in embarrassment when he and Elder Brown found her wearing a robe and slippers, but William thought she looked beautiful. Her crystal blue eyes caught his attention first, then her smile. While most women wore their hair up in pins, hers was down, framing her perfect face beautifully. He had tried and tried to keep his thoughts on the work, but sometimes it became a struggle for William to concentrate with Carrie on his mind.

When he was about to give up hope she might come, Carrie, Eva, and Mr. and Mrs. Drew walked in. William jumped up immediately, welcoming them to their meeting. "Thank you for coming, Miss Drew," he said in a low voice. "I was worried you might have changed your mind."

"I didn't. However, my father read a strange article in the newspaper about Mormons a few days ago, and wasn't certain it was wise for me to come," she said, a little sheepishly. "He finally decided that I could come, only if he and mother came along too."

"I know the very article. I read it myself and found it had a lot of entertainment value, but little truth to it." He winked.

Holding Carrie by the arm, he steered her through the crowd until they finally reached the piano where he reluctantly let go and handed her the music she would be playing. "Hopefully our meeting tonight will straighten out some of those falsehoods written about us in the paper. And thank you again." He patted her hand and made his way to the front of the room.

The cottage meeting went very smoothly. William noted that having a negative article printed in the Burlington Press served to generate public interest in the elders, as many people had never heard of the Mormons and wanted clarification about their "odd" beliefs. He found most to be courteous and truly did seek to know the truth about the Mormons, although there were those whose minds were closed to the truth and chose to believe whatever outlandish piece of fiction the newspaper printed. Those were the people who tried to stir things up, but the elders would very politely answer their accusations and move along, never allowing the meeting to derail.

At the conclusion of the meeting, Carrie accompanied the congregation while they sang *Abide With Me*, after which Mrs. Martha Jacobsen passed out refreshments while the elders continued speaking with people individually, writing down names and addresses of those who wanted follow-up visits. When he finally reached the Drews, William was so fired up about the success of the meeting that he didn't let Mr. Drew's critical appraisal unnerve him in the least. Instead, William shook his hand vigorously and expressed his appreciation for their attendance and especially for allowing his daughter, Carrie, to accompany them on the hymns.

Aaron's eyes widened, clearly taken aback by the confidence of Elder Rappleye. He even agreed to have the elders come over for another meeting.

"Very well. We shall see you again on Thursday evening, then," Elder Rappleye said, trying to contain his excitement.

"Seven should work out fine," Aaron replied. They shook hands, then Aaron and Mrs. Drew turned to leave.

"And thank you again, Carrie, for sharing your musical talent with us tonight," William said, giving her hand a squeeze.

Carrie pinked up. "You are more than welcome, Elder Rappleye. I thought the meeting was extremely interesting and I am so happy that my parents have agreed to learn more about your beliefs."

After also thanking Eva for coming, William watched the Drew family exit the house, his heart beating wildly. *I can't let her get to me,* he thought to himself. *That's not why I'm here.*

The following Monday ushered in another snowstorm and delivered the Monday morning Burlington Free Press newspaper. President Larsen snatched it up and scanned through the pages looking for his well-written article. He finally found it buried with the articles that were, for the most part, trivial. He carefully laid the wet paper on the table then opened it to the article so the elders could read it.

The article began:

> George C. Larsen, president of the Vermont Conference of the Mormon Church has the following to say in answer to an article in the Wednesday issue of the Burlington Free Press, under the heading, *"Begin Campaign against Mormons, mass meeting to be held January 10."* This article contains misstatements, said Mr. Larsen, and for the benefit of those who are willing to hear the

facts of the case, *"I will endeavor to explain the true condition of the Mormon people and the object of the great missionary work that is now being carried on by the Church of Jesus Christ of Latter-day Saints."*

The article went on to explain the Church's position on all of the items in question, quoting scripture and prophets, both ancient and modern. It took up about one and a half columns. It was a decent sized article. The elders all looked pleased about it and prayed it would reach those doubters with ears to listen and hearts to feel. William especially hoped that it would reach Mr. Drew.

Burlington, Vermont
January 1912

It was business as usual at the boarding house. Carrie helped clean up the breakfast dishes, then went about organizing the papers strewn across the desk. She was a meticulous record keeper and hated seeing anything out of order, especially in places as obvious as the front desk of their boarding house.

Scrutinizing an invoice, Carrie jumped when the front door opened.

"Sorry, Miss Drew, I didn't mean to startle you," came a familiar voice.

Carrie looked up to see the very handsome Josiah Taylor grinning at her. "I guess I was a bit wrapped up in these invoices." She neatly pushed the piles aside and gave Josiah her undivided attention.

"It looks to me like you are working too hard. How about we take a walk out back?" Josiah raised his eyebrows.

Carrie looked around. Nobody else was in the room, or even the house. Did he really think she would just leave the desk unattended and take an unchaperoned walk with him? "I'm sorry, Mr. Taylor, but as you can see, there is no one here to mind the desk."

"Then I guess I'll just have to settle for having a chat, if that suits you, that is."

"That suits me just fine," she said. "May I get you something warm to drink? It's a mighty cold day."

"Yes, thank you. I will take tea, if it's not any trouble."

"No trouble at all, Mr. Taylor," replied Carrie.

"But I believe we've been over this 'Mr. Taylor' bit before. Please call me Josiah," he said, giving her a winning smile.

It worked. Carrie felt her knees weaken. "Very well, Josiah," she smiled back. "I will be happy to get you some tea. Please, have a seat."

As she hurried off to the kitchen to get the tea, she remembered how Elder Rappleye made her feel when he shook her hand. How is it that two men can both make me go weak in the knees? she wondered. Well, at least this man is available. It's true, Elder Rappleye can send shivers down my spine, but he is strictly off-limits. Yet, he won't be a missionary forever — at least I don't think he will be. I wonder if Mormon missionaries are like nuns?

These thoughts occupied her while she poured the tea and returned to the front room of the house. Josiah was perusing one of the books he had accidentally knocked over on his first visit.

Traffic through the boarding house was light, making it easy for Carrie and Josiah to have a pleasant visit with each other.

Later that evening, around the dinner table, Mr. Drew brought up a subject that Carrie had been carefully avoiding. "Carrie, my dear, I came across Dr. Hunt at the lumberyard today. He said that you haven't given him an answer to his proposal yet."

Dr. Hunt had been courting Carrie for a few months now, or so he thought. She was inclined to look at their relationship as more of a friendship, as she was not in the least attracted to the much older man.

Carrie's mouth suddenly felt dry. She took a slow drink of water before meeting Aaron's gaze. "Father, I haven't given him an answer because I don't yet have an answer. I know he is a fine man and could give me a good life, but he is twenty years older than I. And besides that, while I do not dislike Dr. Hunt, I'm certain I do not love him. Isn't that important in a marriage, Father?"

Aaron looked thoughtful as she pleaded her case. "I understand, Carrie. Love is a powerful and ideal emotion to have in a marriage."

Carrie could see in her father's eyes a wistful, sad look and realized that he must be thinking of her birth mother, Carrie Foster.

"However," he continued, "one can always fall in love over time."

Now he's thinking about Emily, she thought.

"I just need to know you will marry someone who can take care of you, my dear. Will you promise to give it a little longer? Maybe give him a chance to let you fall in love with him?"

Carrie considered Josiah Taylor and even Elder Rappleye and how each made her feel. She knew she could neither have those feelings for, nor fall in love with Dr. Hunt, but out of love and respect for her father, she agreed.

Josiah came to visit again on Tuesday and Wednesday. Carrie began to feel quite comfortable around him, yet he never called on her for an actual outing, which puzzled her.

Thursday came and Carrie hadn't realized how much she had anticipated seeing the missionaries again — not only to see Elder Rappleye, but also to hear their message.

Just before seven, there was a knock at the door. Carrie took her time walking to the door to answer it, lest she appear overanxious. When she opened it, she was met with a gust of wet, chilly, Vermont air, along with a smiling Dr. Hunt. Her heart sank.

Not wanting to be rude, Carrie invited Dr. Hunt in. She glanced up at the clock and noted the time to be six-fifty. That gave her ten minutes to nicely get rid of the kind doctor.

No such luck. He began to talk all about the exciting world of medicine and especially about anyone in a five-mile radius who had been quarantined for any number of illnesses.

As the clock chimed seven, there was another knock at the door. Carrie looked at the doctor and said, "Oh my, that must be the missionaries. They are coming to talk to me and my parents. I'm very sorry that our visit has to be so short, Dr. Hunt."

Dr. Hunt's mouth turned down in disapproval. "Missionaries ... what kind of missionaries?"

"Mormon missionaries, have you heard of them?" Carrie asked.

"I've read all I need to know about the Mormons in the newspaper. Miss Drew, you would be wise to keep your distance from these so-called missionaries. Nothing good can come from meeting with them." The doctor wore a look that warred between concern and anger.

That only served to put Carrie on the defensive. "So you haven't actually met the missionaries, then," she said firmly.

"Well, no, but it was in the newspaper just last week—"

Carrie cut him off before he finished his sentence, "And this week, did you read the piece in Monday's paper?"

"I didn't need to. That was written by a Mormon, so it can't have much credence."

"Because of the things you read in last week's paper ..." Carrie was beginning to get visibly irritated by now.

Meanwhile, Mrs. Drew had answered the door and let the two missionaries in. They were both standing, hats in hand, in the waiting area watching as the conversation between Dr. Hunt and Carrie unfolded.

"Well, yes," Dr. Hunt answered defiantly.

"So it really is a matter of whom you choose to believe then, is that how it is, Dr. Hunt?"

"Come now, Miss Drew ... Carrie," Dr. Hunt tried to soothe her flaring emotions, "surely you don't believe in those crackpot Mormons. You're a sensible woman. Why I've heard that Mormons have horns and tails and all of the men have several wives."

Carrie had heard enough. She looked up to see the two missionaries watching the argument and was embarrassed until she saw the humor in their eyes. *They are actually enjoying this.*

"I apologize, Dr. Hunt. I'm sure you are right. In fact, we can verify that right now. Elder Rappleye," she said, raising her voice and looking past Dr. Hunt to the missionaries. It was obvious the doctor didn't know they had arrived, as his face began to pale.

"Yes, Miss Drew?" answered William.

"Will you please show us your horns?"

Elder Rappleye began to feel the top of his head, clearly enjoying himself. "Hmm, not here, not there ... how about in back ... no again. They must have fallen off. I'm certain they were here this morning. How about you, Elder Brown? Do you still have your horns, or perhaps a tail?"

Elder Brown stifled a laugh, as did Carrie.

"Or, Elder Brown, what about your ten wives? How have they been faring lately?"

Dr. Hunt apparently had heard enough. He put his hat on and stormed out into the icy, cold, winter night.

"Sad, I was hoping to teach the poor doctor," Elder Brown said, as the door slammed shut.

Everyone burst into peals of laughter. Then Elder Rappleye sobered. "As a rule, we don't usually make it our practice to embarrass or humiliate others and I should apologize—"

Carrie cut him off, "But he deserved every bit of what he got. Now, please come in."

The elders spent a very pleasant evening with the Drews. Even Aaron Drew got into the conversation.

"You're saying that we can see our loved ones after this life?" His eyes grew misty.

"Yes, Mr. Drew, through the sealing power of the temple. But we can teach you about temples next time," Elder Brown said.

After they finished teaching them the message they had prepared, the group gathered around the piano and sang songs together. Carrie noticed, once again, the same peaceful feeling which was present the last time the elders were in the Drews' home.

As Ever Yours

JEANIE R. DAVIS

Burlington, Vermont
February 1912

Elder Rappleye and Elder Brown sloshed through the snow on their chilly walk back to their apartment on Main Street. Thankfully, it wasn't a long walk. William basked in the success of the meeting, especially grateful to have Mr. Drew join in and take an interest.

He couldn't quit thinking about how their evening began, with Carrie's and Dr. Hunt's fiery conversation. "I didn't really think people were gullible enough to believe so many things about us; did you, Elder Brown?"

"No, but I suppose people think that whatever they read in print is gospel truth."

"Not to mention that we have free agency to believe whatever we choose, and there are always those who choose to believe the worst about us." Elder Rappleye paused. "I have to admit, it was quite the thing to see Miss Drew defending us like that."

"Indeed it was. She's something special. I believe she thinks you are as well, Elder Rappleye."

This threw Elder Rappleye for a loop, as he had put his best efforts into keeping his heart at bay all evening. "What do you mean by that, Elder?"

Elder Brown chuckled. "Don't worry, it wasn't anything you did. There was just an unspoken magnetism happening between the two of you. And she could hardly tear her eyes off you during our message."

"Perhaps that was because I was the one doing most of the talking."

"Perhaps," Elder Brown chuckled some more. "She's a beauty!"

"An out-of-our-reach beauty," William quietly added.

As the two missionaries approached the residence that housed their downstairs apartment, the men could hear music playing.

"Do you hear that, Elder Rappleye?"

"I do. I heard Mrs. Warnes got one of those newfangled gramophones ... a Victrola, I think she called it."

The two just stood motionless on the porch listening to the sweet sound. "Do you think it's too late, or should we ask to see it? That's a beautiful song," Elder Rappleye wondered out loud.

"Well, she's obviously awake. Let's see about joining her."

The elders were mesmerized with the Victrola, and Elder Rappleye was quite taken with the song Mrs. Warnes played over and over — *Let Me Call You Sweetheart*.

It was late by the time they decided they'd seen enough of the modern miracle and found their way downstairs and to their beds. But the song kept playing in their heads and both were humming it until they dropped off to sleep.

The next evening, Elder McFarlane arrived from Provo, Utah. It was always nice to add a new face to the group. Elder Brown and Elder Rappleye picked him up from the train station and took him straight to their apartment.

"Welcome to Burlington, Elder McFarlane." President Larsen shook his hand. "You will be boarding at Mrs. Drew's rooming house. After you've had some supper, Elder Rappleye and Elder Brown can walk you over there.

"Try not to fall in love with Mrs. Drew's daughter while you're there," teased Elder Brown. He winced at the sharp elbow to his ribs from William.

After supper, the elders donned their hats, gloves and boots and walked the few blocks to Pearl Street to deliver Elder McFarlane to the Drews.

Carrie was there to greet them. Introductions were made along with some idle chit-chat. Throughout the visit William had the tune, *Let Me Call You Sweetheart*, running through his mind.

They finally shook hands with the new elder, promised to retrieve him first thing in the morning to go tracting, then said their goodbyes.

Another week passed. William was happy about the success they made with the follow-up visits since their last cottage meeting. But they still spent the bulk of their time tracting.

After a particularly cold day out pounding the icy pavement, all four elders congregated for a beef stew supper. William thought it tasted like heaven after being out in the biting cold. "Mrs. Warnes made extra for us. She's a peach," said President Larsen. The others had to agree.

"Elders, I think we need to have a choir practice tonight. How about it?" President Larsen grinned.

Everyone nodded in agreement, as singing was their only pastime besides recording in their journals and writing letters home. They spent time each day studying and praying, but singing was entertainment and they all enjoyed doing it together.

After singing a few hymns, Elder Rappleye made a request, "How about we try that song Mrs. Warnes keeps playing on her Victrola? You know the one, *Let Me Call You Sweetheart*."

He looked to President Larsen, who made most of the decisions. It wasn't a hymn after all. "I think that's a fine idea, Elder Rappleye," he said.

They found their pitches and began. It was easy to remember the words. Ever since Mrs. Warnes bought the record, she played it constantly and everyone in the boarding house could hear it. The men sang at the tops of their lungs and sounded quite good, until there was a knock at their door, which put a stop to the singing. It was Mrs. Warnes.

"Oh dear," President Larsen apologized, "were we singing too loud?"

"Oh no, your singing was fine. It's just this doctor—"

She was interrupted by a man pushing his way through the door behind her. "I'm Dr. Wilder, and boys, you are all under quarantine for smallpox.

You could have heard a pin drop in the once music filled room. "We what?" President Larsen exclaimed. "Nobody here has smallpox, Doctor."

"No, but a woman rooming upstairs does, which is close enough."

William looked around the room and noticed that four more doctors had somehow materialized in their basement apartment. A feeling of despair hit him hard. If they were to be quarantined with someone suffering from the smallpox virus, that meant weeks in their apartment. Plus, there was the distinct possibility that one or more of them would contract the deadly disease.

As the doctors explained to the missionaries that they could not leave the premises, send letters or anything else out of the apartment, let anyone in besides the doctors, etcetera, they heard the sign with the dreaded words,

"QUARANTINED FOR SMALLPOX"
being tacked on the front door.

"We have appointments set up," Elder Brown mumbled.

"Not anymore," one of the doctors who hadn't said anything yet jumped in.

William thought he sounded a little too enthusiastic until he realized who it was ... Dr. Hunt. Ugh. "It's like he's gloating in our misery," William whispered to Elder Brown. "I guess we deserve it after our performance at the Drews." That thought brought a smile to his face — albeit a short-lived smile, once the seriousness of the situation hit once again.

"There will be a police officer posted outside this home, lest you get any ideas about leaving."

Once the doctors took down all of their names, the elders glumly pulled some blankets together for Elder McFarlane to sleep on, since he would not be able to return to the Drews' boarding house.

"I wish there were a way to contact the people we are scheduled to visit to let them know that we won't be able to make it," Elder Brown said.

"And what about the Drews?" said Elder McFarlane. "They'll be wondering where I disappeared to when I don't show up at the boarding house tonight."

There were many unanswerable questions, but the missionaries decided to keep a positive attitude and use their time to study and catch up on journal writing.

"At least we can *get* mail," said Elder McFarlane, trying to look on the bright side. And maybe we can tell the doctor our addresses and have someone, maybe Mrs. Drew, write to our families and explain why we can't write home."

"That's an excellent idea, Elder," said President Larsen.

"Just don't give that information to Dr. Hunt, as I'm sure he will just burn it," Elder Rappleye chuckled.

William and the other missionaries were able to write a letter and Dr. Wilder would copy it onto his own paper, then mail it to each elder's family so they would be informed of the missionaries' condition.

As for the food situation, the landlady gave the missionaries full access to the kitchen where they took turns preparing meals. This was an adventure, as none of the elders had any culinary experience. Potatoes became a staple. They couldn't mess them up too badly.

Burlington, Vermont
February 1912

Carrie, after cleaning up the last of the supper dishes, left the kitchen in search of her bedroom. As she passed the parlor, she heard her mother ask her father about Elder McFarlane. Glancing at the clock on the wall, she realized that it was very late for the missionaries to still be out.

Emily put down her needlework and frowned. "It's really late. Do you suppose he's gone for the night? Surely he would let us know."

"I don't know, Emily. The elders are not generally out past nine o'clock. It's well past ten."

"Do you think I should lock up, or leave the door open for him?"

Before Aaron could answer, there was a knock at the door. It was Dr. Hunt. "I just thought you should know those Mormon missionaries are all under quarantine at Mrs. Warnes' boarding house."

Mrs. Drew's face went from concern to fright. "What are they quarantined for?"

"Smallpox." For being such a serious illness, Dr. Hunt looked not only unconcerned for the welfare of the missionaries, but plain smug.

"That's horrible!" Carrie said, as she entered the room after overhearing the conversation. "Who has it?"

"Don't worry, Carrie, none of your friends, the missionaries, have it. One of the other tenants does, though, so we had to quarantine all of them."

Relief mixed with a severe dislike for Dr. Hunt and his irreverent attitude toward the missionaries flooded Carrie's emotions. "Would you mind keeping us informed of their well-being, Dr. Hunt?" Carrie asked sweetly, trying hard to contain her disdain for the man.

"I will keep you informed. And here, this is for you," the doctor said, handing Carrie a note.

"Is it from the elders?"

"The who?"

"The eld ... the missionaries."

"Absolutely not. They are not allowed to send notes or anything else from that germ-infested apartment. The note is from me. Just read it and consider it, Carrie."

Dr. Hunt left Carrie and her parents stunned. "Can you believe the nerve of that man? He wouldn't mind if all the missionaries contracted smallpox and died." She opened the letter and her jaw dropped.

"What is it, dear?" her mother asked.

"This takes the cake." Carrie's eyes scanned the letter again in disbelief. "Not only is Dr. Hunt rude and unfeeling toward the missionaries, but in this note he apologizes for leaving so abruptly last week and informs me that his offer of marriage is still on the table. As if I would ever marry a man with the manners of a goat!"

Aaron smiled and his shoulders bobbed up and down while his daughter, who was certainly not a little girl anymore, went on about Dr. Hunt. "Well, I have to agree, sweet Carrie, Dr. Hunt showed a bit of promise in the beginning, but I do believe you can do much better than a goat."

His comments lightened the mood for the three of them, as they all began to laugh. Then the concern for the missionaries contracting smallpox set in again, sobering the lot of them.

"I will take soup and bread to the Warnes' place tomorrow," said Carrie.

"I think that is a fine idea. I will help you. Maybe if we keep them well fed, the missionaries can avoid contracting that horrible, disfiguring disease."

It was settled. While the Drews couldn't provide food every day for the elders, they could feed them a couple of times a week.

In the meantime, Josiah Taylor made a few more appearances at the boarding house. Carrie enjoyed his company, but sometimes wondered at his motives. It was customary to visit when there was a chaperone available, which Mr. Taylor seldom did, and he also never asked to call on her.

Carrie expressed her concerns to Eva, as they spent their evenings together quite often. "Why do you suppose Josiah comes by the boarding house so often, yet never calls to court me?"

"It's a mystery to me," said Eva. Maybe you should tell him about Dr. Hunt's proposal and see if that spurs him into action." She gave Carrie a crooked smile.

"Be serious, Eva. I think I should like to get better acquainted with Josiah, but his visits are so short and I'm always a bit worried about being alone with him. He likes to sit very close to me ... but it just feels wrong."

"But he's so handsome, Carrie. I wouldn't mind if he wanted to sit close to me."

Carrie just rolled her eyes and moved on to another subject. "How has work been going at the diner? Is Mr. Rollender still making you take double shifts?"

"Yes, ever since the outbreak of smallpox, we've been working with half our staff. I'm afraid I shall be working breakfast and lunch shifts until the end of winter."

"Just wash your hands a lot, Eva. I don't know what I'd do if you got that horrible disease."

"Oh, I already do. Mr. Rollender has a basin of hot, soapy water that he makes us all scrub in when we get to the diner, and several times during our shift, as well. Do you see how red and raw my poor hands are looking?" Eva held out her hands for Carrie to examine.

"I'm not so worried about your hands as I am your eyes," Carrie replied.

Wrinkling her forehead, Eva asked, "And why is that?"

"You must not see very well because your hands look perfect to me, that's why."

The girls laughed and enjoyed a pleasant visit for the rest of the evening.

The next day was warmer than usual for January. This brought in a few more customers to the diner. Eva, working her second shift of the day, began to tire when the dinner crowd arrived.

As she rounded a corner, prepared to take the order of a family who just took their seats, Eva stopped dead in her tracks. "Afton," she whispered to the other waitress, "can you trade me tables? I'll take this one over here, if you take the one just seated."

Afton gave Eva a questioning look, but then shrugged her shoulders and agreed.

Eva was careful to keep her distance as she watched Josiah Taylor, and what looked to be his wife and small son, perusing the menu. Why, I ought to go give him a piece of my mind, she thought. That certainly explains why he only sees Carrie at the boarding house ... Maybe I am jumping to conclusions, Eva hoped. After all, he could be entertaining relatives.

Just then, she heard the little boy say to Josiah, "Papa, can I get the meat loaf?"

Nope, I wasn't wrong. Josiah Taylor is a snake, and Carrie needs to know it.

Eva didn't follow her impulse and tell Josiah off, as she didn't wish to cause a scene, nor did she want to be the one to break the bad news to his wife. So she stayed out of his line of vision and just seethed in silence. "What am I going to tell Carrie?" she kept asking herself.

Once Eva was off the clock, she thought about going straight over to the Drews' boarding house to tell Carrie exactly what kind of man

Josiah Taylor was, but still couldn't find the words. She decided to ponder on it a little longer. She headed for home instead.

With each step she took toward her home, the angrier Eva became. Finally arriving, she flung the door open and stomped into the house. She didn't even notice the doctors in the parlor speaking with her parents.

"There she is now," Eva's mother said in a worried voice.

Eva peered into the parlor, "What is it, Mother?"

"Oh Eva, Jimmy has smallpox."

Eva's heart sank to her feet. She knew too well what this meant for their family and her little brother, Jimmy. She watched with a heavy heart while the quarantine sign went up on the door and a policeman was stationed outside the house. "I'll not be able to warn Carrie about Josiah for several weeks now," she murmured sadly.

⸺

A few days had passed since Carrie had seen Eva. She thought Eva would come by after one of her shifts at work, as she usually did since she began working overtime. But she hadn't, so Carrie decided to walk over to Eva's house after dinner at the boarding house.

Everything became clear once Carrie drew close enough to see the sign on the Savoy family's front door. A chill ran down her spine. Eva is my dearest friend; I don't know what I will do should I lose her to that dreadful disease.

Carrie returned home and penned Eva a letter expressing that very thought.

⸺

Burlington, Vermont
February 1912

Thirteen days had passed since William and the other missionaries had been quarantined for smallpox. The woman who had been suffering from the disease improved a little bit each day. All looked forward to the quarantine being lifted any time now. They had gotten along well for being in such close quarters and having only a harmonica and a checkerboard as their entertainment. Thankfully, they were allowed to go out to the backyard for some fresh air. Elder Rappleye and Elder Brown took advantage of this luxury and also utilized the barn to get some exercise.

There was a knock at the door. All of the residents of the boarding house knew who it was, as only one visitor ever called on them. "Come in, Doctor Wilder."

"I've come to fumigate your home, Mrs. Warnes."

The clustering tenants all broke into wide grins, as this surely meant they would be set free soon.

"You are very lucky that nobody else has contracted smallpox. A couple of days after I fumigate, barring anyone else getting ill, I will lift the quarantine."

A cheer went up from the residents of Mrs. Warnes' boarding house.

Their celebration was short-lived, however, as not even a full day passed when another of the residents of the boarding house came down with symptoms of smallpox.

Mrs. Warnes knocked on the door to the basement apartment to deliver the news. "I'm sorry to have to tell you this, boys, but I think Mr. Birch now has smallpox. However, there is still hope, as there aren't any pocks on him as of yet and he *is* prone to sickness."

The four missionaries just looked at her as if she'd told them the world was coming to an end. "That can't be," Elder Brown said in a strangled tone. "The doctor fumigated."

"We won't know until we see some pocks appear, but for now, the quarantine remains."

There wasn't even a groan. William looked at his disheartened companions as they moved slowly back to whatever they had been doing.

"And," continued Mrs. Warnes, "... Elder McFarlane, is it?" she asked the newest of the group.

"Yes, ma'am, that's correct."

"You don't look so well yourself. How are you feeling?"

William thought Elder McFarlane had been looking rather pale, but wishful thinking kept him from bringing it up.

"Uh..."

Mrs. Warnes crossed the room and laid a hand on his forehead. Shaking her head, she said, "I'm sorry, son, you're burning up. Did you not notice?"

"I suppose I did. I was just hoping that it was all in my mind. I don't have any pocks. Perhaps it's just the flu."

"Perhaps, but at any rate, you need to be in bed resting, not playing checkers. And whatever you do, stay inside and keep warm."

"Yes, ma'am," said Elder McFarlane.

Once Mrs. Warnes left the room, William and President Larsen went straight to work preparing mustard water for Elder McFarlane to soak his feet in. Then they wrapped him up in blankets and set him by the radiator.

"If you can get a good sweat going, you can possibly get the sickness out of your system," President Larsen said.

It didn't work. Two days later Dr. Wilder returned to find both Mr. Birch and Elder McFarlane with pocks covering their faces.

William gave up his bed so Elder McFarlane could have his own in which to recuperate. This put three men in one bed — not a comfortable way to sleep. They tried sleeping three across the first night, then, after a horrible experience for all, changed things up by sleeping two lengthwise and one horizontally at the foot of the bed.

The doctor returned and gave vaccinations to all of the missionaries. This was almost worse than having the disease itself, as it caused swelling to spread from their inoculated arm across their chest and into their neck and head, making it hard to breathe.

"Elder Rappleye, why are you up?" whispered Elder Brown in the middle of the night, after being vaccinated.

"I can't sleep. I can barely breathe; my head feels as if it will burst and look at my arm — it's tight as a drum." He held up his black and blue, swollen arm. It felt even bigger than it looked, and it looked at least double in size. "I thought I would just walk around a bit to see if I could get sleepy. Sorry if I disturbed your sleep, Elder Brown."

"It's not a problem, Elder Rappleye." Elder Brown held up his bloated arm as if to show his empathy. "With you up walking around, there's more room on the bed." He chuckled softly. "Just wake me when you're tired and I'll take my turn walking the floor so you can sleep."

The men barely slept that night, and things failed to look better in the light of day. It was then that President Larsen was pronounced sick with smallpox. William watched as the once-optimistic elders became more and more discouraged.

By February 13th, the elders had been quarantined for twenty-five days. Elder Rappleye and Elder Brown were still healthy, except for the nasty side-affects from the vaccination. Still, being holed up for so long, especially when they wished to be doing what they were in Vermont to do, was hard.

"Elder Rappleye, you got a letter from home." Mrs. Warnes hoped to cheer William.

It worked. Just when he was beginning to think nobody from home was thinking of him, a letter came. As he read it, a lump formed in William's throat. The letter said many things, but what had the greatest impact and what he needed to hear most were three small yet powerful words, "Exercise your faith". A tear made a path down William's cheek as he read and reread the words of encouragement and comfort written by his mother.

The elders had given blessings to those who were sick at the onset, but with renewed confidence and faith, they determined to administer to the sick once again.

This, coupled with their individual prayers, wrought a miracle. The next time Dr. Wilder came to check on his patients, he declared them all healthy. "I've never seen such a quick recovery as you two have made," he said to Elder McFarlane and President Larsen.

"Perhaps we have been sufficiently humbled," said a weak President Larsen, with a smile.

"I will bring back the formaldehyde to fumigate again tomorrow, and, unless one or both of you boys get sick," he motioned to William and Elder Brown, "you will be set free the next day."

William didn't dare get his hopes up again, as disappointment had visited them before. But by day thirty-one of their confinement, all were declared healthy and free to leave the house.

He had a greater appreciation for his good health after the experience of being quarantined. All expressed their gratitude to the Lord for sparing their lives and allowing them to get back to the work they were sent there to do.

Burlington, Vermont
February 1912

Carrie filled many a cold winter day minding the boarding house and sending letters to her friend, Eva — still quarantined for smallpox. The missionaries, being quarantined as well, were safely tucked away and life at the Drews' boarding house was dull. Josiah Taylor was Carrie's only diversion. He still paid regular visits, but the fact that he never called on Carrie for an outing, or anything besides a visit at the boarding house, was frustrating to her. She enjoyed his company and wanted to spend more time with him — perhaps go to a picture show. She wanted to ask him why he didn't call on her, but she couldn't because it would be very forward and inappropriate.

She was just finishing a letter to Eva when the postman came through the front door. Carrie looked up to see him covered in wet, Vermont snow. She tried unsuccessfully to stifle a laugh. "I see it is still snowing out, Mr. Dunlap. I don't envy your job."

Shaking off some of the snow, the postman shivered dramatically, making Carrie laugh even more. "Sorry about the snow I'm tracking inside. I tried to shake it all off before I entered the house. It's definitely coming down out there. Never worry, though, my dear, your dependable postman will always bring you your mail." He winked.

Carrie was friendly with everyone in the area, but she particularly enjoyed the pleasant and optimistic personality of Mr. Dunlap. "Well, it just so happens that I have a letter for my friend, Eva, ready to be delivered. Your timing is impeccable. Not to mention, my mother just pulled out a batch of her famous oatmeal cookies."

"I thought I smelled something delicious coming from the kitchen."

"Mother fancies herself a bit of a gourmet chef when it comes to pastries and other baked goods. And we are only too happy to taste test any new recipes she tries."

"I believe your mother is, indeed, a gourmet cook." Mr. Dunlap breathed in the sweet aroma that filled the house. "She's never baked anything I haven't loved to sample."

"I will get you some cookies and warm cocoa. That should melt the icicles still hanging from your hair," Carrie teased.

She brought in the goodies and the two sat down to chat. "What have you heard about the houses quarantined for smallpox? Do you know how they are faring?" Carrie was not only interested in Eva's and the missionaries' homes, but also the Romprey's, some nearby neighbors, who had also been quarantined. This especially concerned Carrie, as they had six small children — the youngest, a newborn baby.

"Some of the signs have come down, but I believe the ones you are referring to, if I can tell by the letters you are sending out, are still under quarantine. Your neighbors, the Rompreys, have a particularly bad strain of the disease. I've heard Mrs. Romprey is especially ill."

The news broke Carrie's heart. She liked Mrs. Romprey very much, but even more, she worried about how Mr. Romprey would handle six children were anything to happen to his wife. "That's terrible. I wish winter would end and take all of the sickness away with it."

"Couldn't agree more." Mr. Dunlap emptied the cocoa mug, his tongue swiping across his chocolaty lips. "Oh, before I forget, here is the mail, and I couldn't help but notice that there is a letter in there for you." He dug through his bag and set an envelope in front of Carrie.

That familiar twinkle returned to her eyes, "It's a letter from my Uncle Arthur."

"Is he the one with all of the men's clothing stores — A. L. Foster Company, is it?"

"Yes, that's the one." Carrie clutched the letter, eager to read it.

"To think you are related to someone with so much wealth and prestige. It's almost like you are royalty." He gave Carrie a mock bow.

"Oh stop it, Mr. Dunlap," Carrie laughed.

"I do think it's time for me to leave you to your letter, *Your Highness*," the postman said, getting in one more gibe. "Thank you for the cookies and cocoa. Now I can face the wicked weather that awaits me outside."

Mr. Dunlap took his leave, which allowed Carrie some time to read her Uncle Arthur's letter. The words she read began to blur as tears filled her eyes. "Aunt Josephine is dead," the words wrenched out of Carrie's mouth, along with a loud sob.

"What is it, Carrie?" Her mother rushed into the room.

Carrie numbly handed her mother the letter. "Oh my. I'm so sorry, my dear girl. I know how much you loved her. Your Uncle Arthur must be devastated. He simply adored his wife." She put her arms around Carrie and pulled her into an embrace, hugging her as long as Carrie needed her.

When Carrie had recovered enough to read the rest of the letter, she brightened just a little. "Mother, it says here that my Uncle Arthur and my Aunt Julia, Arthur's sister, would like me to spend some time in Hartford with them. Oh, Mother, do you think I could do it? I've never met my Aunt Julia."

"I think it might be just the thing to help heal your uncle's aching heart. Carrie, you are a bit of sunshine wherever you are." She gave Carrie one more squeeze. "Let's talk to your father about it over supper tonight."

Eva was always happy to hear from Carrie and had the doctor write a few notes back to her in return, but she never ventured informing Carrie about seeing Josiah Taylor with his wife and young son at the diner. There would be a scandal if word got out. The Taylors were well known in the area. No, she would just have to wait until the quarantine was lifted to give Carrie the news. Thankfully, only two of Eva's family members contracted smallpox ... so far. She just prayed the quarantine would end soon. It was miserable being cooped up away from civilization.

Over liver and onions that evening, Carrie shared with her father the news of Aunt Josephine's death and the invitation to visit Hartford for a few weeks. "I know I would not be able to go yet, with all the sickness here and the number of people we are taking meals to — they are relying on us — but I think maybe in spring?"

Aaron appeared to be mulling it over while he ate a couple of bites of liver, smacked his lips and wiped his mouth. "I think we could spare you for a few weeks in the spring, if you would really like to go, Carrie."

"Oh, thank you, Father. I do wish to know my Aunt Julia. I wonder if she is anything like my birth mother."

"No one is more like your birth mother than you, my girl." Aaron's voice had grown soft and a bit husky.

Carrie glanced at her mother and saw that she was looking down at her plate in silence. "Mother, please do not think that because I am curious about my birth mother's family, that I love you any less. You have taken care of me my whole life long and I love you as if you gave me birth." She placed a gentle hand on top of Emily's.

"And I love you as well," Aaron said, planting a soft kiss on Emily's cheek.

"It's settled then." Emily gave herself a shake, as if ridding herself of her insecurities and smiled at the two people she loved most in this world. "You should go to Hartford with your uncle and aunt in the spring."

By the end of February, most of the people Carrie worried about were out of quarantine. All except for the Rompreys. The disease was too much for Mrs. Romprey and she eventually succumbed to it, leaving Mr. Romprey a widower and their six children, including baby Raymond, motherless. The disease was still making its rounds through the rest of the family. The Drews did what they could for the Rompreys, but until the quarantine was lifted, they couldn't help as much as they would have liked.

The missionaries were back to holding street and cottage meetings and Elder McFarlane was finally able to return to the Drews' boarding house.

When the elders returned with him, Carrie was so relieved that she ran to give them hugs. As William stumbled back a step, she realized that elders weren't allowed to show any physical affection to young ladies while serving a mission. She settled for a handshake, apologizing the whole time. "I'm just so happy that you are all right."

"Please don't apologize, Miss Drew. You are a sight for sore eyes. We are fine. Elder McFarlane, however, wasn't as lucky as Elder Brown and I were." William hurried to add, "But he's all right now."

Carrie looked from William to Elder McFarlane and felt tears prickling in the backs of her eyelids. Elder McFarlane looked like he'd been through a war, what with the pock scars covering his thin face. Carrie silently cursed the dreaded disease as she looked at the poor man's blemishes.

Elder Rappleye and Elder Brown hadn't gotten the disease; thank the heavens above, thought Carrie. She hadn't known until that moment just who was sick in the missionaries' home. They looked a bit pale from being inside, but otherwise seemed no worse for the wear.

"Miss Drew," Elder Rappleye stirred a cup of hot cocoa, "we are having a cottage meeting Thursday evening. I wonder ... would you be willing to sing a solo for us?"

He hesitated long enough that Carrie knew he'd struggled to work up the nerve to ask.

He continued, "You have a beautiful voice and I know it would add to the spirit of the meeting if you would agree to sing."

Her face warmed at the compliment. "I expected to be asked to play the piano as I have done before, but sing a solo? That's something I'm not accustomed to doing. I'm not much of a singer, but if you really want me to, I suppose I can do my best."

"That's where you are wrong, Miss Drew, you are a very good singer. Elder Brown and I can both attest to that."

Looking at Elder Rappleye doubtfully, she asked which song they would like her to sing so she could practice.

At the conclusion of their visit, Elder Rappleye took Carrie's hand to shake and thanked her for her willingness to help with the upcoming meeting. Her petite hand was so warm in his much larger hand that, as he looked intensely into Carrie's blue eyes, she sensed that he wished he could do more than shake it. A shiver ran up her arm and straight to her heart as she wished the same thing.

"Thank you for your kindness, Miss Drew," he said, still holding her hand and her gaze.

"You're most welcome." Carrie willed her heart to remain calm as she lingered in the clasp of his hands. But the familiar thud in her chest that accompanied his touch only accelerated.

As the elders were leaving, Josiah Taylor approached the boarding house. Carrie, having a view of all three of the men, couldn't help but observe the stark contrast. The missionaries had an aura about them that drew her in. It always felt good to have them in her home. Josiah Taylor, on the other hand, seemed to carry a dark countenance about him that Carrie had never noticed until that moment.

"Good day, Carrie," Josiah spoke in his friendliest voice.

"Hello Josiah, how are you doing today?" Now that Carrie could sense a very real difference in the demeanors of the men, she wasn't certain what to make of it — or what to make of Josiah Taylor. She felt as though she should be on her guard — from what, she didn't know.

Josiah made his usual conversation. They talked about the weather, the quarantines, his business and such. Since there were no other customers to tend to at the moment, they seated themselves on the settee. Josiah slipped his arm around Carrie, which she found a bit too familiar.

She decided to hang propriety, come out and ask him a few personal questions. After all, he was taking liberties she wasn't certain she was okay with.

"Josiah, why do you come here?"

"Why, I thought it was obvious. I come to see you. Would you rather I not come?"

"It's not that. I enjoy our visits."

"I thought so." Josiah lowered his head, his eyes on Carrie's lips.

Carrie was appalled and promptly pulled away before he was able to succeed in his goal. "Stop!"

"You just said you enjoy my visits. And Carrie, you *are* old enough to be with me without a chaperone. Please don't tell me you've never kissed a man before."

How did this get so turned around? Carrie was seething now. Do I explain, or just throw him out? "You have twisted my meaning if you thought, by my question, I was asking you to kiss me."

"Come now, Carrie, we have known each other long enough to—"

She cut him off. "We have known each other several months, but you have yet to even take me on an outing."

"I know how busy you are here. I didn't think you could go out," Josiah said in his defense.

Carrie looked around. "Does it really look busy to you? And even if it is busy, my mother handles things quite efficiently when I'm not here."

She wasn't certain that she really wanted to go out with Josiah after what had just passed between them, but she still waited to see what his response would be.

Josiah looked at his pocket watch and gasped, "Oh my, I have spent longer than I should have on my lunch break. We'll continue this conversation when I next visit."

Carrie just sat there. Somehow she had known he wouldn't give her the answers she needed. She silently stood up and saw Josiah out.

Closing the door behind her, Carrie slumped down to the floor, wondering what to make of the strange visit.

Burlington, Vermont
March 1912

The sun made an appearance on Thursday, making the evening warmer than previous nights. The snow stopped coming down and moonlight glistened across the blanket of white earth, which was good for the missionaries. They were certain that if it had kept snowing the way it had been, no one would dare venture out of their warm homes to attend a cottage meeting.

The three elders greeted people as they entered the home, while President Larsen made sure things were ready for their presentation.

More people showed up than expected. "I guess they missed us," Elder Brown whispered to Elder Rappleye.

"Or maybe they wanted to see how we looked after a month in quarantine," Elder Rappleye chuckled.

"Or, consider this," Elder McFarlane chimed in, "perhaps many of them were confronted with their own uncertain existence and, therefore, truly do want to hear our message tonight."

That bit of insight from Elder McFarlane sobered the other two as they looked at their pockmarked comrade's face.

"And if they don't wish to, they should," he concluded. "It was, indeed, a wake-up call for me. I can only imagine going through that horrible illness without the knowledge we possess of the plan of salvation."

The others agreed. While it was frustrating to be kept under a guard's watch for thirty-one days, it was also very frightening to be faced with the prospect of never returning home to see their loved ones again. This knowledge was what prompted the elders to pick "Eternal Life" as their chosen topic for that night's cottage meeting.

The Drews were among the first to arrive, as Carrie promised to sing at the onset of the meeting. They exchanged greetings and the missionaries showed them to their seats.

The meeting was called to order and after an opening hymn and a prayer, President Larsen announced a special musical number to be performed by Miss Carrie Drew.

Carrie was a petite five feet tall and very slender. William couldn't help but notice how small she looked standing in front of all those people. I hope I didn't ask too much of her, he thought.

The accompanist began and Carrie stood erect. As she began to sing the song, *I Know That My Redeemer Lives*, a sweet spirit entered the room. Her voice was like an angel, William thought, a lump forming in his throat.

Everyone else seemed to feel it, too. The room fell completely silent, except for her beautiful, singing voice. As Carrie sang the final note, there wasn't a dry eye in the audience. William composed himself enough to look up and meet Carrie's gaze. He nodded and tried to smile his thanks, but felt his eyes betray him as a tear found its way down his cheek. He would never forget how beautiful she looked and sounded as she sang about her Redeemer.

The song accomplished its purpose. With that sweet spirit thick in the room, the stage was set for the message the elders had prepared. Still struggling with his emotions, William was happy he wasn't billed as the first speaker.

The meeting went well. At the conclusion William sought out Carrie to thank her for singing. He had to wait in line, however, as many others had the same idea. Finally, William made it to the front of the line. He took Carrie's hand in both of his and said in a low voice, "Don't you ever say that you can't sing, Miss Drew. I've never heard that song sound so beautiful. I can't thank you enough." He stopped there, lest he become emotional again. He gave her hand a squeeze, then stepped away so others could speak with her.

There were plenty of people waiting to talk to William and the other missionaries, as well. Their message seemed to have struck a chord with those in attendance. They were able to make several appointments to meet with investigators. William could hardly stop smiling; so happy to again be back doing missionary work.

It was mid-March and the time had come for missionary transfers. William had mixed feelings. He was comfortable in Burlington and the prospect of being transferred felt like leaving home again. He loved the people here. Still, it was always a bit exciting to go to a new area and meet new people. What William had learned, thus far, was that there were good people everywhere he had served — sometimes ignorant, sometimes rude, but for the most part, decent, well-meaning people.

There were six elders in Burlington now. Elder Snow and Elder Madsen arrived while the others were under quarantine. William was happy there were at least two missionaries in the area who escaped the smallpox epidemic; although, without any leadership available, the two hadn't accomplished much in the way of missionary work.

All together now, the missionaries held a meeting to receive their new assignments. William, Elder Madsen and Elder Brown were billed for Sherbrooke, in the province of Quebec, Canada.

They were given very little notice of the transfer, and so made quick work of visiting all of their Burlington friends — now more like family. Knowing they would return at the end of summer made it easier to say goodbye.

William's heart ached as he said his goodbyes to Carrie. He wished he could give her a hug or even tell her of his feelings for her, but he couldn't — and he didn't.

The very next day, the elders were on a train bound for Sherbrooke, stopping only in St. Johns, then Montreal. They finally arrived at their destination on Thursday, March 14, 1912.

The first order of business was to find a boarding house. Country work wouldn't begin until later in the season. Therefore, they needed a home base. Thankfully, they accomplished this without too much trouble. As soon as their belongings were settled, they went straight to work tracting.

"The snow is even deeper here in Canada," commented Elder Madsen, trying to keep his balance on the white sidewalk.

"That it is," agreed William.

Before Elder Brown was able to put in his two cents worth, he suddenly disappeared, sinking into a watery hole up to his knees. "Oh my, and it's colder here, too."

The three of them chuckled as they hurried back to the boarding house so Elder Brown could change his soggy trousers, ribbing him along the way about being swallowed up in the hole. They also took the opportunity to warm up before hitting the streets again.

"Did you hear that?" asked William, cupping his ear to the door. "Someone is out there going on about Mormons."

All three men quieted in order to hear the conversation.

"Those Mormon missionaries are sent by the devil himself, Mrs. Alcott. You must be careful with them staying here under the same roof as yourself," came the voice just beyond their bedroom door.

"It's almost as if he is talking so loud in order for us to hear him," Elder Brown said.

"It's impossible to not hear him." William grimaced.

"As your pastor, I will be keeping an eye on you, Mrs. Alcott. I don't want them filling your head with stories of this Joseph Smith character."

He had the elders' full attention now as he listed a number of untruths about Joseph Smith and the Church in general.

William had heard all he could take. Stepping out of the room, he cleared his throat. "It is kind of you to look out for Mrs. Alcott's well-being, Pastor. I feel certain that, however, if you're intent on spreading rumors, you would like to know the truth about those things you seem to be quite unclear about."

The pastor, whether he wished the elders to overhear him or not, surely didn't want to be corrected by them. Fumbling over his words, he began reciting, once again, all the things he had just told Mrs. Alcott.

The three missionaries couldn't get a word in until he was finished. Then they calmly pointed out his errors. Their discussion went on for another two hours.

When the pastor finally took his leave, William said, "I doubt he will change his views about the Mormons; nor will he stop warning people about us. But at least we had our say."

"Of course he won't change his views. Being a pastor is his livelihood. If he ever admitted that his information was incorrect, he would have to close up shop," added Elder Brown.

Elder Madsen, the newest missionary in the group, was still a bit flabbergasted at the whole situation. "Do you come across many people as narrow-minded as the pastor?"

Elder Rappleye and Elder Brown chuckled. "Oh you're just getting a small nibble of what is to come, Elder Madsen," Elder Brown replied.

As news of Mormon missionaries proselytizing on the streets of Sherbrooke got out, William and his companions were disheartened to see more and more anti-Mormons surface. The elders went as far as taking it up with the mayor, as they had been threatened with being prosecuted — for what, they weren't sure — but the mayor's only advice to the three was to pack it up and leave town, stating they had quite enough religion in Sherbrooke.

"Look at this, Elders." William pointed to a newspaper article in the morning paper he was reading over breakfast.

The heading was bold,
"CITY COUNCIL IS AFTER THE MORMONS"
William read it aloud. "One of the features of the meeting was a petition, submitted by Mr. T. J. Parkes, asking the Council to take immediate steps to stop the Mormon elders from working in this city. In supporting his petition before the Council, Mr. Parkes said that the movement threatened the sanctity of our homes, the very heart of

our national existence. These Mormon elders believe in the Book of Mormon, and the Book of Mormon believes in plural marriages. In his opinion, the Mormon propaganda was one of prostitution, and cases had been reported where young women had been inveigled to Utah where they were maltreated—"

"That's hogwash!" interrupted Elder Madsen. "Read what the petition says."

William dropped his gaze down to the formal petition and read,

> *To His Worship the Mayor and the Aldermen of the City of Sherbrooke:*
>
> *Gentlemen, May I ask you to take some steps to stop the propaganda now being carried on by the so-called elders of the Mormon Church in this city. So far as their religion is concerned, I have nothing to say, but as their tenets aim directly at the root of our present civilization by destroying the sanctity of the home-life, I think the matter well within the purview of your Council and could be dealt with either by a reference to the City Attorney or the Chief of Police.*
>
> *Very faithfully yours, THOS. J. PARKES*

Elder Madsen looked like he wanted to punch something.

"This isn't the first time this has happened, nor will it be the last, Elder Madsen," William said calmly. "We just need to keep on tracting until they force us to leave. If we're lucky, it won't come to that."

Burlington, Vermont
March 1912

Carrie hummed a happy tune as she stood on tip toes to dust the top shelf of a bookcase.

"Why so happy, Carrie?" asked Emily, as she passed through the room.

"It's Eva." Carrie put the feather duster in its resting place and gave Emily her full attention. "She finally has a free night. That means she's coming over. I haven't seen her since her family was quarantined."

"That was several weeks ago, wasn't it?" Emily paused to recall when she last saw Eva.

"Yes. Then, once she got out of quarantine, she worked double shifts to cover for others who were still sick. Plus, after not working for so long, she really needed the money."

When Eva arrived at the Drews' boarding house, she was welcomed with warm hugs and smiles from Carrie and her parents. After the Drews inquired about the Savoy family's health, Eva pulled Carrie aside.

"Carrie, can we speak in your room?"

"Of course. Is everything okay? You look worried about something."

"Yes, I just really need to talk to you."

After Eva and Carrie closed the bedroom door and situated themselves comfortably on the bed, everything Eva had been holding in all month about Josiah came tumbling out.

Carrie's mouth grew slack — stunned. "He has a wife and child? You're certain?" Her face lost all color. "Eva, he tried to kiss me just two days ago."

Now Eva appeared to be stunned. She looked at Carrie and saw something akin to an expression made after eating spoiled food. "Are you all right, Carrie? I didn't want you to get hurt by that snake, but I couldn't tell you any sooner because of the quarantine."

"I'm all right. His kind words and flattery made me feel good, but there was always something amiss about his character that I couldn't quite put my finger on. Now I know what it is." Carrie grabbed the nearest pillow from her bed and lobbed it across the room. "He has some nerve. I shall have to think on how I will handle it if he ever returns."

"Why wouldn't he return, Carrie?"

"I sort of skewered him with questions about why he never took me out, and after his failed attempt at a kiss, he became defensive and left. It's all for the better, I suppose. Oh Eva, I've just been so lonely without you, and now the missionaries are gone—"

"What? Which missionaries are gone?"

"That's right, you wouldn't have heard. Elders Rappleye, Brown and Madsen are now serving in Canada."

"Canada!" Eva began to sniffle. "Would it be improper to write to him ... I mean them?"

Carrie's face broke into a slow grin, "Him? Him who?"

Eva's face turned positively beet red. After sputtering about, she finally came clean. "Elder Rappleye! Oh Carrie, I think I'm in love with him."

Carrie's eyes widened. "How in the world can you be in love with Elder Rappleye? You've only been around him a handful of times, and never since before the quarantines."

"I don't know." Eva shrugged. "He's just so handsome and kind, and did I say handsome?" Her eyes took on a dreamy look. "I want to marry someone just like him one day."

Carrie, amused by this, also felt a twinge of jealousy. She didn't think Elder Rappleye held any special affection for Eva, but did he for her? She certainly felt sparks fly when he looked into her eyes, especially after she sang at the cottage meeting. She opted not to say a word about that experience lest Eva break down into a fit of the vapors.

"You know, Eva, Elder Rappleye hails from way out west in Wyoming. It's a long way from the city in rough and rugged country. Do you think you love him enough to pack everything up and move out to the middle of nowhere?"

"I would go anywhere for Elder Rappleye." Eva exhaled a long sigh.

"Well, at least I know that being under quarantine hasn't dampened your spirits," she teased. "As far as writing to Elder Rappleye, or any of the missionaries, perhaps you should wait to see if they write to you first."

"But that might not ever happen. I should declare my love now, so Elder Rappleye knows how I feel."

"Eva, that's not a good idea. Remember they are here on the Lord's errand and cannot court the women they meet. If you write anything at all, it should be words of encouragement to help them remain focused."

Eva frowned. "If he writes to you, you'll tell me, will you not?"

"I promise," Carrie said, squeezing her friend's hand.

⌒

Services were held for Mrs. Romprey on a cold, rainy day, which felt appropriate. The family had recovered from smallpox, but the lot of them looked so forlorn. Carrie's heart ached for them.

Mrs. Drew approached Mr. Romprey, who looked, by far, to be in the worst shape. He was holding onto his youngest child — just a baby — almost as if he were a rag doll. "I wonder, Mr. Romprey," Emily began, "if perhaps you could use some help with your children now that they are motherless?" She gently held her hands out to Raymond, the little tot in his father's arms.

Mr. Romprey stared at Emily for only a moment before handing the child off to her. "I would very much appreciate the help. Most of the young'uns are fine, but I don't do so well taking care of Raymond here. If you could just care for him for a while ... you know, until I get back on my feet ... after being quarantined and all. I would much appreciate it."

Carrie knew her mother longed to rear more children and would be only too happy to help out with Raymond. Emily had been unable to have children of her own, but with Carrie, then Clara and now Raymond living under her loving care, her need to nurture could be satisfied.

Aaron seemed to come to the same conclusion as Carrie, as he gazed up to the heavens and smiled his thanks. "God truly works in mysterious ways," he whispered.

What the Drews thought would be days taking care of Raymond became weeks, then months. Carrie worried that her mother would find it difficult to relinquish the baby, once Mr. Romprey wanted him back. Taking care of Raymond wasn't an easy task, as he ate a special diet for his delicate system, but Carrie watched as Emily became equal to the task and clearly loved Raymond as her own.

"Aaron?" Emily whispered one evening as she held the slumbering baby Raymond.

Aaron looked up from his newspaper. Carrie looked up as well.

"Why do you suppose Mr. Romprey hasn't inquired about his baby? Certainly he's missing him by now. It's been several months."

"Are you becoming weary of caring for Raymond?" Aaron looked concerned.

"Oh no, Aaron, it's not that. I have grown to love Raymond a great deal. I guess I'm worried that Mr. Romprey will come to claim him after I have lost my heart to the boy."

"Perhaps it's time to pay Mr. Romprey a visit and see how things stand?"

Emily nodded her head slightly. "I'm sure you are right."

The following morning, Carrie and Emily walked to the Romprey residence. Emily's hand shook as she reached up to knock on the door. "What if Mr. Romprey wants Raymond back, Carrie? I mean, look how healthy he's become under our care." She carried Raymond protectively on her hip. Carrie watched as the boy clung to Emily. Emily kissed him on the head.

Mr. Romprey opened the door. His health looked to be improved, but not his disposition. He looked down at his son as if he were a stranger.

Once inside, Emily seemed to muster up the courage to ask the question that was hanging in the air. "Mr. Romprey, will you want Raymond back in the near future?" Her voice trembled. "It's just ... I worry about him becoming too attached."

Mr. Romprey lowered his head as if ashamed before he answered, "Since my wife passed away, life has been harder than I expected — as I'm sure you can imagine. If you are agreeable to keeping Raymond, it would be most helpful."

"Adopt him?" Emily's face lit up.

"No, nothing legal like that, mind you, just ..." He lifted his shoulders and held his palms up, fingers splayed. "Keep him."

Carrie was confused and felt certain that Emily was, too. "But what if you change your mind? After all the months Mother has cared for and loved Raymond, it would *devastate* her."

"I promise to never change my mind. Just raise him as your own. I just don't want to get into the legalities of it all. It's obvious he is happy with you. He doesn't even seem to recognize me."

Emily let out a sigh of relief. "Oh, thank you, Mr. Romprey. Carrie's right. I do love him and will rear him as best I can."

As time passed, Mr. Romprey never did ask for Raymond back. In fact, he appeared to be relieved to be rid of another mouth to feed. Carrie thought him quite heartless to act as if the boy never existed, but she was happy that her mother could raise another child, this one from infancy.

As the days warmed, Carrie looked forward to her trip to Hartford, Connecticut. She had never been to her Uncle Arthur's home. Judging by his fine clothing and his motorcar, she imagined it to be a grand place.

In his last letter, Arthur had asked Carrie if sometime in mid-April would be a good time for him and Julia to pick her up and bring her back home with them for an extended stay.

She wrote him back:

"Uncle Arthur, mid-April will work out very well for me to go with you and Aunt Julia to stay at your home in Connecticut. I very much look forward to the trip. Let us say Monday, April 15th?"

And so it was settled. Carrie danced about her work, daydreaming about her upcoming stay in Hartford, as well as meeting Julia, and possibly others in her birth mother's family.

A couple of weeks passed before Josiah Taylor came to the boarding house again. Carrie was ready.

Armed with the information Eva had provided, she invited Josiah to sit down before she started her well-practiced statements.

Carrie's lip twitched, struggling to keep her many emotions in check. "I think I understand, now, why it is that you've not called on me for an outing, Mr. Taylor."

"Carrie, why so formal? I thought we'd gotten past that."

"No, I believe it is proper for me to call you Mr. Taylor, seeing how you are married and have a family."

Josiah's face flushed. "H ... how did ... I mean, what are you talking about, Carrie?"

"Please don't try to deny it. And please don't come back." She stood up and exited the room, passing her mother, who entered, piercing Josiah with a searing look.

Carrie could hear Josiah rush to the rack where his coat and hat were hanging. Then, the door shut. She had done the right thing, she knew, but hearing the door close that final time hurt.

"Carrie, I'm pretty sure we are done with Mr. Taylor," her mother called out.

Carrie came back to her mother's side, a little bit teary. "And I had thought he was going to be someone special."

Her mother wrapped her loving arms around Carrie and said, "There is someone very special out there for you, my girl, and you will be so happy that you waited for just the right man. I feel it."

"Thank you, Mother. I'm sure you are right."

Sherbrooke, Canada
April 1912

Fortunately for the missionaries, Mr. Parkes' petition to curtail their efforts fell flat and the elders carried on their work. William realized that as long as there were men and women willing to dedicate time and energy to spreading the Gospel of Jesus Christ, Satan, the adversary, would put people such as Mr. Parkes in their path to thwart the work. William had also come to know that that was no reason to throw in the towel. No, William might get discouraged now and then, but his fire never burned out. He had witnessed miracles as he watched people's lives change in response to the gospel while he served his mission, and his testimony grew stronger.

"Why are the streets so crowded today?" Elder Madsen tried to edge his way through the mass of people to see what the attraction was.

Just then a train whistle blew. "It looks like they are trying to get near the tracks," said William. "There," he pointed, "there's an empty spot. Let's take a seat and see what the commotion is about."

Elder Rappleye, Elder Madsen and Elder Brown crowded together on a grassy knoll near the tracks.

Elder Madsen narrowed his eyes at the scene before him. "What do you suppose? I've never seen —"

"I believe it's a funeral." William squinted into the morning sun.

"But on a train?" Elder Madsen looked confused.

"The engine is draped in black and purple — aren't those mourning colors?" observed Elder Brown.

"Yes, and didn't we read that the president of the Grand Trunk Railroad, a Mr. Hays, I believe, was killed in that horrible accident on the Atlantic Ocean?" William's forehead creased as he recalled the article he'd read documenting the disaster.

"Ahh, now it makes sense. I guess it's appropriate to have his funeral procession on the tracks instead of the road," said Elder Madsen.

A few weeks prior, the news had spread fast; there was a terrible accident in the Atlantic Ocean. A magnificent passenger liner from Britain, the RMS Titanic, had hit an iceberg and sunk, killing over 1,500 people.

It was a tragedy, to be sure, but a bit surreal for the elders, since they were far removed from the accident. Now, however, seeing the funeral procession of Mr. Hays play out before their eyes, the whole terrible event became real.

The elders sat in reverent silence as the engine and the car carrying Mr. Hays' body slowly made its way down the tracks. Men removed their hats and women wept. Hays had been well-respected and would be missed.

"Do you remember what the obituary said about Mr. Hays in the newspaper? You know the last thing he said to ... I believe it was a colonel?" Elder Brown scratched his head.

Elder Rappleye thought for a minute before recalling the quote. "I think he was quoted by a Colonel Gracie as saying something about three big ocean liners all spending their time and money one-upping each other. They all want to be the most luxurious and fastest. He said that sooner or later there will be a disaster."

"He got that right. Now he's dead," said Elder Brown. "I wonder if that was some sort of premonition."

Once the crowds cleared, the elders made their way back to the boarding house for their noonday meal. It felt somewhat disrespectful to start tracting again immediately, while people were still grieving.

A few days later the three elders took some time to walk down town to pick up their laundry and mail. It was always nice to have errands to run on such a pretty, spring day. After all, most spring days in Sherbrooke were rainy and cold.

After retrieving their mail, Elder Rappleye and Elder Brown were perusing their letters when they realized Elder Madsen wasn't behind them.

"Who is Elder Madsen speaking with?" Elder Rappleye turned to take a few steps toward the lagging missionary.

"I'm not sure."

"Oh no, it can't be ... " William stopped in his tracks.

Who?... Who can't it be?"

"Look at the building they are standing in front of. The Sun Life building. Isn't that where Mr. Parkes, who tried to get us run out of town, works?"

"Elders!" hollered Elder Madsen. "Do either of you have any literature on you?"

William looked at Elder Brown. They both wore the same confused expressions. "I have some, Elder Madsen," Elder Brown hollered back.

"I have a bad feeling about this, Elder," William said.

Mr. Parkes was overly friendly, bending over backwards to apologize to the elders about the petition and explaining that he was sure it was just a misunderstanding. "Please let me make it up to you boys. May I purchase one of your books of literature?"

Elder Brown dug one of his books out of his bag and handed it to Elder Madsen, who then handed it to Mr. Parkes.

"Oh, dear, I don't have any money with me. Will you please just come up to my office so I can get some coins?"

William began shaking his head, clearly nervous about following Mr. Parkes anywhere, but he couldn't just stay there while the other two walked into a den of lions. "It's okay, Mr. Parkes, you can just have the book."

"Nonsense. I work in this building right here. Come on in. It will only take a few minutes." The kindness dripped off his tongue like syrup. The elders followed him.

William noticed three people sitting in Mr. Parkes' office. Not working. Just watching and waiting. *I wonder why three employees are just sitting here doing nothing.* The hair on the back of his neck stood up.

In the meantime Elder Brown had opened one of his letters from home and was looking at a view of Salt Lake City.

"Whatcha got there?" Mr. Parkes asked, feigning interest in Elder Brown's pictures.

"These are views of where I'm from." Elder Brown held the picture up proudly.

"Those look mighty fine. How much will you sell them for?" Mr. Parkes asked.

"Oh, these are not for sale."

"Fiddlesticks! You can surely get more, can't you?"

"Well, I suppose I can, but—"

"Then I'll take these three," Mr. Parkes said, pointing at three of the pictures. "I'll pay you a quarter for them."

"Here, you can just have them. Like you said, I can get more."

"Come now, I know you boys could use a little extra money. Just take my quarter."

"But they are not worth more than a nickel. Just take them."

"I insist!" Mr. Parkes shoved the quarter into Elder Brown's hand and took the three pictures of Salt Lake City. "Now, I must get back to work. You boys have a good day."

As the elders parted company from Mr. Parkes, William had a feeling of foreboding. Evidently, Elder Brown did as well. "Do you two feel like we were just hornswaggled?" he muttered as they exited the building.

The other two just nodded their heads in agreement.

After the elders got home and had a small meal, there was a knock on the door. It was the High Constable calling. He had with him a written warrant for Elder Brown and Elder Madsen for selling merchandise without a license.

"I knew it was too good to be true." Elder Brown slapped his hand hard on the nearest wall. "Mr. Parkes won't give up until he's driven us out of town."

"Come with me, boys. Your trial is set for two o'clock."

They entered the courtroom and saw Mr. Parkes there, looking smug, along with the three people he had conveniently planted in his office to serve as witnesses of the transaction.

The elders attempted to explain to the judge what Mr. Parkes had done to ensnare them and how they didn't wish to take money for any of the literature or the pictures, but did so at Mr. Parkes' insistence. The judge just shut them down.

"You can either pay a fine of five dollars plus the court fees, or spend thirty days in jail. Which will it be?"

"How much are the court fees?" mumbled Elder Brown.

"They come to thirty-three dollars."

The whole thing looked ... smelled ... rotten to the elders. The fees were exorbitant! But through some miracle, by pooling their money, they were able to come up with just the right amount to pay the trumped-up charges.

This didn't please Mr. Parkes at all. "Your honor," he said, "I have another complaint to put in about these men."

The judge lowered his bushy, grey eyebrows. He was beginning to look fed up with Mr. Parkes' use, or abuse, of the judicial system. "Mr. Parkes, I believe we've been here long enough today. You men are excused." The gavel hit the wood and the matter was closed.

The elders walked back to their boarding house penniless, but happy they didn't have to spend the next month in jail. "When have we ever carried so much money on our persons?" asked Elder Madsen.

"Never," answered Elder Rappleye as he yanked the apartment door open. "And I don't believe it to be a coincidence, either."

"A month in jail would have been worse than the month we spent in quarantine," chimed in Elder Brown.

"There is no doubt about that," agreed Elder Rappleye.

"How long until we are able to do a country trip do you think?" Elder Madsen plunked himself down on the sofa.

"Soon. Once the weather has decided to stay warm instead of being fickle, we will embark on our country work." Elder Brown followed Elder Madsen's lead and collapsed onto the sofa, adjusting his position after feeling a hard spot where a spring had popped through the cushion.

"I don't mind saying that it will be nice to get away from this area," sighed Elder Madsen.

They all agreed.

Burlington, Vermont
April 1912

Carrie flew to the window of Mrs. Drew's boarding house. Sure enough, the motorcar she heard coming down the street was Uncle Arthur's. Her bags were packed and waiting by the front door. Carrie was ready for a new adventure, and this would be a fine one, she thought. She only wished her Aunt Josephine were still alive. That would make the trip perfect.

"Uncle Arthur." Carrie walked into Arthur's arms as he pulled her into a bear hug.

"The older you get, my sweet girl, the more you look like your mother." Arthur held Carrie back to take a good look at her.

"Uncle Arthur, I'm so sorry about Aunt Josephine."

Arthur's eyes misted and he pulled Carrie back into an embrace. "Winter has been hard on a lot of people."

Carrie could attest to that, as she had seen an unusual amount of quarantine signs in the neighborhood over the past several months — including the ones posted on the homes of the missionaries, the Rompreys and the Savoys.

"Having you spend time at my home will do me some good. I'll have to stop feeling sorry for myself and show you the town." Arthur cleared his throat to compose himself once more. "Oh, and I nearly forgot Julia."

Julia, Arthur's sister, moved from beside him and extended her arms to hug Carrie. "Hello, Carrie. I'm so happy to finally meet you. Arthur has nothing but good things to say about you."

Carrie blushed a bit before responding. "Uncle Arthur is much too kind, I assure you."

She noticed that Julia's eyes were also misting up. Oh dear, I must have said something wrong, she realized.

Noticing the concern on Carrie's face, Julia was quick to reassure her, "I'm fine, Carrie, it's just that my brother is right. You look so very much like my sister — your mother — it kind of took my breath away. I've missed her dearly. I shall love getting to know you better in the weeks to come. I'm so happy you have agreed to spend some time with us."

Carrie relaxed her shoulders. "I look forward to our time together as well," she added with a smile.

After saying her goodbyes to her mother and father, Carrie, Arthur and Julia were on their way to Hartford, Connecticut.

Having never been so far away from home, Carrie couldn't help but be excited as she watched the scenery from the roofless motorcar. And Arthur kept up his tradition of spontaneously handing her ten-dollar bills along the way.

When they approached Arthur's home in Hartford, he looked back at Carrie, clearly awaiting her expression. She didn't disappoint. Her jaw dropped as her eyes took in the most magnificent Tudor-style mansion she had ever seen. It was beautiful, as were the lush grounds surrounding it.

"Oh my, Uncle Arthur. I never imagined your home to be so enormous."

Arthur just grinned, obviously happy to see the excitement dancing in her eyes.

Carrie took to Julia right away and couldn't help but wonder about her birth mother. Over some toast and orange juice one Sunday morning, Carrie decided to brave the waters and ask. "Aunt Julia," she began, feeling shy, "were you and my mother close?"

Julia put a warm hand atop Carrie's and gave it a squeeze, as if to tell her that her questions were welcome. "Your mother and I were very close when we were young. But after I married and moved away, we grew distant. I've always feared she resented me."

Carrie narrowed her eyes in confusion.

"You see," Julia continued, "when our mother died, Father sent Carrie — your mother, that is — to live with some relatives she'd never met before in Barre. I offered to have her come live with us, but Father insisted she needed more parental role figures than Frank and me." Julia wiped her mouth with a monogrammed napkin and sat silent for a moment. "I don't believe she knew I offered to have her." She shrugged her shoulders and her lips turned down into a frown. "But enough of that. Arthur and I are having a grand time spoiling you. You are just the diversion he needed. Tomorrow we have a wonderful shopping trip planned, so rest up today."

The next day Julia and Arthur took Carrie uptown to shop, as promised. When they reached Fox's Department Store, Arthur said, "Carrie, I want you to pick out a new outfit — anything you want. The only stipulation is that you don't check the price tags."

"Oh, no, Uncle Arthur, I couldn't. That is much too generous."

Julia grabbed Carrie by the arm. "Yes you can, Carrie. Arthur is good for it. Let's have some fun."

Hesitant at first, Carrie began trying on dresses, but she never failed to look at the price tags until her aunt scolded her. "Stop doing that, Carrie! Pretend everything in here is free. What would you choose then?"

That was all it took. Carrie let go of her hesitation and simply enjoyed being treated like royalty.

The shopping spree resulted in a beautiful lavender, silk dress, with shoes to match, along with a hat complete with peacock plumes. Carrie had never felt so pretty.

Over the next days and weeks Carrie continued her adventures. While the three of them traveled about the state, Carrie met many other relatives she hadn't known previously. She never knew there were so many Fosters. She found most of them delightful, but a few seemed to put on airs, which didn't impress her in the least. That was something she loved about Uncle Arthur. Although very wealthy — a self-made millionaire — he didn't act as if he were any better than Carrie's humble family in Vermont.

She was enjoying her visit immensely when a letter came in the mail addressed to Arthur, but was really a note to Carrie. After Arthur looked it over, he handed it to her, a frown on his face. "It looks like your trip is going to be cut short."

Carrie nervously took the note and began to read it. Her mother was ill. It didn't appear to be anything serious, thank goodness, but still, she knew how hard it had to be for her mother to take care of Clara and Raymond while trying to recover from an illness. "It sounds like I'd better return to Burlington." She frowned.

"I will let the chauffeur know that we will need to leave tomorrow," said Arthur. "Chin up, sweet girl. We have had most of the summer together. I have loved having you here, and I'm certain your family sorely misses you. In fact, I have to wonder if your absence is the real ailment your mother is suffering from," he teased.

Carrie arrived home safe and sound the following evening. Her mother, still weak, was on the mend from a bout of rheumatism. Carrie had been so caught up in the new experiences she was enjoying, as well as meeting so many relatives, she hadn't realized how much she really missed her family in Burlington. She was very happy when she opened the door to find her parents, along with Clara and little Raymond all anxiously waiting for her there. It had been a glorious vacation, but she knew this was where she belonged — with her little family at the Drews' boarding house on Pearl Street.

After unpacking, Carrie handed her parents a roll of ten-dollar bills. They gave her a questioning look. "Uncle Arthur is a generous man," was all she said.

Life was slowly getting back to normal for Carrie. Her mother fared much better now that she had returned. Little Raymond seemed to have grown to twice his size while Carrie was away. Then there was Eva. She positively lit up with smiles at her dear friend's return.

There was one person Carrie missed, however, whom she hadn't considered missing, since he had left Burlington before her ... Elder Rappleye. "I wonder what he is doing right now," Carrie pondered as she prepared for bed one night. "I hope his time in Canada is over soon and that he hasn't forgotten about me." She couldn't help wondering if he and Eva had been communicating. The thought of it caused her to wince.

Canada
1912

W illiam had definitely not forgotten about Carrie — could never forget about Carrie — but he was doing his best to put all of his focus into his missionary efforts. The elders had been serving out in the country for the past month or so and finding some success with preaching the gospel, but little success from Mother Nature as she insisted on pelting the Canadian landscape with moisture nearly every day. Sometimes the one thing that kept William going was the knowledge that he would soon be returning to Burlington; to the Saints that treated him like family; to old missionary friends; and most of all ... to Carrie.

Before embarking on their country trip, the elders shipped their trunks to Burlington. The plan was to tract their way back to Vermont on their journey. Therefore, they would not be returning to Canada. William had some good experiences in Sherbrooke, but for the most part, he found there a general prejudice against the Mormons and he would not miss the area ... especially Mr. Parkes.

The men had most recently been staying in the town of Newport, Vermont. It was a beautiful area near Lake Memphremagog. Here, they had experienced some wonderful gospel discussions and several successful open-air meetings. At one particular meeting, attendees accumulated to the tune of two hundred souls. The elders couldn't be happier, nor could they remember ever being so well received since their transfer to Canada. This was also beneficial in securing meals and beds for the night, as many people were interested in hearing more of what the elders had to say.

The town of Newport came alive in the summer. Visitors came from Canada and other surrounding areas to visit the lake. William had never lived in a city that attracted tourists. He found it fascinating to watch the number and variety of people coming and going through Newport.

It came as a great surprise when two men passing through Newport happened to be friends. In fact, they were also missionaries serving in the country.

"We heard you three were here in Newport." Elder Williams pumped Elder Brown's hand up and down. "Elder Mason said we just had to look for the only men in town still wearing dress suits instead of bathing suits." He laughed and the others joined in.

"Yeah, Elder Williams and I thought it would be nice to spend Independence Day with friends, so we tracted our way to Newport."

William had to admit that he found having two additional friendly faces among their group refreshing.

July 4th burned hot, just like the fireworks it would surely end with. The five elders thought it would be a nice day to take an excursion on the Lady of the Lake boat. With excitement for something other than missionary work, for a change, the elders headed to the water.

As they approached the docks, they came upon a notice that read, "No free excursions on July 4th. Boat rides $1.00 per person."

"A dollar for a boat ride?" gasped Elder Mason. "That's two weeks' worth of suppers at the diner!"

The others agreed the boat ride was out of the question.

Instead, they found a shady area near the lake and spent a lazy day enjoying the scenery while they looked forward to the fireworks in the evening.

Unfortunately, Heaven decided to put on its own fireworks display. It was as if dark clouds crept in undetected, bringing down sheets of water, drenching the elders in the process. They sloshed their way through puddles of water back to their apartment and ended up spending the evening talking religion with their landlady and her friends.

On July 5th, the elders split back into their original companionships and tracted their way out of Newport. Elders Rappleye, Brown and Madsen headed toward Derby Centre. It was not an easy walk in the heat and humidity.

"When it's not raining cats and dogs, it's nearly one hundred degrees in the shade." Elder Madsen mopped his brow with his handkerchief.

The others nodded, but this was country work and there was nowhere to go but forward, so press on they did.

At last they reached Derby Centre. The weary men set up for an open-air meeting.

The turnout was good. Elder Brown was delivering a compelling summary of the Plan of Salvation to the captive audience, when one man, who had been elbowing his way closer to the front of the group, turned around and yelled, "I've heard enough of these Mormons. I have a bucket full of rotten eggs. Let's pelt them!"

Another man yelled, "Better yet, let's tar and feather them."

William shook his head. Will men such as these, he wondered, ever realize how very ignorant they reveal themselves to be when they act like that?

Elder Brown looked back at William. They exchanged a knowing look and Elder Brown proceeded as if nothing had happened.

The man who stirred things up stood there gawking at the elders, no doubt wondering how they had the audacity to go on in spite of his threats.

The elders continued on with their presentation, each taking a turn to speak and to answer questions for as long as they had anyone left to listen. No rotten eggs were thrown, neither were they tarred nor feathered.

"Elder Rappleye, how did you know those men wouldn't make good on their threats?" asked Elder Madsen at the end of their meeting.

Did you see any eggs, or tar, or feathers?"

"No, but they could have had them stowed away somewhere. You two didn't act alarmed in the least."

"People like those men are usually all talk, no eggs," William quipped. "The longer you do the work, *His* work, the thicker your skin becomes and the stronger your faith grows. Besides, it would have given us something to write home about had they really tarred and feathered us." He chuckled.

It was too late to find a place to sleep for the night, but one lady offered the elders a couple of quilts and pointed them in the direction of a barn. They found some newly mowed hay and tucked under the quilts for the night.

"Is it strange that I am getting used to sleeping on hay?" Elder Brown pulled the quilt up to his ears.

"At least it cools down at night and the barn will keep us dry should it rain." Elder Rappleye sighed.

Snoring came from the dark lump to William's left. Quietly laughing he said, "I think Elder Madsen likes the hay as well."

"Elder Rappleye, do you ever wonder if it's all worth it? I mean we've been arrested, we've had horrible lies written in the newspapers about us, and we've been threatened with rotten eggs, tar and feathers. I just wonder if the work we are doing will make a difference in the larger scheme of things."

William reflected on his Patriarchal Blessing, given to him as a young man. One paragraph resonated in his mind as Elder Brown spoke. William read his blessing often. He had this part memorized: *"You shall in your day and generation perform a great work in the building up of the Kingdom of God upon this earth. You shall go forth to the nations of the earth and preach the gospel of the Son of God, and you will be an instrument in the hands of God in bringing many souls to Him."*

"No," William said, ending his contemplation, "I never wonder if it's worth it. We may not have had tremendous success in Sherbrooke, but we plant seeds everywhere we go. Remember the open-air meeting that brought two hundred people to us in Newport? Remember the baptisms of Brother and Sister Blair and the Griffin family in Burlington? Every seed we plant has the potential to grow and I'm happy to have been called to help plant those seeds. So, in answer to your question, no, I never wonder. I know it is worth it."

The quiet, darkness and spirit in the barn after William's powerful words created a most reverent feeling. Silence hung in the air. Even Elder Madsen quit snoring.

"You're right, Elder Rappleye. I know beyond doubt that this gospel is true, and I am honored to share it with others. I don't know why I ever let discouragement enter my mind. It is one of Satan's tools."

"It's hard not to get discouraged, but think of it this way. Why does Satan work so hard to thwart the work we are about? I believe we encounter so many obstacles because what we are doing is vitally important and Satan does not want us to succeed. But in the end we will be triumphant, that is, if we never give up. After all, Joseph Smith prophesied that the gospel shall roll forth until it fills the earth. I believe we are playing a small part of that prophecy just by being here."

Elder Madsen was awake now and the three continued their conversation well into the night.

The next morning, as the men brushed the hay from their clothes, Elder Madsen remarked, "I never knew a smelly barn could feel like such a sacred place as it did last night. It's an honor to serve with both of you."

William and Elder Brown agreed that the feeling was mutual. Missionaries shared not only their time with each other; they shared their fears, their successes, and oft times their testimonies. The camaraderie and brotherhood between them grew strong as they served together.

Burlington, Vermont
July 1912

The bell on the front door jangled, announcing the arrival of a guest to the Drews' boarding house. Carrie looked up to greet whom it was when her face spilt into a huge smile and tears sprang to her eyes. It's William — Elder Rappleye — she hurried to correct herself . She felt sheepish for thinking of him as William, but she caught herself doing it more and more often. Her first impulse was to run into his arms, but she knew that wouldn't be appropriate, so she settled for a warm handshake.

"This is my new companion, Elder Walters. Elder Walters, meet Miss Carrie Drew." William's eyes sparkled when they met hers. "We have been assigned to stay at your boarding house."

Emily walked into the room and, like Carrie, not only looked as though she wanted to, but did run straight into Elder Rappleye's arms to welcome him back to Burlington. "We've missed you so," she said. Then, as if she had forgotten she held a tot on her hip, she hefted him up higher in her arms and introduced Raymond to the elders. "This is the newest member of the Drew family. His name is Raymond," she announced with a huge smile.

Raymond immediately took to Elder Rappleye, holding his now chubby, little arms out for him to take. William smiled his willingness to comply, as he pulled the little boy into his own strong arms. "This feels like home. There is always a little one for me to spoil in Cowley." He grinned, but Carrie noticed his voice hitch and realized how much William surely missed his home.

"Mrs. Drew," William said, still holding little Raymond, "this is my new companion, Elder Walters. We were told to inquire if you have a room for let; maybe one for the next couple of months?"

Mrs. Drew's face lit up, but then, in the same instant, fell. "All of our rooms are full at the present time, but one will be opening up in the next day or so."

Carrie spoke up, "They may have my room until another becomes available. I'll sleep with Clara."

"Are you certain, Miss Drew? After all, we have become quite accustomed to sleeping in barns, and I must say, there's just nothing quite as refreshing as waking up to cows bellowing because their udders are near explosion." Elder Rappleye chuckled, his eyes dancing with merriment.

Carrie chortled. "I wondered where that smell was coming from." She pulled a sour face and plugged her nose dramatically. "Please feel free to bathe before you sleep in my bed."

It was almost more than William could take, sleeping in Carrie's bed. He could smell her sweet scent all around him. This may not have been a good idea. He pulled the covers close to his nose and inhaled, then let out a deep sigh. *How am I to concentrate on missionary work, when I can think of nothing but Carrie? Hopefully a room will open up soon.*

In early morning the men crept quietly out of Carrie's room, so as not to disturb her or the other residents on the second floor, which was generally reserved for the Drew family members. They wanted Carrie to have access to her room and wardrobe as soon as she was up and about.

The smell of sizzling bacon wafting up the stairs told them they were not the first to arise. It was a welcome aroma after many months of eating mostly bread and vegetables from farmers' gardens.

As they were finishing a hearty breakfast of bacon and fried eggs, the boarding house telephone rang. William looked up in surprise.

"That's new," he said to Elder Walters. "I wonder when they got a telephone. Sure would have been nice to have back when we were quarantined."

It was a call for the elders. Mrs. Drew motioned for one of them to take it. William obliged.

After a somber conversation, he hung up the phone. "Elder Walters, we need to go out immediately."

"Is something wrong?" asked Emily, seeing the concern on William's face.

"That was a call from the Besnetts. Do you know them?"

"Yes, I am well acquainted with them. Are they not well?"

"We began teaching them just yesterday. It seems their baby granddaughter is sick, so sick that they believe she may not live until we reach their home. That was Mr. Besnett asking us to come administer to her and give her a blessing. We had better get over there quickly."

Emily looked distraught, but wasted no time asking more questions. She helped them gather their things and rushed them out the door.

It was only a few blocks to the Besnett's residence, but if the baby's life was in danger, there was no time to lose. William hoped that Mr. Besnett exaggerated about the condition of his granddaughter.

Mr. Besnett must have seen the elders approaching. He had the door open and ushered them through the house to a small bedroom. There was a young woman sitting on the edge of a bed next to her little one, weeping. The elders drew closer to the child. Mr. Besnett wasn't exaggerating; the baby was gaunt and lifeless. The woman looked up, and through her tears tried to explain that her daughter had had a fever for a few days, but appeared to be doing better yesterday. This morning, however, the baby, who looked to be about one year old, was listless and unresponsive; her dark lashes lay in stark contrast against her pale, white cheeks. "Is there something you can do for her?" she asked, her eyes pleading.

William knelt down and touched the child's face, gently moving a lock of hair from her eyes. "We can give her a healing blessing, if you will allow it."

"Yes, yes. I know I am not of your faith, but if you can help my baby, I will forever be in your debt."

Together, Elders Rappleye and Walters took the baby in their arms, anointed her with oil, sealed the anointing, and then gave her a blessing to be healed. The spirit of God was strong as the blessing was pronounced upon the child.

When William completed the blessing and laid the baby back onto her bed, there wasn't a dry eye in the room.

Mr. Besnett looked especially pleased. "I can feel God's presence. I know she will be healed," he cried out in his thick French accent.

The elders stayed for only a few more minutes, assuring the Besnetts that they could call on them at any time, afterwhich they took their leave.

The warm sun fell on William's shoulders, cheering him as he and Elder Walters left the Besnett residence. With the urgency of the situation, he had been aggrieved by the mood in the home. That, coupled with the pungent odor of ointments and herbal remedies, had made him queasy. The morning summer air cleared his head.

Carrie and Mrs. Drew watched through the window for the missionaries to return. When they arrived, Emily demanded a full report. The elders obliged.

"Do you think she will be healed?" Carrie twisted her fingers together as if wringing out her concern.

"I felt very strongly that the child has not completed her mission here on Earth, but so much depends upon the faith of those caring for her. Honestly, there was a very powerful feeling in the room and I do believe she will recover," answered Elder Rappleye.

As the missionaries prepared to head out tracting for the day, the telephone rang again. Once more it was for the elders. "It's Mr.Besnett again. Oh, I hope it's not bad news." Emily handed the phone to Elder Rappleye.

His face lit up as he listened to Mr. Besnett. "That is wonderful news," he said. "Please continue to keep us informed." He replaced the phone on the receiver.

Turning back to face the others, he had a captive audience. "Mr. Besnett wanted us to know that his granddaughter is awake, laughing and even drinking broth."

There was a collective sigh of relief in the room.

"I thought she would be healed, but considering how very ill she was, that was some kind of miracle healing," Elder Walters said.

"With enough faith, miracles still do happen." Elder Rappleye smiled and breathed a deep sigh, clearly relieved.

The two elders turned to leave for another day of tracting. "Oh, ... uh, Carrie, we tried our hardest, but there may still be some hay in your bed," William said with a wink.

They exited the house, and Carrie sank to the nearest sofa. "Mother, why is it that there aren't more men like Elder Rappleye? If I should ever meet a gentleman half as kind as he is, I will marry him on the spot."

Mrs. Drew sat down next to Carrie and pulled her daughter into a motherly embrace. "I can't disagree with you, my dear girl. He's one of a kind ... but so are you."

The weather was still very warm as July melted into August; therefore, the elders were still required to be out doing country work. While William would have preferred to stay at the Drews' boarding house every night, they couldn't do that just yet. So they packed their grips and embarked on another country trip heading north.

One of the first towns the missionaries stayed in, St. Regis, looked promising for a street meeting. So, seeking out a City Council member, Mr. Wilson, the elders obtained permission to preach on a town corner.

Elder Rappleye began the meeting and gained a lot of attention from the gathering crowd. There were at least one hundred townsfolk listening to what William had to say. It was exciting to have so many gathered there.

William was caught up in the spirit of the meeting, when a police officer muscled his way through the crowd and told him to stop. William paid him no mind and continued to preach. Angry now, the officer grabbed William by the shoulders, turning him around so that he was facing the officer, and forced William to give him his full attention.

"I said stop your preaching!"

"But officer, we received permission to be here from Mr. Wils—"

"I don't care who gave you permission. *I'm* telling you to stop!"

The townspeople who witnessed the exchange became angry. One man began yelling, "Let the men preach! We want to hear what they have to say!"

Then another started to hoot at the officer. Before long the entire congregation of townsfolk was hooting at the officer.

Elder Walters asked William in a low voice, "What should we do?"

William shrugged his shoulders. "I've never heard a gathering hoot at anyone before. Let's just see how it plays out."

The angry people hooted the officer right out of the group. The elders watched, both amazed and amused at what was happening.

Once the policeman was gone, the audience pressed the elders to continue with their preaching. William didn't feel right about just ignoring the officer, so instead he began passing out literature and talking to people one on one, answering their questions.

All in all, the elders felt good about the meeting, even with all the hooting.

They continued tracting north up through Canada, preaching the word, passing out tracts and other literature, asking for food and places to sleep and often finding themselves in a barn. Very much like their previous country trips, there were many people who opened their hearts and their homes to the men, and others who did not.

On September 6th the elders took a train to Plattsburg; then they traveled by boat to Burlington. It was good to be home.

Burlington, Vermont
September 1912

Rain, rain, rain, and more rain! That was the only way to describe the month of September in Vermont. Carrie could see no end to it. On top of that, Elder Rappleye and Elder Walters moved out of the boarding house and back into the mission headquarters apartment. Carrie had been so happy when the elders returned from their country trip, but now they had moved out. Thankfully, they came over nearly every night to take their meals at the boarding house, and they most always stayed to sing with the Drews.

One particular evening around the dinner table, the subject of religion came up. "What church do you attend, Carrie?" William eyed her curiously.

A little embarrassed, Carrie answered, "The church on the corner, Methodist Episcopal. But I must confess that I don't attend very often."

"Why is that?"

"I cannot agree with everything they, or so many other churches believe."

"Like what?" William pushed for more.

"Well, I suppose I am a strange sort of person, as I can't agree with what the churches teach about baptism and also the personality of God. I believe we should be baptized by immersion, as Jesus was, and I also believe God to be a man."

Carrie noticed the elders look at each other then look back at her, smiling. "So, I suppose you two elders think I am a strange person as well?" Her face fell. She felt disappointment emerging.

Elder Rappleye chuckled. "The only thing strange about you is that you have always been a Mormon and just didn't know it." The other two elders present nodded in agreement. "Would you like to attend our Sunday meetings?"

"And we would love to teach you more, here in your home, as well," Elder Walters was quick to add.

"That's right. With the quarantines and our country trips, we haven't had any gospel discussions with you since last winter," William reminded the Drews.

Carrie very much wanted to attend their meetings. She already felt close to the members of the church in Burlington, as she helped with many cottage meetings. Now she needed to understand the doctrine.

"Should you decide to be baptized, however, that will have to wait until it warms up again, as our baptisms take place in Lake Champlain," William said.

Carrie saw a wistful look cross William's face, as if realizing that should that happy day arrive, he would likely be transferred elsewhere. Their eyes locked for a moment and she wondered if he were communicating to her how much he wished to have the honor of immersing her in the waters of baptism.

As if snapping out of a trance, William continued, "There is always such a spiritual feeling at baptisms... "

Carrie's mind wandered. There was just something about William. She found him more than physically attractive. She also loved the light in his eyes and the spirit she felt in his presence. Her heartbeat quickened at the thought. Being baptized by him would make the event all the more special.

When she forced herself back into the conversation, William was still talking. "But for now, we would be happy just to have you attend our Sunday meetings."

"We meet at the Blair's home for our Sabbath meetings," Elder Walters said. "You are all welcome to attend," he added, addressing Mr. and Mrs. Drew and thirteen-year-old Clara.

"As are you, my little friend." William pinched Raymond's cheek.

Raymond had taken such a liking to him, holding his arms up for William to hold him every time he walked in the door, that William began calling him his *little friend.*

"And I'll bring my friend Eva. I'm sure she will wish to be included." Carrie's eyes sparkled with excitement.

"In the meantime, here is some literature you can read about our beliefs." William pulled some tracts out of his well-worn bag and handed them to Carrie.

After the elders left for the evening, Carrie plunged into the tracts and the *little book*, as the elders referred to it, full of Gospel information. She read and read until she had read all of it, but it wasn't enough. Until now, Carrie hadn't realized how hungry she was for sincere understanding where religion was concerned. Everything she read rang true. She felt a burning in her heart and her testimony began to grow. I feel as though I know this; like I've learned it before — another place; another time. A chill ran up her spine.

Carrie began rummaging through cupboards and drawers. "Where's that Book of Mormon the elders gave us all those months ago, Mother? Do you know?"

Mrs. Drew pulled the book out of a desk drawer in the parlor. "Have you finished reading all the other literature they gave you, Carrie?"

"Yes, and you should read it too, Mother. I believe it is the truth. How long have we known the missionaries? And just now we are learning what they believe? Sometimes I think they are almost too polite about not being pushy."

"Or maybe it's a matter of timing, Carrie. If you are correct, and what they are preaching is the truth, perhaps God was waiting for us to be good and ready before he had his message delivered to us."

Carrie noticed Aaron listening in on the conversation and gave him a look, inviting him to voice his opinion. She valued it.

He accepted the invitation and spoke up. "While I don't disagree with you and, quite honestly, find the elders to be forthright and upstanding men, I am old and more than a little fixed in my ways. If I were to ever consider joining a church, it would most likely be the Mormon Church, but as you well know, Mormons don't drink coffee, nor do they smoke tobacco. Those are two things I would have a hard time giving up." He smiled, but it didn't quite reach his eyes.

Carrie gave her father a squeeze. She realized he was right, but vowed that one day he would be converted, as well.

"We've come to say our goodbyes." Elder Rappleye stood at the Drews' front door with his new companion, Elder Wood. Noting the confused expression on Carrie's face, he went on, "We've been given a new assignment in Newport."

Carrie frowned her disappointment that they were leaving so soon. "But you've only been home ... I mean back in Burlington for a month." She blushed.

"We'll be *home* by Thanksgiving," William said, his eyes twinkling at her faux pas. "Carrie, please keep attending the Sunday meetings," he added in a reverent, almost pleading voice. She let him pull her as close as he could — not close enough, in her estimation — while clasping her hand for a farewell handshake. He appeared to be blinking back tears before finally looking down at her.

Carrie was less successful as tears spilled down her cheeks. "I will." Her voice began to crack.

Carrie did attend the Sunday meetings. She also read the Book of Mormon, which she loved. Her testimony intensified through her studies. Mrs. Drew also began to read the Book of Mormon, although at a somewhat slower pace. She still had little Raymond and thirteen-year-old Clara to care for.

Carrie wondered if anything would ... could come of her feelings for William. "It's probably just a passing affection," she told herself. "Yet it just gets stronger as time goes by, even when he's not here." Then frustration always set in as she realized that once his mission was over, Elder Rappleye would go back to being William Rappleye on a farm in Cowley, Wyoming — over a thousand miles away from her.

As Ever Yours

Carrie kept busy at the boarding house. A year or so before, her mother had hired a French girl who helped with the cooking and cleaning. As of late, she had been on an extended vacation, visiting family in Quebec, so Carrie had plenty to do. She also picked up a position selling tickets at the local cinema. Between jobs, her newfound interest in the Mormon Church, and, of course, Eva, Carrie's days were never dull.

Eva never let Carrie forget that she was still in love with Elder Rappleye. This declaration always made Carrie feel ill at ease. After all, Carrie had no claim over Elder Rappleye, and he hadn't, of course, proclaimed his feelings for her, but she felt there was something there and was certain he felt the same way. She wondered how to react to Eva when she went on so. Still, remaining quiet about her feelings felt a mite deceitful, so Carrie decided to brave a hint about her own love for a certain elder.

Following Sunday services a few weeks after the elders had been transferred, Eva began going on about how much she missed Elder Rappleye.

Carrie had spent plenty of time thinking of just the right way to approach the subject so as not to offend her dearest friend. "You are right, Eva. Things are just not the same without Elder Rappleye here. I'm afraid I am as smitten as you are. It's too bad for me, however, since you are so beautiful. I don't stand a chance," she teased.

"You are in love with Elder Rappleye, too?" Eva's jaw dropped in astonishment.

"Well, *in love* is wording it a bit strongly, I guess, but I will admit that he is one of the kindest men I have ever met."

"And the most handsome, too." Eva's eyes took on that familiar dreamy gaze. "Well, good, we can pine together over a man we can't have."

Carrie felt a burden of guilt lift. At least she knows, and she doesn't seem to be bothered by it. And, for all I know, William might prefer Eva to me. Carrie forced a smile and gave her friend a squeeze.

CHAPTER TWENTY-FIVE

Newport, Vermont
October 1912

William breathed the crisp, autumn air deeply. "Vermont in October is like paradise," he murmured as he and Elder Wood made their way to their rented boarding house room.

They'd had a long and somewhat successful day of tracting. William was tired, but not too tired to watch the sun set.

The Vermont weather had cooled, creating a vision of rich gold and sparkling rubies before him. As the sun descended, rays of light twinkled through the leaves of the numberless maple trees, adding warmth to the already dramatic color. The view was magnificent. William had to stand still and soak it all in. It was as if strokes from God's own brush had recently wisped through the area, splashing color atop color.

Pulling William out of his reverie, Elder Wood turned and asked, "Are you coming, or should I just go on into the house?"

"Go on in. There is nothing like this in Cowley, Wyoming. I wish I had a camera and could capture the beauty of this place. For now, I will just have to be satisfied to observe."

Instead of going in, Elder Wood seemed to drag his thoughts out of the work they had been doing all day long and watched the sun descend slowly, dissolving into a deep red sea of color. "Sometimes I get so caught up with the pressures of the day, I forget to enjoy our surroundings," he said in a low voice, as if not wanting to disturb the peaceful moment.

"It's a simple thing, but I can't help but think of the many opportunities I have had because I answered the Lord's call to serve. The places I've been, the people I have met, and this." William motioned to the last ray of sunlight sparkling through the autumn leaves.

Elder Wood merely nodded.

The elders' time in Newport and surrounding towns kept them busy and was surprisingly successful. It helped that they had a rented room to return to each evening, especially with the weather turning wintry. They could spend more time teaching doctrine when they didn't have to be appealing for a bed every night.

Time passed quickly in some respects. Staying busy on the Lord's errand helped keep William's mind off Carrie. Before he could get too homesick for his Vermont family, as he'd come to think of the Saints and dear friends there, he found himself, along with Elder Wood, on a train bound for Burlington just in time for the Thanksgiving holiday.

Stepping off the train platform, William thought to himself, Carrie is right, this feels like home to me now. There's nowhere else I'd rather spend the holidays than here.

They spent Thanksgiving with the Drews, where the elders were currently boarding. William couldn't help but smile when he breathed in the aroma of the roasting turkey. Nothing beats my mama's cooking, but turkey smells just as good in Vermont as it does in Wyoming.

The food was delicious and the company even better. Carrie, William couldn't help but notice, seemed even more delightful and beautiful with the added glow of the gospel. He was so happy to hear she'd been attending the Sunday meetings with the Saints, as well as studying the scriptures and other literature he'd left for her.

William never let his tenderness for Carrie rise to the surface. He wasn't in Vermont for that reason, although it wasn't always easy to keep his feelings in check, especially living under the same roof. The elders kept busy tracting the surrounding areas, visiting the Saints and holding cottage meetings. They spent many evenings gathered around the piano, as Carrie accompanied the elders and her family in singing their beloved songs. This was William's favorite time of day. He relished every moment in Carrie's presence.

Christmas was vastly different for William this year. He couldn't help remembering the previous Christmas as he and his companion celebrated with the other Vermont elders at Mrs. Warnes' boarding house, stuffing themselves with rich foods and sweets. He'd been so homesick for family and his mother's cooking. Now William didn't feel homesick at all. He was surrounded by friends who had become dear to him, and he and Elder Wood received several invitations for Christmas dinner.

Along with the delicious Christmas foods came presents. Packages from home were always more than welcome, but William also received many presents from his Vermont family. Handkerchiefs and neckties were the standard. They were most useful for missionaries. And though it wasn't unique, William's favorite gift came from Carrie — a silk handkerchief and a tie. "I don't think I will ever use this one to blow my nose." He smiled, carefully folding the handkerchief up for safe keeping. Smelling her perfume on it, he wondered if he should keep it buried somewhere so it would not distract him.

Winter not only brought the holidays, but also the familiar quarantines. Last year it was smallpox making the rounds. This year it was measles and black diphtheria plaguing the people of Vermont. Thankfully, neither disease found the elders this time around.

Quarantines hampered the missionaries' ability to teach and hold cottage meetings. The Blairs, who generously opened their home for the Sunday and cottage meetings, were under quarantine with black diphtheria. The elders visited them frequently over the back fence, careful not to get too close. They moved their meetings to the Griffin's house and tracted homes that didn't have the dreaded quarantine sign attached to the door.

William was feeling content until January 23rd. That's when the letter came. President McFarlane received it from the Eastern States Mission Headquarters and called the elders in to hear the message it contained.

As President McFarlane began reading, his voice caught and he handed the letter to Elder Anderson to finish.

It read, "Elders Rappleye and Anderson have been transferred to New Jersey and East Pennsylvania, respectively." The room was silent. He went on, "They are to report as soon as possible, provided they can be spared."

President McFarlane wiped a hand across his face, missing a few errant tears. In a husky voice he said, "You are free to go as soon as tomorrow, though I'd like to keep you forever."

William always knew he couldn't stay in Burlington forever, but still, the letter seemed to pierce his very soul. How could he leave these men, who were like his brothers? How could he leave the Saints, who were so faithful in a place where Mormonism wasn't widely accepted? How could he leave Carrie? *How could he leave Carrie?*

He and Elder Anderson just went through the motions as they packed their trunks in preparation to depart the next day. When they finished, it was still early enough for them to make the rounds to bid farewell to all those people dear to them.

This time William would not be returning. He would serve out the rest of his mission in a different place, with different people. Logically, William knew this was to be expected and he should be happy for a new experience, but it truly felt as if he were leaving his home in Cowley, Wyoming, all over again. It hurt.

After visiting with all of the Saints, William and Elder Anderson returned to the Drews' boarding house, where they spent the rest of the evening with the Drew family and Eva Savoy. They ate supper, sang all of their favorite songs, visited together, but it just wasn't enough. William could not believe they were leaving the very next morning.

He longed to tell Carrie how much she had come to mean to him, that he had known from the moment he met her that he loved her, but he knew he must not. Once again, he had to settle for a handshake.

"I will write to you," William said softly as he held Carrie's petite hand in his much larger one.

Carrie, unable to hold back the tears, nodded. "I would like that." She watched as the two men lugged their trunks to catch the streetcar, which would deliver them to the train that would take them far away.

Thankfully, for William's sake, the trip to Camden, New Jersey, which was to be his next assigned field of labor, took the missionaries through several historical regions. This gave William little time to miss his Vermont family, especially Carrie, as he discovered his country's rich heritage.

Being born and reared in the West, William had only learned in school about the places he was now experiencing first-hand. I only wish my family could see what I'm seeing, he thought.

Their nine-day journey took them through Boston, where William eagerly devoured any and every piece of American history available. After all, it was Paul Revere's birthplace as well as where he made his famous ride. Then, of course, there was Bunker Hill. The elders even took a side trip to Lexington.

Then it was on to New York City. William had never imagined, let alone seen, so many motorcars. The Brooklyn Bridge alone had four streetcar lines, one team line and two walkways.

They also visited the Woolworth Building. It was 55 stories high — the tallest building in the world, and it wasn't even finished yet.

It was February 2nd by the time William made his way into the mission headquarters in Camden, New Jersey. He and Elder Anderson had been separated and sent to different locations when they departed New York. William's new companion was Elder Faucett.

Burlington, Vermont
January 1913

Carrie couldn't help herself. She knew William would take several days to get to his new location, and even then perhaps not have time to write, but she still eagerly awaited the postal deliveries each day. She was thrilled, then, that just four days later she received a postcard from Boston bearing William's signature.

It was a simple thing, a picture of the tower where the lantern hung during Paul Revere's great ride. There was nothing of a personal nature written on it, just facts, but then it was signed,

As ever yours,
William E. Rappleye

William had sent Carrie postcards before, while he was in Sherbrooke, but they were always signed very impersonally. Sometimes they said, "Good luck," or "Your friend." But *"As ever yours"* felt so much more personal. Carrie's eyes glistened as she read and reread the card, especially those last three words.

She took the postcard up to her bedroom and placed it on the nightstand. Her eyes scanned the room, taking in the many photos and name cards of the missionaries she had met and corresponded with since her family bought the boarding house on Pearl Street. Some of the men were married with families of their own. She admired them for leaving their loved ones to serve the Lord. Others were like William — younger, single. She realized just how many Mormon men she had become acquainted with over the past few years. There was definitely something different about them. They led clean lives in every way. Their language was never vulgar, their clothing was always laundered and pressed — not expensive — just well cared for, and they were such hard workers — dedicated to their callings. Most of all, these men all had something about them — a glow, or an aura — that separated them from anyone else Carrie knew. There was a light in their eyes that drew people to them. She identified it as the light of Christ, borne from having the gift of the Holy Ghost. She wanted that light.

The Book of Mormon Carrie had been reading began to look well-used. She read it every evening before bed and some nights she couldn't put it down. There was power within the pages. She treasured it.

"Well, Elder Rappleye," she murmured. "You've got me wanting what you and the rest of the elders possess ... a testimony. I need to know that what you are about is the truth. I need to feel the power of God burn within my heart. Everything you have ever preached makes sense to me, yet I need to not just believe it, but know and feel it to be true."

She picked up the worn Book of Mormon. The marker, William's name card, held her place in the book of Ether — so close to the end. As she thumbed through the book, her eye caught William's writing on the inside cover. "How did I not see this before?" she wondered.

The words he wrote were simple, but poignant.

> *"To my friends, the Drew family,*
>
> *I pray that as you read the words in this book, you will feel the power and truthfulness in its pages. I testify they are true. I know that Joseph Smith restored the Gospel of Jesus Christ to the earth in these latter days; the same Gospel that existed when Christ and his Apostles were living. This book is a testament of Christ and I know that if you read it with a sincere heart, you will know it to be true. Please read Moroni 10:4, get down on your knees and ask God if these things are not true. Then you will also know.*
>
> *Your friend always, Elder William E. Rappleye."*

A chill made its way down Carrie's spine. Not wasting any time, she flipped to the last page and read Moroni 10:4 for herself.

> *"And when ye shall receive these things, I would exhort you that ye would ask God, the Eternal Father, in the name of Christ, if these things are not true; and if ye shall ask with a sincere heart, with real intent, having faith in Christ, he will manifest the truth of it unto you, by the power of the Holy Ghost."*

Aha. The answer to the question Carrie only dared ask herself, "How do I know it's true?" She reverently closed the book then lowered herself to the braided rug on the floor beside her bed and uttered a prayer; a plea to know if the things she had been studying and learning from the elders and in the church meetings were true. At first she felt tentative about her request, but the longer she prayed, the bolder she became. If she were, in fact, entitled to know the truth for herself — not what a preacher or missionary told her to believe — but the truth straight from God, she would stay on her knees until she got an answer.

At first, Carrie felt nothing, but continued to pray. Then, remaining on her knees, she waited for an answer. It was subtle when it began, but the burning within Carrie's heart grew to a near explosion. With tears streaming down her cheeks, Carrie looked up to the Heavens and thanked God for answering her prayer. From that moment on, Carrie knew her life would never be the same.

The next morning, the routine of daily living returned, but it felt different to Carrie. Now there was meaning to everything she did. She viewed the people around her as children of God and she knew He had a plan for her. Carrie wanted nothing more than to know what that plan was. But first things first. She needed to be baptized.

Hearkening back to one of her last conversations with Elder Rappleye, she realized that baptisms were performed in Lake Champlain, which was freezing during the winter months, and in reality, didn't warm up enough to wade into until June. "Well, then, June it will be," she said to herself, feeling more than a little disappointed about having to wait. "I shall begin preparations now by visiting the missionaries and getting a baptismal date on the calendar."

The next week Eva scrutinized Carrie as if sensing something different about her. Carrie had always been happy and the sort of person everyone liked to be around, but now there was an added spring in her step, not to mention a light in her eyes.

"What's going on with you, Carrie?" she probed, while helping her and Emily with the dinner dishes.

"Huh? What do you mean?"

Eva's eyes narrowed. "I can't put my finger on it, but something is different about you."

"I've noticed it, too," Emily added.

Carrie blushed, not comfortable about being the topic of their conversation.

"Does it have anything to do with how long you spent up in your bedroom last week?" Emily prodded.

So it's true, Carrie thought, once you have a testimony of the Gospel, it shows. "Well, perhaps it does." She kept her head down, hiding a smile. She handed Eva a plate.

"What in the world happened in your bedroom last week?" Eva put the plate down and turned Carrie to face her. "You can't just leave it at that. Please share. I must know."

"Well, it's kind of personal—"

Before Carrie could finish her sentence, Eva was shutting her down. "Who do you think you are talking to? We share everything."

"And I'm your mother. I deserve to know, as well."

"Very well, then. I will tell you what happened, but please don't laugh, or think I'm silly. All this means a lot to me."

After securing promises from both women, Carrie, her mother and Eva made themselves comfortable in the parlor where Carrie proceeded to tell them about her experience. If she thought either of the women would laugh at her, she was mistaken. Both Eva and Emily listened in rapt attention, and by the time Carrie finished, both were touched to the point of tears. Carrie felt relief and happiness to have someone to share her experience with. Plus, she felt that in some way, her testimony could help Emily and Eva find their own.

"May I borrow your Book of Mormon when you are finished reading it, Carrie?"

Carrie looked up into Eva's tear-stained face and felt a lump form in her throat. "Of course you can. In fact, I finished it two nights ago. I'll get it for you now." Then she turned to Emily. "Mother, did you read it when the elders first gave it to you?"

Emily shook her head, looking down as if she were ashamed. "I confess that until you asked for it, I completely forgot we had it."

"Well, then, after Eva reads it, it will be your turn."

Emily looked doubtful. "Carrie, you know I don't read well. I can't possibly read a book like that."

Carrie nearly forgot her mother could neither read nor write when she married Aaron. Thankfully, Aaron had overlooked that shortcoming and married her anyway, much to the chagrin of his family. In the years that followed, Aaron spent time teaching Emily to read, but it never came easily to her and the Book of Mormon would definitely be a challenge. "Perhaps Father could read it to you. And if he won't, I will." She pulled her mother into a tight embrace. "I just want you both to know what I now know."

The next time Carrie was able to meet with the missionaries, they penciled her in for a baptism for June 19th, 1913. It seemed a lifetime away, but Carrie would use the time to learn everything she could about the Gospel. She wanted to be good and ready to enter the waters of baptism when the time came.

She couldn't wait to tell William what had transpired since he left Burlington. So with pen and paper in hand, she dedicated an evening to writing every detail of her own personal conversion, not leaving out anything. His words, after all, had prompted her to get on her knees and pray about it. She made sure to thank him for that. Then, mimicking his own words, she closed the letter,

As ever yours,
Carrie

Camden, New Jersey
February 1913

Camden, New Jersey was nothing like Burlington, Vermont — at least for the missionaries. The Saints were devoted and the elders there shared the same special camaraderie, but William sorely missed the men he had grown so close to in Vermont. He missed the Vermont Saints, who kept the faith despite the doubters they lived amongst. He missed the evenings spent singing around a piano, which had become a regular pastime for the elders in Burlington. Most of all, William missed Carrie.

"I think the Lord knew what he was doing when He transferred me away from Carrie," William concluded. "My feelings were just getting too intense for me to focus on what I was sent here to do."

The sad realization didn't make the separation any easier, but William moved forward, keeping the work of the Lord in the forefront of his mind, while tucking Carrie away, for now.

He did send postcards and letters to Carrie, as well as many of the other Vermont Saints, including Eva Savoy. Then he looked forward to getting correspondence in return.

The work was much the same in Camden as it was in Burlington. The missionaries spent most of their time tracting and holding cottage meetings. They also met with the Saints regularly.

"I've never been so cold in all of my life." The words were barely understandable, as Elder Faucett's teeth chattered.

William nodded in agreement, too cold to attempt to speak. The pair had been tracting for several hours and were ready to call it a day.

That is, if their frozen bodies could make it back to their boarding house.

William thought his fingers might never thaw, and he was nearly certain he suffered frostbitten toes. February was brutally cold. Both he and Elder Faucett took turns suffering nasty colds. Reflecting back on the year previous, however, William realized that they were lucky to only have sore throats and runny noses. The images of Elders Larsen and McFarlane with pock marks covering their bodies still haunted William.

Finally home, William began to shed his coat, hat and scarf, only to realize that their room wasn't much warmer than the outdoors. Just then, there was a knock on their door.

"I'm sorry it's so cold in your room. I meant to have this heater running before you arrived home. Better late than never." The landlady handed over an oil heater, looking a little chagrinned. "Oh, and here's your mail."

William promptly forgot about the chilly room, thanked the landlady and grabbed the mail. Besides the letters for Elder Faucett, there was a letter from home, a letter from Eva Savoy, a postcard from Elder Brown and finally — there it was — a letter from 137 Pearl Street.

Once the heater was pumping out warm air, the men settled in to read their long awaited letters. It was the first mail delivery since they had moved into the boarding house in Camden, so both elders had been anxiously watching for news from their loved ones.

William didn't even have to think about which letter to open first. He carefully tore open one end of the letter from Carrie and pulled it out. As he began reading Carrie's account of her personal conversion to the church, a lump formed in his throat and tears burned in his eyes. Willing them away so he could read the letter to completion, he took a couple of deep breaths, looked away for a moment, then continued. What he read was everything he had been praying for. His love and admiration for Carrie only increased as he read her sweet testimony. "Yes, it's good I've been transferred. I do not think I could restrain myself from pulling you into my arms if we were together right now," he whispered to himself.

"What's that, Elder Rappleye?" Elder Faucett looked up from his letter to see William swipe at his eyes. "Is everything all right?"

William hadn't spent much time yet with Elder Faucett. Certainly not enough to open up and tell him about Carrie, but he wanted to share the good news with somebody. "Everything is fine, Elder Faucett. I just learned that a dear friend of mine is getting baptized. I only wish I could be there for it."

William read the letter again and again. He couldn't remember ever being so happy.

By the time the mail was read, the room finally began heating up and William felt good — inside and out. As he reached to pull out a blank piece of paper to write a letter in reply to Carrie's, Elder Faucett reminded him that they hadn't yet eaten supper. As if on cue, William's stomach growled and he hesitantly gave up the pen and followed Elder Faucett down to the kitchen.

The dining area was average size — bigger than that of a regular residence, but smaller than a cafeteria. There were other diners eating their supper when the elders took their seats at one of the two long tables. William sorely missed eating with the Drews at their boarding house, or even with the Warnes at their place. Here in Camden, he knew no one and no one knew him. There is a comfort in being among friends.

William could hear a conversation going on behind him. Two men were talking about Mormons. It was hard to ignore what they were saying when they were sitting within earshot of the men. From his vantage point, William couldn't tell if the men were regular boarders at the house, or just taking their supper there. His companion, however, sat across the table from William and had a perfect view of the two. "Elder Faucett, what can you tell me about the two men behind me?" he asked in a near whisper.

"I believe I've seen one of them before — he probably boards here. I'm certain I've not seen the other. I would never forget his long beard. The one with the beard keeps motioning our way, as if he's talking about us."

"He is talking about us. And none too politely, either." William continued to eat in silence so he could hear the conversation.

It was a pretty much one-sided conversation, the bearded man doing most of the talking. "That Joe Smith was nothing but trouble. He was a horse thief and a kidnapper — snatching young girls for his own personal pleasure. He got what was coming to him. The Mormons say he was martyred, but he was definitely murdered — a fair punishment for his sins."

William was nearly to his boiling point listening to someone speak so disrespectfully about a man whom he had learned to love dearly, from atop the knee of his father. His own grandfather knew Joseph Smith personally and would have done anything for him, not out of fear or for some reward, but out of love and respect and a firm testimony of what Joseph taught. Tunis Rappleye, William's grandfather, had become a bit of a legacy in his own right, blazing the trail from Nauvoo, Illinois to Salt Lake City, Utah. He'd sat at the Prophet Joseph Smith's feet and learned the Gospel from him directly. He knew, and William knew, that there was no truth to the lies some ill-informed people spread about Joseph Smith.

William had heard the Mormon Church misrepresented many times — sometimes out of ignorance, sometimes out of malice — but to hear this personal attack on Joseph Smith — accusing him of the most heinous of crimes — just began to feel a little too personal for William's comfort.

Inwardly he was praying; praying with all his might that he would know how to handle the situation. Should he turn around and declare the truth, or should he hold his tongue? He didn't want to cause trouble for the landlord of the boarding house.

The man's voice rose behind him, breaking into William's intense prayer. "He was possessed of the devil, and so are the rest of them Mormons."

William took a deep breath and calmly turned around. "I assume you are speaking about me and my companion here?"

The bearded man's face reddened.

William continued, "I won't try to change your mind about Mormons because it is quite clear your heart is set in hating us, but I would kindly ask you to refrain from speaking about a man that my grandfather rubbed shoulders with and would vouch for, if he were here. A man who never asked to become a prophet, yet willingly took up the task when called upon, and even gave his life for the cause. A man whom I have personally prayed about and know to be a man of God. If you could please be respectful enough to allow us our beliefs as we allow you yours, I would be most grateful." He then, just as calmly, turned around and continued eating.

The bearded man sputtered off a few more hateful comments toward the missionaries, then stalked out of the room.

Elder Faucett observed in amazement. Being fairly new in the mission field, he had not encountered a direct (or semi-direct) assault on his beliefs. "How did you stay so calm, Elder Rappleye? I couldn't hear what they were saying, but by your response, I realize it was quite slanderous. I think I would have either left the room in fear, or lost my head and let him have it."

"Well, I wasn't exactly praying over my food," chuckled William. "I was begging the Lord for help and once I opened my mouth, *He* did the rest. I only hope that the other gentleman can forget all those nasty lies he was being told."

"It sure seems like Satan tries harder to destroy our church than any other." Elder Faucett took a drink from his glass of water.

"He has good reason. Why would he care about stopping anything but the truth?"

"Good point."

William looked behind him to see the lone diner still sitting at the table with a dazed look on his face. William turned fully around and said softly, "I'm sorry if that upset you. It's just that it was very difficult for me to hear such ugly things said about a man whom I highly revere and respect. I hope you'll forgive my intrusion on your conversation."

"Actually," began the man, "I would like to hear more about your beliefs. I'm boarding here, as I believe you are. If you have the time, I would like to hear what you have to say."

Relief washed over William. "Of course we have the time. We would be honored to share our beliefs with you. Your friend's words didn't poison you against us, then?"

"No, no. He's a windbag. He pretends to know everything about everything. But when you spoke, I heard truth. I would like to hear more of it."

William and Elder Faucett returned to their room rejuvenated. "We tracted in freezing temperatures all day long and got no appointments," said Elder Faucett as he moved close to the small heater. "Then, we go to dinner and end up with a very good prospect. And all because you spoke up."

William was much too humble a man to feel he deserved all the credit, but he did offer up a very sincere prayer of gratitude for the Lord's help in guiding his words and actions that evening.

Burlington, Vermont
February 1913

Dear friend Carrie,

I am overjoyed about your news. Not only that you have set a date for your baptism, but even more, that you have received your own personal witness of the truthfulness of the Gospel. I've often felt that same burning, however, not while praying to know if the Church is true. I guess I always just knew. My father taught my siblings and me that sometimes our testimonies grow over time — step by step — and other times there is a much bigger spiritual manifestation — like the one you had. One day I asked my father why I hadn't had such an experience as yours. He asked me if I had doubts about the truthfulness of the Gospel. I told him no, and he just laughed and said, 'Why does the Lord need to manifest to you something that you already know?' I knew he was right, but sometimes I wished I could have had an experience like yours. While reading your letter, however, I found I had a similar burning as you described. The spirit of God is in your testimony.

Carrie looked up from the letter and let her gaze land on Elder Rappleye's photograph, which was propped up on her nightstand. "You are completely oblivious to the powerful light of the gospel which you possess on a daily basis, aren't you, William," she whispered. She couldn't help thinking back to the time she saw William and Josiah Taylor standing next to each other and how starkly different their countenances were. "Your testimony shines brighter than any other that I know."

Carrie continued reading about William's adventures in New Jersey. William always asked Carrie to give his regards to her family, and he never failed to inquire about little Raymond, referring to him as his *little friend*, which brought a smile to Carrie's face. She'd never forget how Raymond took to William so readily. Then he signed the letter,

As ever yours,
William E. Rappleye

She read and reread the letter, especially the first paragraph. She was so grateful for the gift William and the other missionaries had given her — the gift of truth and light.

Carrie pulled a hatbox from under her bed where she had been storing William's postcards and letters. She retrieved the postcard she had received the week previous on Valentine's Day. On the front of the card it read, "To My Valentine" in fancy colors and lettering. Then, on the opposite side, it was just signed, "From ?" Every time Carrie looked at the card, it made her giggle. She wasn't sure why. She really should have wanted William to say something romantic on the card, but true to form, he very appropriately refrained from doing so. In fact, if she didn't know his handwriting so well, she might not have known who sent the card. She ran her fingers across the words that were actually embroidered on a piece of cloth, then attached to a postcard — "To My Valentine." For now, that's all she needed to know.

The next morning didn't stray from the cold, damp, Vermont weather, but despite the frigid temperature, the sun managed to shine. "Carrie?" Emily stood at the bedroom door and softly called to her daughter. "Are you feeling okay, dear? You didn't show up to help with breakfast. That's not like you."

Carrie could hear her mother's voice, but struggled to open her eyes. "Mother?"

The grogginess in Carrie's voice must have alarmed Emily. She rushed to her bedside and laid her fingers on Carrie's forehead. Carrie could see panic in her mother's face.

She began to rise. "I'm sorry Mother. I must have overslept. I started feeling poorly last night. I'll get up and be down as soon as—"

"No, no," Emily cut her off, gently pushing Carrie back to the lying position. "You stay in bed. I'll call for the doctor."

"Doctor?" Carrie couldn't seem to think clearly enough to comprehend why she would need a doctor. "I'm sure I'll be fine, Mother. I just overslept is all." A wave of dizziness caused the room to spin as she tried once more to sit up.

"Carrie, you're burning up. Promise me you will stay in bed while I call for the doctor."

Carrie was reluctant until a fit of coughing possessed her, causing her to choke on the phlegm rising in her throat. Emily found the pitcher of water on Carrie's basin and poured her a glass. Once the coughing subsided, Carrie promised she'd stay down; she then promptly laid her head back on the soft pillow and closed her eyes.

Carrie awoke next to Dr. Hunt poking something into her mouth. "How long has she been like this?" he asked her mother.

"Well, she has had a cold and a bit of a cough for the past week, but I didn't think it was anything to become alarmed about. She appeared to be okay at supper last night."

Carrie lay barely aware of what the doctor was saying or doing as he pulled a thermometer out of her mouth. "103 degrees." Dr. Hunt frowned. "This isn't good." He then listened to her chest and the concern on his face only intensified. "It's as I suspected. I hear a rattle in her lungs. I'm certain Carrie has pneumonia."

Emily began to weep into a handkerchief. Pneumonia had claimed the lives of many people the Drews had known. "What can I do to help her, Doctor Hunt?"

"There isn't a cure, as yet, but I'll prepare some opium for her cough and a mustard plaster for her chest. Do you have a hot water bottle? If so, use it wherever she complains of pain."

Carrie, barely aware of the happenings around her, tried to force herself to focus. She observed her mother listening intently to the doctor. Emily's legs began to wobble and Carrie feared she might collapse.

"I'll check in on her in a couple of hours. For now, just keep her comfortable." With that, he stood to leave. He paused at the door, "It wouldn't hurt to pray for her, as well."

The next few days were a blur for Carrie. She would become conscious every once in a while, just long enough to realize that she was gravely ill. She would hear people speaking in hushed tones, so as not to disturb her, and nothing they said sounded good.

She was fairly alert when the doctor came on the third day. He took her temperature, asked how she felt, and then just shook his head. Carrie tried hard to hear what he was saying to her mother. It was obvious that he didn't want Carrie to hear. She caught bits and pieces; enough to know that he held little hope for her recovery.

"Mother," Carrie's voice was raspy and her throat sore. Emily was to her in seconds. "Mother, please get the missionaries. They'll know what to do."

Emily looked at her with doubt in her eyes, then must have realized that Carrie hadn't been this lucid in days and with her temperature reaching 104, it made no sense that she was coherent now.

"I mean it, Mother. I know they can help me."

Doctor Hunt let out a scoffing grunt.

"Unless, Doctor Hunt, is there anything else you haven't tried on me? From what I've overheard, it doesn't sound as if you hold out much hope for my survival."

"I've done everything within my power, Carrie." Dr. Hunt crossed the room and knelt at Carrie's bedside. "I just don't want you to get your hopes up about the Mormon missionaries being able to perform a miracle and save you."

"Very well. If I'm likely to die anyway, I have nothing to lose. Please, Mother, send for the elders."

Carrie barely got the words out of her mouth when she began coughing in earnest once more.

The doctor shook his head, told Emily that he would be back to check on Carrie in the morning and took his leave.

Emily stayed with Carrie to comfort and reassure her. "Your father is getting the missionaries, Carrie. They will be here soon. You know they are all fond of you and will wish to help. I only wish they were still boarding with us."

When the elders arrived, Carrie was resting fitfully — not fully conscious of the happenings around her. She felt hands being placed upon her head; a blessing being pronounced on her. By the time the prayer was finished, Carrie felt her body relax. Still barely aware, she heard President McFarlane's gentle voice.

"Thank you, Mr. and Mrs. Drew, for calling on us. We all have a soft spot for your daughter and shall fast and pray for her. I will get word to Elder Rappleye, as well. I know he will want to be included in praying for her recovery. With our faith combined, miracles happen."

Emily and Aaron thanked the missionaries and showed them out. "We will keep you informed of any changes," said Emily.

Camden, New Jersey
February 1913

"Do you have any consecrated oil left, Elder Faucett?" William creased his brow in concern, examining his empty oil container.

"Why, is someone sick?"

"No, but I am completely out of oil, and if we were called to administer to someone, unless you have some, we wouldn't be able to do it."

Elder Faucett pulled out the small vial where he kept his oil and inspected it. "It looks like I am out, as well."

"We need to go to the mission office and have some oil consecrated to replenish our supply," William said with some urgency.

"Why are we in such a hurry to get the oil, Elder Rappleye?"

"I don't know. I just feel like we need to go to the mission office right away."

"So, it's not necessarily about the oil. You just feel like we need to go to the office, then?"

"I suppose so. Either way, I really do think we should get over there quickly."

"I've learned to never doubt your intuition, Elder Rappleye."

The two bundled up in their coats, hats and gloves and headed to the mission office.

President Davis, who presided over the area where William was now serving, looked up to see the two missionaries come through the door. "Welcome, Elder Faucett, Elder Rappleye. To what do I owe the pleasure of your company today?"

"Hello, President Davis. We came to get some oil consecrated," said William.

"Well, that's only half true," added Elder Faucett. "Elder Rappleye here felt a prompting to come by today. Is everything okay?"

President Davis' smile flattened into concern. "As far as I know. Oh, wait, this letter just came for you, Elder Rappleye. It's from President McFarlane of the Burlington Mission area."

William tore the envelope open and began to read.

"Elder Rappleye, is everything all right?" asked President Davis.

"It's Carrie ... uh, Miss Drew. She's gravely ill with pneumonia. The doctor doesn't expect her—" William quit reading. He *had* to quit reading. This could not be true. Carrie had just committed to be baptized. She had been happier than ever in her last letter.

"Elder Rappleye, I don't know who this Miss Drew is, but she's obviously someone very important to you," said President Davis.

William, unable to speak, just nodded. Finally finding his voice, he said, "I am going to fast and pray for her. I would welcome any of the elders in this area to join me. Miss Drew is scheduled for baptism in June. You are correct; she and her family are very dear to me."

"I will call on all of the area missionaries to fast for Miss Drew." President Davis laid a reassuring hand on William's shoulder.

"This must be why you felt so compelled to come here today, Elder Rappleye," said Elder Faucett.

William, feeling numb, nodded in agreement.

The elders began fasting immediately and continued for the next two days. William wrote a letter to the Drews, asking that they let him know of any changes. He had prayed fervently before, but never in his life had he felt the need to spend endless amounts of time on his knees.

Finally, just over a week later, a letter came from the Drews' address. William ripped it open and began reading.

Dear Elder Rappleye,

Thank you for fasting and praying for our Carrie. President McFarlane said that faith combined produces miracles, and he was right. Carrie is still very weak, but she is improving every day. Doctor Hunt is baffled — though one would expect that. He had us all convinced that Carrie was beyond saving. I do believe it was the Priesthood blessing she received, as well as your faith and prayers that healed her. Aaron and I cannot thank you enough. Carrie will write as soon as she is able.

Warmest Regards, Mrs. Aaron Drew

William dropped to his knees and offered a prayer of gratitude. If ever he had wanted a prayer to be answered, it was this one.

Once the scare of losing Carrie had passed, William felt more himself again. He hadn't realized how emotionally drained he was from worry. Now he could fully concentrate on missionary work.

February began to thaw into March. It wasn't vastly warmer, but any rise in the temperature could be counted as an improvement. William felt grateful that he and Elder Faucett had only suffered from colds this winter. Especially since their little room heater proved to be less than efficient. Warm weather couldn't come soon enough for the two of them.

They had both acclimated to the area well. Sunday meetings were held at the Doughty's home, just as they were held at the Blair's in Burlington. William enjoyed the Doughty family. They had several children, but the one who claimed William's attention most often was little Albert. Everyone referred to him as "little" because he was the youngest of the Doughty brood and, although he tried to keep up, was often found trailing behind his siblings. William admired the little guy's tenacity, as he never gave up or became discouraged. He just kept on trying. William often told Albert that someday his determination would pay off, then he'd swing Albert onto his broad shoulders and race the other kids, making Albert the winner.

William and Elder Faucett had just finished breakfast on a mildly warm Saturday morning, when the boarding house phone rang. The landlady, Mrs. Pruett, answered and motioned to the elders to come. William took the call. It was President Davis.

"I have some bad news," President Davis began. "Little Albert Doughty from Sunday School has fallen into the Cooper River and they are having a hard time getting him out. Could the two of you come down and help?"

William felt the blood drain from his face. "Of course we can. We'll leave right away." He hung up the phone and relayed the conversation to Elder Faucett.

The two scuttled out in a hurry, anxious about little Albert.

"Did President Davis say if there is any chance the boy is still alive?" Elder Faucett panted, trying to match William's long strides.

"No, but by the sound of his voice, I'm quite certain he is not." William swallowed hard, trying to keep his emotions at bay. He had grown to love little Albert.

As they approached the river, it was quite obvious that the boy was dead. Sister Doughty sobbed against her oldest daughter, while Brother Doughty fought the frigid water with a few other men trying to retrieve the body of his young son.

"He's snagged on something," hollered Albert's father, "but he's too far out for me to reach him. The water is moving too fast. Maybe if we form a human chain by holding onto each other we can reach him." He glanced at the shore and spied the two elders. "The missionaries just arrived. They can help us."

The elders were to the river in seconds, ready to offer their assistance.

They tried every way imaginable to reach the boy, but nothing worked. William couldn't quit looking at the lifeless body, bobbing up and down with the current. The sight sickened him, but he was so grateful to know in his heart that Albert no longer possessed that body and was somewhere far better.

Finally, one of the Doughty's neighbors showed up with some grappling hooks. This proved to be effective. After five hours in the water, little Albert Doughty's body was pulled from the river.

Over the course of the day, William had learned that the Doughty boys were innocently playing next to the river when the watchman yelled at them. This frightened the boys and they began running. Little Albert couldn't keep up with his older brothers and tripped on an exposed tree root and tumbled into the river.

What bothered William most about the story was that there were men working nearby, including the watchman, who witnessed the whole scene and did nothing to help. William's heart ached for Albert's family.

"There's a lesson in all of this," Elder Faucett said to William.

"And what is that?"

"If you think about it, if we just stand by and do not teach people what we know about the restored Gospel of Jesus Christ, it's like watching them drown spiritually."

William agreed that it was a good analogy, but he wished more than anything that little Albert hadn't died in order for the lesson to be learned.

Three days later William was honored to dedicate the grave of Albert Doughty.

Burlington, Vermont
March 1913

It took an entire month for Carrie to fully recover from the illness she had suffered, although her turn-around from going downhill to up was definitely a hairpin turn — sharp and fast. All who understood how truly sick she had been knew what a miracle it was that she had pulled through. Her father sat by her bedside occasionally to read her correspondence and just soak up precious time with his daughter.

"You know, Carrie, you have cheated death twice now."

"How so, Father?"

"Do you remember the story I told you about your birth? The doctor was ready to put a cloth over your nose and bury you with your mother. Two pound babies just don't live. You are a miracle child. And you continue to be so. I'm certain that God has a mission for you to accomplish here. He has spared your life — twice."

"Father, never forget your part in saving me the first time around. I would not be here had you taken the easy way out and let the doctor have his way. I owe you my life. Maybe God does have something in store for me. I don't know. But I'm going to do my best to find out."

Aaron bent down and kissed his daughter on the forehead. "I love you, Carrie. Oh, here's a letter from Elder Rappleye." Aaron placed the envelope on Carrie's nightstand. "You probably don't want me to read that one to you." Aaron chuckled as he exited the room.

Carrie carefully opened the letter from William. She hadn't had the strength to write to William or anyone else in weeks. She knew her mother had sent word of her recovery, but she wasn't sure to whom.

She read William's account of how President McFarlane had let him know of her illness; how he and several other missionaries fasted and prayed for her and that he received word from her mother that she was steadily improving. Carrie was grateful to her mother. She wouldn't want William to think she had just stopped writing for no good reason.

After reading the letter, she carefully slid it back into the envelope, unwilling to set it aside for now. She drifted off to sleep with the letter securely between her hands.

Before long, Carrie was back on her feet again, bustling around the boarding house, helping with meals and such.

When Doctor Hunt gave Carrie her final examination, he couldn't hide the surprise in his eyes. "You seem to have no lasting effects from the pneumonia, Carrie. You are a lucky girl. I've never seen *anyone* as sick as you were *live*, let alone come out completely unscathed."

"I'm pretty sure luck had nothing to do with it. I'd rather say I'm blessed, Doctor."

"Call it what you will, I'm just happy you are doing so well."

"Thank you, Doctor Hunt. I am, too." She smiled sincerely at the doctor, realizing he would never admit the missionaries' role in her recovery.

Time seemed to be marching in place as Carrie anticipated her baptism in June. She only wished the lake would warm up sooner so that she could expedite things a bit, but after the especially cold winter they had experienced, there was no hope for that to happen.

Eva burst through the kitchen door to find Carrie tidying up. She had an announcement. "I've decided that I want to be baptized, too."

Carrie hoped Eva might have had an experience similar to her own personal conversion. Eva hadn't said she had and Carrie didn't want to ask something so personal. So, giving her friend a hug, Carrie expressed how happy she was that Eva had made that decision.

She brought two glasses of lemonade to the table and sat down to have a friendly chat. Dare she ask about William?

"Have you received any letters from Elder Rappleye lately?" That seemed innocent enough.

"Yes, I got one just last week. How about you?"

After comparing notes, Carrie realized that William was sending letters to both her and Eva at the same time. I suppose he doesn't want to hurt anyone's feelings, she thought. And who knows? William might be in love with Eva and *I'm* deluding myself. Carrie sincerely hoped not. She also reasoned that if Eva was writing to William, he was far too polite to just ignore her. Of course he would write back. She only wished she could read some of their correspondence.

"Carrie?"

Carrie jolted out of her reverie. "Sorry, Eva, I don't know where my head was. What were you saying?"

"I asked if Elder Rappleye told you about his trip to Washington, DC?"

"Yes, he did. That was quite the thing, wasn't it? To go to Washington to see Woodrow Wilson inaugurated and end up in the middle of a Women's Suffrage Parade. And from the pictures I saw in the paper, there were thousands of people there."

"Elder Rappleye's lucky. He and his companion have not only been to Washington, DC, and seen the outgoing as well as the incoming president of the United States, but they also went to Philadelphia, where they saw several historical sites." Eva watched her drink as the pulp swam around in her cup.

Carrie laughed. "It makes you wonder if they are doing any missionary work."

"He'll come for our baptisms, won't he?"

"Eva, I don't think it works that way. They were able to go to those historical places because their whole district went and the sites are very close to New Jersey, where the missionaries reside. Elder Rappleye can't just say he has to travel to Burlington for a baptism, then up and leave."

Eva looked as if she might cry. "I really thought he would come. I miss him."

"I miss him, too." Carrie squeezed Eva's hand.

Emily took more time to make the commitment to be baptized. It was a life-changing decision. But after having Carrie and Aaron read to her from the scriptures as well as the literature William left, she felt quite certain baptism was the next step.

This delighted Carrie. Now, if only her father would take the leap of faith. She felt certain he believed the Mormon doctrine to be true; however, she knew her father well enough to know that he was somewhat stubborn and stuck in his ways. "All in good time, Father, all in good time."

Thursday, June 19th finally arrived, rainy and cold, but that didn't dampen Carrie's spirits. She told the missionaries that she didn't care how cold it was inside or outside of the lake — she had waited long enough.

Together, Carrie and Elder Matthew Madsen entered Lake Champlain. The frigid water didn't bother Carrie in the least. All she could feel was the warmth of the Holy Ghost reconfirming to her that she was making the right decision. The proper words were uttered and Carrie was lowered into the water — washed clean from all sins. Carrie had never felt so happy and clean. Tears blended with her already wet face.

Elder Madsen hurried Carrie up to the bank of the lake, where Emily was waiting with a towel. He turned his attention to Eva. "Are you next, Miss Savoy?"

Carrie smiled at Eva as she toweled herself dry. She felt lighter than air.

"I do want to be baptized next—"

Before Eva could finish her sentence, a loud clap of thunder and a streak of lightning sent them all scurrying away from the water.

"Can we wait until the weather improves?" shivered Eva, her teeth chattering.

"Of course," said Elder Madsen. "It is dangerous to be in the water in the midst of an electrical storm."

The rainy weather continued for two more days. Finally, on Sunday, June 22, 1913, Eva Savoy and Emily Drew were baptized members of the Church of Jesus Christ of Latter-day Saints.

Emily had suffered from severe rheumatism and headaches for several years previous to her baptism, but would tell anyone who asked that after coming up from the waters of baptism, she never suffered from either again.

Directly following Eva's and Emily's baptisms, all three, including Carrie, were confirmed members of the Church of Jesus Christ of Latter-day Saints and given the gift of the Holy Ghost.

The only thing that would have made Carrie's baptism better — besides sunny weather — was if William could have baptized her. For now, she would have to settle for giving him a full account in a letter.

When Mr. Dunlap arrived to deliver the mail, Carrie was ready and waiting to send her letter off to Camden, New Jersey. Mr. Dunlap chuckled as he exchanged her letter to Elder Rappleye for one to Carrie postmarked from Camden. "It seems you are keeping the postal workers quite busy between Burlington and Camden."

Carrie smiled and nodded to Mr. Dunlap. He began some small talk, but must have realized she was more interested in the contents of the letter he had just delivered than socializing. "I'll just be on my way, then," Carrie heard him say.

As soon as the door shut behind Mr. Dunlap, Carrie quickly opened the letter. It was puzzling to get a letter from Elder Rappleye at that time, as he generally waited for hers to arrive before responding.

It was a short message, and it looked as if he had written it in a hurry.

Carrie,

> *I don't have much time to write, as I have been given very short notice of my departure. However, I wanted you to know that I am being released as a missionary. My papers were handed to me on July 1st. I will be leaving Camden as soon as possible. It will be a long journey home to Cowley, Wyoming, but I will write as soon as I arrive.*

As ever yours,
William E. Rappleye

"That was four days ago." Carrie reread the letter to make sure she hadn't misread the date. "That means my letter won't find him in Camden." She thought about running after Mr. Dunlap, but realized he was long gone.

Carrie's heart ached. Until that moment, she honestly did not know how much she truly loved William. She felt empty inside. A tear slid down her cheek as she realized that she most likely would never see him again.

Camden, New Jersey
June 1913

June 1st, 1913. It had been two full years since William Rappleye became Elder Rappleye. Thumbing through his mission journal, William realized how lucky he had been. When first embarking on this journey, he was nervous to visit a strange part of the United States — strange to him, anyway. He was also concerned about how he and his message would be received. Now, two years later, William was in love with the Eastern states, he was enamored with the people he had met along the way, and he had a deep appreciation for everything he had experienced — both positive and negative. If nothing else, he had grown from the negative. William had seen and done things he never would have done had he not answered the Lord's call to serve.

Then there was Carrie. A smile played on William's lips when he thought of sweet Carrie. He counted meeting and becoming acquainted with Carrie Drew as one of the greatest blessings of his mission. And if he never saw her again … the smile disappeared and William shuddered … he still considered himself a better person for having known her.

"Elder Rappleye," President Davis's voice jolted William back to the present, "I just learned that James E. Talmage, of the Council of the Twelve Apostles, is expected to arrive this afternoon. We need to prepare for his visit."

William had been serving directly with President Davis for the past two months. He snapped to attention at the president's announcement. It was no small thing to meet an apostle of the Lord. There really wasn't much planning to be done, however. Just some tidying up.

Meeting one of the Twelve Apostles — one more blessing to add to my growing list. William's smile returned.

The apartment was straightened and a bedroom readied just in time to welcome the apostle. Before long, all of the missionaries serving in the area were congregated and ready to hear Elder Talmage speak to them.

After listening to the wisdom Elder Talmage imparted to the missionaries, all present were invigorated. This helped William because he was aware that his release was coming soon, but knew not the exact date. Oftentimes, missionaries who were nearing the end of their missions would get restless and their work proved to be less than effective. William began to understand this emotion. At times it was difficult to keep his heart in the work. Now, after hearing Elder Talmage's inspiring message, he readied himself to move forward without thinking about when his release date might be.

On June 19th, however, William's mind and heart were far from the work he had in front of him. They were, in fact, in Burlington, Vermont, with Carrie. William gazed out the window at a mother bird feeding a worm to her chicks in a nearby tree. He envisioned Carrie dressed in white for her baptism, then being lowered into the sparkling blue Lake Champlain. His heart swelled when he thought about all of the blessings in store for her as she made the commitment to take God's name upon her. What he wouldn't give to have been present.

The train whistle blew. William couldn't believe he was actually headed home. There would be plenty of stops along the way — none of which included Burlington, Vermont. He was disappointed about that, but very excited to see his family again.

William's traveling companion, Elder Anderson, was returning to the West as well. Their first stop: Palmyra, New York. They took their time and relished visiting the home of Joseph Smith, the Sacred Grove and the Hill Cumorah. There was so much Mormon Church history in the area. William broke off a small piece of bark for a souvenir from the tree Joseph Smith prayed beneath when he received the well-known "First Vision" — a key factor in the restoration of the Mormon Church.

After spending several days in New York, he and Elder Anderson parted ways, and William's next stop was Chicago. He didn't have as much to do in Chicago, so after just a couple of days, William was back on a train bound for Denver, by way of Kansas City.

Nell Rappleye Broadway, William's older sister, lived with her husband, Dr. Broadway, in LaSalle, Colorado. William spent several days there, reacquainting himself with his young nieces and nephews.

Finally, after what seemed like an endless amount of time on trains, William arrived in Cowley, Wyoming on July 23rd, 1913. His mother and father, as well as several of William's siblings, nieces and nephews, were there to greet the newly returned missionary. "What a sight for sore eyes!" William beamed. Cowley might still be wild country, but it's home. His mother wasted no time pulling him out of his ruminations about home as she wrapped William in a bear hug.

The next day, William and his father lazed on a blanket of cool, Wyoming grass. "What are your plans, Son?"

Laura, William's mother, was busy scurrying around, laying out picnic food on a long, wooden table for their dinner. It was the 24th of July, a day of commemoration and celebration for the Mormons.

On that day in the year 1847, Brigham Young and his trailblazing companions (Tunis Rappleye included) entered the Salt Lake Valley and uttered the famous words, "This is the right place," meaning, this is the place we will make our new home, a refuge from the persecution that has plagued us for years.

"Well, I figured you could use some help on the farm. Then after harvest season, I'm not certain what I will do. I'll need to find a job." William rubbed his chin.

Frank smiled, obviously happy to have his hard-working son home and willing to help out. "Your brother, Roy, is working in Montana on the railroad. He said they are always looking for help, if you are interested."

"That sounds like it might be worth looking into."

Laura frowned, "William's only just home one day, Frank, and you're already planning to send him away?"

"The boy's got to eat." Frank stood up to fill his plate with delicious fried chicken, potato salad and watermelon. "But for now, let's just enjoy your homecoming and the next few weeks that we have together. It's sure good to have you back in Cowley, Son."

William had been home for a couple of weeks now, and as much as he tried to suppress his feelings, they would not go away. After spending many nights on his knees, William knew he had to follow his heart. So, pulling out a notepad and pen, he began writing.

Dear Carrie,

I have arrived home safely. Cowley is vastly different from the Eastern states, but it is home to me and I am happy to be back. I hope this letter finds you and your family doing well. I miss you all very much. The letter you mailed in the beginning of July finally made its way to my home. I'm sorry about that; I had little warning of my departure.

Carrie, I need to confess something to you. I love you and I have for some time now. It was inappropriate to profess or act upon those feelings while I was serving as a missionary, but now I feel compelled to make them known to you. I do not know if you have similar feelings toward me, but I must ask — will you marry me? If the answer is yes, I will send you train fare to Billings, Montana as that is where I will be working very soon. If the answer is no, please do not feel you have offended me in any way. I will just count myself blessed for having known you.

Hopefully ever yours,
William

William sealed the letter and put it on the small table next to his bed. "If I still feel like it's the right thing to do in the morning, I will mail it," he spoke aloud, not knowing if it were to God or to himself he was talking.

Morning came early on the farm, but William didn't forget about the letter. As he headed out the door to help his father in the hayfield, William handed his mother the letter. "Ma, would you mind mailing this for me?"

Laura gave him a puzzled look. "Who is Miss Carrie Drew?"

William's lips tugged into a smile, "Hopefully, my future bride." He winked at his mother, who was wearing an astonished look. The screen door creaked as it swung shut behind him. Before she was able to collect herself enough to ask any more questions, William was gone.

If William thought working out in the hayfield was labor intensive, he realized it was nothing compared to the grueling work of building a railroad. He rose at five o'clock in the morning to care for eight head of horses before work, then put in ten hours on the grade, as well as driving the load wagon. After all that, William would walk five miles to the town of Fergus to see if he had received any mail. It would all be worth it if the letter he was waiting for had arrived.

It didn't take long before William was rewarded with a letter from 137 Pearl Street. He barely contained his excitement as he nearly ran the five miles back to his camp near the town of Hilger, Montana. His fatigue was all but forgotten.

By lamplight, he read the letter.

Burlington, Vermont
August 1913

Carrie's hands began to tremble as she read the latest letter from William. She clutched a chair to steady herself.

"What is it, dear?" Emily squinted, trying to read over Carrie's shoulder.

"It's William ... I mean Elder Rappleye. He asked if I will marry him."

"He what? But he's in Wyoming. You aren't considering it, are you, Carrie? I mean, he will expect you to leave Vermont and move to the West with him."

Carrie smiled at her mother. "Do you mean for me to stay here with you and Father forever?"

"Yes. I can't even imagine living without you here."

The sincerity in her mother's reply surprised Carrie. "Mother, you know I can't stay here forever. I wish to have a family of my own someday. I thought you liked Elder Rappleye."

"I love Elder Rappleye as if he were my own son, Carrie, that's not what I'm worried about. I just can't lose you." Tears formed and began to make a path down Emily's face. She took ahold of Carrie's hand. "Do you want to marry Elder Rappleye? Do you love him?"

Carrie paused before she looked earnestly into her mother's face. "Yes, Mother, more than ever. I do love him. I think I always have."

The crease in Emily's face only deepened at hearing Carrie's confession.

"What if you came to Wyoming with me? You, Father, Clara and Raymond. We can all go to Wyoming together." She rushed on, "William said it's wild country, compared to what we're used to, but he loves it there. I'm sure we could learn to love it there, too."

Emily dried her eyes on her apron and furrowed her brow in contemplation for a moment. "Let's talk to your father about it tonight at supper." She pulled Carrie into a squeeze.

By the beginning of September, the Drew family's boarding house was sold and their belongings were being crated and shipped off to wild Wyoming. Carrie could hardly contain her excitement about the move. She knew it would be an adjustment for the whole family, but the thought of becoming Mrs. William Rappleye gave her butterflies.

There was a rap at the door. Carrie opened it, expecting to find one of the many men hired to crate up their belongings.

"Eva! I haven't seen you in an eternity!" Carrie pulled Eva into an embrace.

Eva didn't say anything and stood stiffly as Carried hugged her.

"What is it, Eva? Are you well?"

Eva burst into tears. "I thought he loved me, Carrie," she said between sobs. "I really thought he loved me. But it was you he loved."

Understanding registered on Carrie's face. Suddenly aware of her friend's disappointment and broken heart, her eyes began to mist up. "Oh Eva, I'm so sorry. I honestly didn't know that William loved me until I received his letter once he returned home. I never meant for you to get hurt."

"But you can't leave me, Carrie. You are my dearest friend. You can't leave me and marry the man I'm in love with."

"Did William write to you, Eva? Did he explain things?" Carrie was certain Eva had wasted no time in writing William to divulge her secret love for him once he was released from his mission, or quite possibly just before then. Eva was the type to wear her heart on her sleeve.

Eva's tears weren't letting up. Carrie handed her a handkerchief and guided her to the settee.

"Of course I wrote to him, Carrie. I told him how I felt about him, but when he wrote back, he very politely told me that he loved me like he loves his sisters. That's something I never wanted to hear. Oh, Carrie." Eva blew her nose. "Now you are leaving me and marrying the man of my dreams."

"Eva, we will keep in touch, I promise! I'm so sorry if I ever misled you. I've always loved William too, but I didn't realize just how much until he asked me to marry him. Now, I can't imagine a life without him. Please try to be happy for me, my dear friend. I will sorely miss you." Carrie pulled Eva into a tight embrace. This time Eva didn't resist.

Clenching her teeth as if still fighting the urge to wail out loud, Eva nodded her head. "I will always want the best for you, Carrie. You have been like a sister to me, and I love you for that. I guess it just came as a surprise. I suppose I should write Elder Rap— ... William a letter of congratulations. I promise to try and be nice," she said through hiccups from crying.

"Thank you, Eva. I know this is hard for you. I promise to be your friend forever."

On October 8th, 1913, five weary travelers arrived in Billings, Montana: Carrie, Aaron, Emily, Clara Benoit and Raymond Romprey — a family pieced together by circumstance, yet a family still the same.

It didn't take long to spot William. He was the man wearing the grin from ear to ear. However, he did look quite different donned in heavy boots and work clothes — nothing like his missionary attire that the Drews were accustomed to seeing him wear.

As William made his way to his soon-to-be family, Emily sighed. "I thought he was a fine-looking man before. Now he's ruggedly handsome."

"Hush, Mother! He'll hear you." Carrie's eyes twinkled, betraying her stern warning.

William finally reached the group and this time, when Carrie opened her arms to pull him into an embrace, he walked straight into them.

"*Ahem*, you're not married yet," Mr. Drew said.

They all laughed, but the two still clung to each other as if years instead of months had separated them.

"When do you have to return to work ... uh ..." Carrie had never called William by his given name to his face and seemed uncertain with the abrupt change in protocol.

"He chuckled. To you I am William, or Will, as most people around here call me. And, never."

"Never ... never what?" asked a baffled Carrie.

"I quit my job here in Montana. I never have to go back to work on the railroad. I will find something else. Something better suited for a married man, when that time comes. We will probably still need to live in Billings, at least during the winter; there are no jobs beyond farming for me in Cowley. For now, I will take you to my home. My folks are anxious to meet you all."

William had described Cowley, Wyoming to Carrie as being quite different from Burlington, Vermont, but he guessed she never imagined just how different it would be. He chanced a sideways look at her as they approached the Rappleye homestead. Her eyes widened as if she'd been transported back in time. William's heart began to twist. By the time he was ushering the Drew family inside, he was near suffering a panic attack.

The Rappleye's home, a log cabin, had a very rustic appearance, with a bed in each of the three rooms and a kitchen, much like the early settlers lived. It made sense as the Rappleyes were among the early settlers of Wyoming. Still, what was home to William would be backward to Carrie and her family. William began to question his logic for proposing to her. What was I thinking? She must be positively mortified, he thought to himself. He wiped clammy hands on his pants.

William, recognizing the shock registering across the Drew family's faces, hurried to make introductions — hoping to get their minds on something other than the house. "Ma, Pa, this is Aaron and Emily Drew, Clara and Raymond. And this is Carrie."

After all who were present at the time in the Rappleye home were properly introduced, they settled in for a visit. William breathed a sigh of relief when he saw how well they all seemed to be getting along. He whispered to Carrie, "I guess I should have warned you about the dirt floors and the oil cloth ceilings."

That may have been the wrong thing to say. Carrie looked like she would either laugh or cry when he said it. William wasn't sure. But then she held her head high and whispered back, "Your home is lovely. I can tell there is a lot of love in your family. Besides, a little dirt never hurt anyone."

William reached over, squeezed Carrie's hand, and gave her a grateful smile.

The two returned their attention back to the conversation at hand.

"You can stay with us until you can find a place of your own to live," Laura Rappleye generously offered. We don't have much to offer in the way of luxuries, but what's ours is yours."

"Thank you for your hospitality," said Aaron. William realized they really didn't have any choice in the matter. Once they had made the commitment to live in Wyoming, there was really no turning back.

A week passed before the Drews were able to secure some rooms in William's married sister's and brother in-law's home, Clara and Jack Snell. They lived very near the Rappleyes.

William and Carrie spent most of their days buying furniture for the Drews' new abode and helping them move their belongings, which had finally arrived from Burlington. William was determined to make his future in-laws as comfortable as possible.

He was well aware of the sacrifice the Drews had made in relocating to Wyoming. After enjoying some of the modern luxuries while on his mission, currently inaccessible to his family, William knew what it was like to step back in time — nothing about it was easy. He never, in his wildest imagination, expected the entire Drew family to pick up and move west, but he was pleased they did and wished to ease their burden.

Frank and Aaron got along famously. They spent many evenings in deep conversation. William overheard his father ... well, being his father — blunt and to the point — just like his name. "Now that you're out here living among many more Saints than in Vermont, don't you think it's about time you were baptized yourself, Aaron?"

William, who was just passing through the house with a box laden with goods, stopped, frozen in his tracks and turned to look at Aaron.

"I know you are right, Frank, but I don't suppose I can still hang onto my pipe."

William nearly dropped the crate he was carrying, as he took a step backward.

Both men burst into laughter. William let out a sigh of relief. This is just what Aaron needed all along, he thought — someone his own age to help him make the commitment of baptism.

The two couldn't have been closer in age unless they were twins. Both Frank Rappleye and Aaron Drew were born in the year 1848, yet had vastly different backgrounds. They seemed to enjoy regaling each other with stories of their upbringings. William was so grateful for the instant bond between them. Laura Rappleye was several years Emily's senior, but William was gratified to see them getting on well, too.

⁓

"Aaron Edward Drew, having been commissioned of Jesus Christ, I baptize you in the name of the Father, and of the Son and of the Holy Ghost, Amen." William's eye's glistened as he lowered his soon-to-be father-in-law into the lake water.

In line next was fourteen-year-old Clara Benoit. Coming out of the water, she wore a smile from ear to ear. William would never have guessed that Clara was not born into the family. She often told him that she never regretted her decision to leave Vermont for the wild Wyoming country. And she especially didn't regret wishing to become a member of the Church.

"My turn, my turn," Raymond yelled as he rushed toward the water.

"Hold on, little friend." William was quick to grab Raymond before he dove head first into the frigid water. "You will have a turn, but not for a few years yet."

Disappointment was written all over Raymond's face, but once the cold water from William's wet clothes seeped into his own, Raymond began to shiver. "I guess I can wait a while 'til it warms up ... like in ten years." William chuckled and ruffled the boy's hair affectionately.

It was November 2nd, 1913 when Aaron Drew and Clara Benoit were baptized and confirmed members of the Church. "My family is beginning to feel eternal," Carrie beamed. "Isn't it about time we took our vows?" she asked William when they found time to take a walk together.

"It is indeed," William said, pulling her into his arms and kissing the top of her head.

Carrie shivered from the sensation. "When?"

"I need to help Pa get enough wood cut and coal stored for the winter, and then we can be married."

"Why can't we be married in the temple? Now that my folks are both members of the church, they could all participate in the ceremony."

"We will be sealed as soon as possible, Carrie. There's nothing I want more, but you have only been a member of the Church since June. There is a rule about getting a temple recommend, the paper that allows one to enter His holy house. You must be a member for a full year."

"But why?" Carrie found a tree stump to stand on, making herself nearly eye level with William, who normally stood a foot taller than she.

William smiled and put his hands around her tiny waist. "I suppose the Lord wants to make sure anyone going through the temple understands and is truly committed to the Gospel and is not just there for a wedding or something. It makes sense when you think about it. But don't worry. We will make it to the temple. We made it this far and I love you more every day."

"I had my doubts when I first saw Cowley, but Will, I would marry you even if we had to live in a tent and eat Wyoming grass." Carrie's blue eyes sparkled.

William's breath caught and, as if he couldn't help himself, wrapped his arms around her waist and placed a tender kiss on her lips. "Our wedding best be sooner rather than later." He smiled devilishly.

CHAPTER THIRTY-THREE

Billings, Montana
November 1913

On November 28th, final preparations were made for the journey into Billings, Montana. The plan was for the couple, William and Carrie, to get married and find a place to live. Then, William would find a job.

There were many hugs, kisses and tears shed as family members bade the happy couple farewell. "I will write every day," promised Carrie. The train whistle blew and off they went.

They secured two rooms at the St. Paul Rooming House in Billings. Then, William and Carrie set out to buy some suitable clothes for the wedding. They spent the remainder of the evening, which there really wasn't much of, in nervous anticipation for the events of the following day.

It felt odd to be married by someone not of their faith, but since they could not yet be sealed in the temple, it didn't really matter who married them, as long as it was legal.

After a bit of time and effort, William and Carrie found someone to join them in holy matrimony. Reverend Henry North, of the First Congregational Church, performed the ceremony. *"I now pronounce you Husband and Wife."*

"I've waited the better part of the last two years to hear those words," William whispered to Carrie as he slipped a wedding band on her slender finger.

Carrie looked up at her husband, tears streaming down her cheeks. "I love you, Will."

"You may now kiss the bride," the Reverend continued.

William pulled Carrie into his arms and did exactly what the Reverend suggested.

At precisely three-thirty in the afternoon of November 29th, 1913, Carrie Drew and William Rappleye became Mr. and Mrs. William Rappleye. A new chapter in their story had begun.

William found work at a sugar factory in Billings, Montana. It didn't last long, as it was only a winter campaign, but that suited the newlyweds just fine. After several months away, they were both anxious to see their families again, and there would be plenty of work on the farm back in Cowley to keep William busy beginning in the spring.

⟡

"Oh, no you don't." William rushed to pull Carrie away from the wagon bearing their few belongings, freshly delivered from Billings.

"For Pete's sake, Will, I can carry in a few items without hurting myself."

"Not in your condition, and not while I'm right here to do it myself. Now go have some lemonade. Mama just made a fresh pitcher full." William kissed Carrie on the forehead , then bent down and whispered something about keeping his mama out of trouble to her barely bulging stomach.

Carrie laughed as she swatted William away. "You act as if I'm an invalid. I finally feel well enough to function like a regular person."

"All the more reason for you to rest; I don't want you feeling ill again."

Some time in January Carrie had begun to be nauseated and tire easily. It wasn't like her. She had always been a hard worker at the boarding house. After a few weeks of feeling sick, William talked her into seeing a doctor.

"It looks as if you two will need to find a larger home," the doctor said with a wide grin. "Mr. Rappleye, your wife is with child."

William could hardly contain his excitement. "When will our child arrive, Doctor?"

"By my calculations, Mrs. Rappleye should be ready to deliver her baby in mid-October."

Word spread quickly, once Carrie and William reached Cowley. Everyone congratulated the happy couple ... everyone except Aaron.

"Father, I wish you could be happy for me. William and I are overjoyed to be expecting a baby," Carrie pleaded to her father.

"You know the reason I struggle with your news, Carrie," Aaron said gently. "I just can't bear the thought of what happened to your mother happening to you. What if her condition is genetic? What shall I do if I lose you? What will William do?" Intense sadness reflected in his eyes. "I can honestly say I've never seen a man more in love with his wife than William is with you. It's a somewhat painful reminder of how I felt about your mother. You could never understand what I lost the day you were born."

Tears rolled down her cheeks. When Aaron looked up, he clearly realized the pain he had caused and rushed to rectify it. He pulled Carrie into his arms. "I'm sorry, sweet girl. You are in no way to blame for what happened to your mother. And I thank the Lord every day that you are still with me. Please forgive me for speaking of it."

"Father, there's nothing to forgive. I do understand your misgivings, and you're right. I cannot know your loss, but I want so badly to be a mother. You yourself said I have cheated death twice now. Just maybe the good Lord has a mission for me. I surely hope he didn't send me away from our comfortable home in Vermont for me to perish in this wild country. I have faith that I will be all right. Please try to be happy for me — for us. You are to become a grandfather, after all."

Aaron loosened his grip on his daughter and held her back to look at her. "I am happy for you, Carrie. I will cling to my newfound faith to see us through the fear of losing you. I love you, my darling girl." He kissed Carrie on the forehead.

"Thank you, Father. I love you, too."

The months passed slowly, as they always seem to do when one is anticipating the arrival of a new baby. William was busy farming, which was a nice change from working nights at the sugar factory. The couple resided with William's parents in the log house with the dirt floor and the oilcloth ceiling. It was a cozy fit.

The summer of 1914 was quite unforgettable for the Rappleyes. One of their cows became bloated from eating too much alfalfa, resulting in its death. William, being resourceful, butchered the cow for the beef, then fed a helping of the meat to their pig. The sow was a wedding gift from William's father and was plump with baby pigs nearing their time of delivery. Unfortunately, the pig choked on the beef and also died.

These deaths seemed to be an omen for what was to come next; things far worse than the loss of a cow and a pig. First William's father, Frank, had a stroke and was incapacitated for most of the summer. His wife, Laura, accompanied Frank to Colorado to be cared for by his son-in-law. Then Aaron, too, had a stroke.

Carrie was beside herself with grief. Her father, the one constant in her life since her birth, was no longer himself. He lost his ability to move around physically, making him bedbound, and his speech became slurred and incoherent. Carrie spent many long hours sitting at her father's bedside, reading and occasionally singing his favorite songs. At times she felt he was with her as he would look deep into her soul and relay a message of love and tenderness, but most often Aaron's eyes were empty. He eventually became completely unresponsive.

Both Aaron Drew and Frank Rappleye completed their Earthly missions in September — eleven days apart — just weeks before the arrival of their grandson.

Carrie and William mourned the loss of their fathers, while Laura and Emily mourned the loss of their sweethearts and life companions. The only solace they found came through knowing they would all be together again one day. Emily and Carrie were especially thankful that Aaron had been baptized just months before.

On October 19th, Carrie's labor began. The household was still in mourning for the loss of two very fine men, Frank and Aaron, thus the arrival of a child was a bright spot in an otherwise very dark time.

William paced nervously as Carrie's labor intensified. "I should be with her," he said to his mother, who kept a light conversation going, trying her best to keep him calm.

"William, the father's place is not in the birthing room. I truly don't believe men could stomach watching a birth."

"I'm a farmer, Mother. I've been present for many births, albeit, they were animals. What if she has the same problem her mother had? I'm going in. She might need me."

Before he could shoulder his way past the women into the room where Carrie lay, however, William heard the cry of his new son. Relief washed over him ... that is, until the words he heard next.

"She's hemorrhaging! Get as many towels and rags you possibly can!" the doctor barked out.

William was to Carrie's side in seconds, head bowed over her and praying. "Stay with me Carrie. I can't lose you."

Barely able to remain conscious from loss of blood, Carrie looked into William's eyes and said, "I won't leave you. It's not my time." Then her eyes closed. Somehow her declaration made William feel better. Yet he kept her feeble hand in his and continually felt for a pulse.

The bleeding finally stopped and Carrie's heart was still beating. No one present dared to be relieved just yet. It was as if time stood still as William, Emily and Laura all held their breath in anticipation of what would happen next.

"I believe we were able to stanch the bleeding in time to save her life." The doctor swiped at his brow with his forearm and dropped some blood-soaked cloths into a bucket.

Carrie awoke to find William's pale face looking down at her. "Where's my baby?" she whispered.

William's eyes filled with grateful tears. "He's just in the next room. Clara has him. He's beautiful, Carrie." He bent down and kissed his wife, so grateful she had pulled through.

Once the baby was cleaned up and quietly nursing, the doctor sat down with the new parents to explain what had happened. "We call it a ballooned uterus," he said. "You're likely to have the same occurrence should you have any more children."

"Then she shall not have any more children," Emily spoke quite vehemently from across the room.

"Mother, that decision is not yours to make. It is between Will and me, and I do wish for my new baby boy to have a playmate."

Emily began to protest until William laid a gentle hand on her arm, then turned to Carrie and asked, "How did you know you would live through the hemorrhage, Carrie?"

"In my Patriarchal Blessing that I received just days ago, I was told I would be a mother in Israel and that I have much work to do for my family that has not yet received the gospel. I cannot do either of those things if I'm dead."

William squeezed Carrie's hand. "No, I don't suppose you can."

The couple decided to name their new baby boy Foster Drew. Foster, after Carrie's birth mother, Carrie Foster, and Drew in honor of her father, Aaron Drew.

In the quiet of their log cabin room, warmed only by a low burning fire, Carrie rocked her baby. "I never thought I could be so happy," she said softly to her husband, who was kneeling next to her, caressing the baby's head. "I only wish my father could have lived to meet his grandson."

"I do believe your father was present when Foster was born. He was praying for you right alongside the rest of us. He would be proud of you, Carrie. You are a woman of great faith." William's hand left the baby's head and reached up to turn Carrie's face toward his. "Thank you for coming west for me. Thank you for living in conditions much less comfortable than you are accustomed to and, most of all, thank you for becoming my wife. I love you, Carrie."

"Your tenderness and patience never cease to amaze me, William. It is I who have been blessed." Tears formed in her eyes. "What you have given me is eternal."

A few days later, when he knew Carrie would be all right, William headed back to the fields to finish the fall harvest. The work had been overwhelming with his father now gone. When he pulled out his dinner pail to eat his noon-day meal, he found a piece of paper folded up alongside his sandwich. It read:

To my darling,

> *'Tis not the wall of stone without*
> *That makes the building small or great,*
> *But the soul's light shining round about*
> *And the love that stronger is than hate,*
> *And the faith that overcometh doubt—*
> *Even in a log house,*

Your loving spouse

"I really did marry an angel," William said to himself, wishing he could still be at Carrie's side. Unfortunately, time and money didn't permit William to be where he wanted to be, and he knew his sweet wife was being well attended to by Laura and Emily.

He whispered a prayer of thanks for his wife and their healthy new son, then tucked the note safely away.

As Ever Yours

Cowley, Wyoming
1915

Emily Drew had taken up baking doughnuts and was selling them out of the log cabin during the summer. Carrie explained to her mother on numerous occasions that she was not selling the pastries for enough money to cover her costs. Emily, not having a head for business, was so happy baking and selling her goods, she didn't seem to hear what Carrie was saying. Thus, William picked up the bill and allowed his mother-in-law to go on baking.

"She's suffered a lot since moving west, Carrie," William replied, after Carrie began apologizing for her mother's lack of business sense. "Let her have this if it makes her happy."

One of William's most endearing traits, in Carrie's estimation, was his unfailing generosity and desire to make his loved ones — as well as hers — happy. "I married a good man," she told herself.

During that time, one of the elders from William's mission, Alonzo Barrett, came to stay with the Rappleyes for a time. He was so impressed with Emily's delicious cooking that he offered her a job in Logan, Utah. "It is for a fraternity at the university there. If you can bear cooking for hungry college students, the job is yours."

"I'm flattered," Emily said, "and I do like the possibility of living somewhere more civilized than Cowley, Wyoming, but I don't want to leave you, Carrie." She took a slow bite of a doughnut while deliberating the possibility of moving to Logan.

"Nor do I want to see you go, Mother, but it is a good opportunity for you. Besides, Will and I shall be moving back to Billings for his job at the sugar factory soon."

After much pondering and prayer, Emily took Clara and Raymond and moved to Logan. Shortly thereafter, Carrie and William moved to Billings for the winter campaign at the sugar factory.

At the end of the campaign, William was offered a job to help build another sugar factory in Lovell, Wyoming. He and Carrie packed up once more and moved their little family to Lovell. After completion of the facility, William was hired as a foreman at the sugar factory. This relieved Carrie, as she did not look forward to moving back to the log cabin in Cowley, especially now that her mother and family had moved away.

By the spring of 1916, Carrie grew large with child again. She was due to deliver in August. "Will, before this next little one comes along, I would really like to go to the temple and be sealed," she said over supper one warm evening in May.

They had planned on being sealed a year after their wedding, but with the deaths of their fathers and the birth of little Foster, they had to reevaluate the situation.

Carrie, with a look of determination, broached the subject. "I know we are low on funds, but isn't this one of those things that is important enough to take out a loan?"

William looked up from his plate to see his wife's beautiful face. Being sealed to her for eternity needed to be a priority. "You're right, Carrie. I'll go to the bank tomorrow and see about getting that loan."

William fidgeted with the buttons on his suitcoat, more than a little nervous about asking for a loan to go to Salt Lake City to be sealed to his wife in the temple. None of the bankers he knew in Lovell were of the Mormon faith; they wouldn't know why a trip such as this one would be worth borrowing money for. Still, he had to try.

"Good morning, Mr. Rappleye. How can I help you today?" Lovell was a small town and most everyone knew most everyone else who lived there.

"Hello, Mr. Whitlock. I came to enquire about taking out a loan..."

Before William could get the rest of the sentence out, Mr. Whitlock was patting him on the back and nodding his head. "If your name is William Rappleye, I don't need any collateral. Your word is good enough for me. How much do you need?"

During the short time William and Carrie had lived in Lovell, William's good character had become well-known. He was a man of honesty and integrity.

William was pleasantly surprised by Mr. Whitlock's positive response. He obtained the money needed, then bought train tickets to Salt Lake City, and off they went. Will, Carrie and little Foster were finally going to the temple.

On their wedding day, William thought Carrie to be the prettiest woman he had ever seen. Today she was even prettier. Yes, she had been living in more unforgiving circumstances, given birth and nearly bled to death, was rearing a toddler, and now was nearly seven months pregnant. But when William looked at Carrie across the altar in the Salt Lake Temple, it took his breath away. She looked like an angel. He would finally be sealed to her, not just for this life, but for eternity. Tears were burning in his eyes only to be met with a reflection of the same in her eyes. This was how it was meant to be. He didn't just love Carrie for now, he loved her for forever.

When temple workers brought little Foster in to bind him for eternity to his parents, the tears of gratitude spilled over. Finally, on June 8th, 1916, they became a forever family.

The three stayed in Salt Lake City for a few days before continuing their journey to Logan, Utah to see Emily, Clara and Raymond. While there, they attended the Logan temple and were able to do the necessary temple work to seal Carrie to her parents. It was an uncomfortable journey for Carrie, being large with child, but she knew without a doubt that it was right.

Carrie and William were at peace. Being sealed to each other and their loved ones for eternity leant a feeling of permanence to the couple.

It was good to get back home — even if home was a tiny house in desolate Lovell, Wyoming.

"I don't think I've ever felt so completely happy, Will." Carrie took in her surroundings. William relaxed on the sofa and baby Foster napped on a blanket while a cool breeze whispered through the window.

The house was not, nor would ever be, the modern Vermont home she had left behind, but it was hers and William's and she loved it. Her eyes met William's. He was looking at his wife as if she were the most beautiful creature on earth.

"Come sit with me, Carrie." William's voice grew husky.

She readily complied, snuggling up next to him.

William pulled her into his arms. "Why'd you do it, love?"

"Why'd I do what?" Carrie asked, tilting her head up to look into William's eyes, their heads so close they were nearly touching.

"Why were you willing to leave your beautiful home in Vermont and come all the way out here for me?" The love in his intense gaze spoke volumes.

"William, don't you know me by now? All the money in the world couldn't entice me away from you and this life." She waved her hand, indicating their home and baby. "Like you always tell me, this life is but a short time in the grand scheme of things. We, you and I, are in this for the long haul — for eternity, and there's no one I'd rather spend it with. I'm surprised you would even question that."

"I guess I just keep wondering how I got to be so lucky." William leaned in and gave his wife a tender kiss.

Carrie whispered against his mouth, "No, love, *I'm* the lucky one."

Once settled, William's mother came from Cowley to Lovell for a visit and to help out when the new baby arrived.

Carrie was shelling some peas for dinner when a couple of them fell to the ground. Before she could get to them, twenty-one-month-old Foster had scooped them up and popped them in his mouth. The unwashed peas were covered in bacteria, which soon made little Foster deathly ill with cholera infantim.

Carrie and William were again facing the possibility of losing a loved one — this time, their baby boy, whom they cherished.

The disease ate away the lining of little Foster's bowels and even infected his mouth, making it near impossible for him to swallow his medicine. A once robust baby, he was now skin and bones.

"Mother Rappleye, can you send someone for William at the factory? I believe I am beginning labor."

Laura looked alarmed. She and Carrie had been working tirelessly to take care of Foster. Now was not a good time to have a baby. Unfortunately, she could not will Carrie's labor to stop. Laura wasted no time fetching both William and the doctor and soon both were at Carrie's bedside caring for her as she labored and delivered another baby boy.

Circumstances couldn't have been worse. Carrie bled profusely, as predicted by her doctor in Cowley. Foster was nearly dying from cholera, and the new baby wasn't breathing. The doctor seemed to be in a panic, dipping the baby in hot water, then cold, and thumping him on the back. "This baby cannot die! The other baby is so sick; I fear we will lose them both." The words tore out of the doctor's mouth like a knife ripping through William's heart. His entire world could crumble, all within a moment's time.

He was busy helping his mother stanch the bleeding, when he looked up to see Carrie's face go from pale to ashen, as she slipped from consciousness. "Don't you leave me, Carrie," he choked out. "You're a fighter and you still have work to do."

A tiny cry pierced its way through the commotion, like a flower in a dust storm. Everyone stopped what they were doing to look to where the doctor stood, sweat rolling down his bald head, but grinning from ear to ear. "He made it. You have a healthy son."

Carrie seemed to internalize what was happening as she began to stir.

Once the baby was out of danger, the doctor returned his attention to Carrie. Feeling for a pulse, he took over where William had been sitting. Bloodied towels littered the ground. "You say this happened the last time she gave birth?" He directed his question to William.

"Yes. The doctor in Cowley called it a ballooned uterus hemorrhage."

The doctor just shook his head. "You're lucky she lived."

That didn't help William feel any better, but just as the last time she had given birth, the bleeding slowly ebbed until it stopped, and Carrie's heart was still beating.

On August 28th, 1916, William Morris Rappleye was born. Named after his father, William, and grandmother, Laura Elizabeth Morris Rappleye. The family simply called him Bill.

Carrie finally came to consciousness, but felt very weak for some time after Bill's birth. Caring for a sick toddler and a newborn was nigh impossible for one so sick herself — especially when William's mother had to leave. William hired a girl to help, but she turned out to be very unmotivated and inexperienced so they let her go. Somehow Carrie managed and, despite all the forces which prevailed against her, she pulled through yet another impossible situation.

It wasn't until after Thanksgiving that Foster began to recover from the cholera. Many prayers of thanks were said when Foster could finally lift his head. He had hovered near death for so long, but Carrie knew he would pull through. Once again William credited his recovery to his wife's faith.

To their dismay, however, once on the mend from cholera, Foster's immune system was so battered that he immediately contracted dropsy, a disease that prevented him from passing fluids. He went from being skin and bones, to becoming so filled with fluids that Carrie could hardly lift him. The doctor instructed her to keep Foster near the stove with a very hot fire in order for him to perspire as much as possible. He feared that if Foster didn't pass the fluid from his body, he would simply burst. Carrie and William couldn't bear the thought of their precious, little toddler facing such a horrible fate. They were careful to heed the doctor's counsel in the matter.

One night, a very weary Carrie gently lay her sleeping newborn in his cradle and retired to her bed for the night. Foster slept in a baby buggy, near the hot stove, per the doctor's orders. William, having worked a long, hard day as well, already dozed when Carrie got in bed. He snaked an arm around her waist and snuggled her close. She immediately fell asleep as she always did when William held her.

Out of nowhere, she heard a voice. In the fogginess of sleep, Carrie couldn't tell if she were dreaming. Then she heard it again. She sat up bolt straight, waking William in the process.

"What is it, Carrie? Are you all right?"

"I need to move the buggy."

"You what?" William was still trying to clear the cobwebs from his head.

"I need to move the buggy," she said, scurrying out of William's arms and the warmth of their bed. She moved quickly into the kitchen where the buggy was still standing, just as she had left it. She pushed the buggy forward a few feet, until she felt the panic in her heart subside, then returned to her room. She gave William a look that said, "I just do what I'm told," and snuggled back into bed.

Only a few moments later William and Carrie were again awakened, this time by a crash coming from the kitchen. They rushed in to find that Foster and the buggy had tipped over. The little boy lay sprawled out on the cold floor. If Carrie hadn't moved the buggy, he would have landed on the hot stove. Cold shivers ran up Carrie's spine as she thought about how close she had come to ignoring that still, small voice.

The very next night, Carrie was awakened again. She heard water dripping. This time it was good news. She found a puddle of water beneath the buggy. Foster's fluids were finally draining. William had given Foster many blessings during his illnesses, and in each one he was told his health would be restored. Finally, Carrie thought, those blessings are coming to fruition.

It took several cycles of Foster's little body refilling then draining before he was cured of the illness, but it did eventually happen.

When life began to take on a semblance of normalcy, Carrie, rocking baby Bill to sleep, posed a question to William. "Why do some people suffer so many trials, especially when they are trying to do everything God expects of them?"

"William thoughtfully looked at his dear wife and answered, "I believe God only gives us trials that we are capable of handling. In a way, he is molding us — chiseling off the rough edges by making us stronger through our trials. Carrie, you are the strongest person I know, with faith to match your strength. The trials you have suffered have made you even stronger because you have allowed God's power to work within you. You are an example to so many — especially me. I love you, Carrie."

A tear slipped down Carrie's cheek. She knew William had suffered the same trials as did she. He never left her alone, always lending his strength. She felt she could do anything with Will by her side.

Lovell, Wyoming
1917

To my Darling,

> *I love you dear, I love you well,*
> *I love you more than words can tell.*
> *The world to me is always spring,*
> *And I can only laugh and sing.*
> *If you would leave me now, dear heart,*
> *The sunshine and my heart would part,*
> *And all that would be left for me,*
> *Would be to rise and follow thee.*

xxxxxxxxxxxxxxxxxxx Carrie xxxxxxx

William read the note from his wife over and over, still overwhelmed by the love he felt for her. "She really has no idea how much she means to me," he whispered, as he tucked the note safely back in his dinner pail. "I only wish I could express it as she does so eloquently through verse."

Despite, or perhaps as a result of, the adversity that seemed to plague the couple since the summer of 1914, William and Carrie were molded together in an unbreakable bond. They were two caring and loving people who touched many lives around them as their own love increased.

Another move took the small family of four to Greybull, Wyoming, where William accepted the job of foreman on a newly purchased ranch. Carrie was also put to work as the cook for the workers there.

If Carrie and William thought Cowley to be wild country, they were in for a big surprise when they traveled to Greybull. It definitely qualified as an unsettled, uninhabited piece of earth.

They were given a small, two-room house to live in at first. Water had to be lugged in and Carrie had to keep a vigilant eye on her boys, what with rattlesnakes and scorpions slithering about. A large tent was pitched behind the house for the men to sleep in. These were the men Carrie prepared three large meals for each day, as well as made up their beds in the tent and generally cleaned up after. The work was exhausting, but Carrie never complained

As she dished beef stew up for the men one cool spring evening, she looked around the room, bewildered. "Where is my husband?"

"William never leaves the ranch until he can't see no more, ma'am. And now that it's stayin' light later 'n later, I 'spect he'll work straight through dinner," answered the man they all called Eddie.

Carrie shouldn't have been surprised. She knew her husband and his work ethic. That was one of the things she admired most about him, although she wouldn't mind if he had a bit less work to do so she could spend more time with him.

Eventually, a larger house was constructed on a bit of an elevation, which lent itself to a nice view of the valley. Carrie and William were able to move their little family into it. In the back part of the house was a bunk room, which took the place of the tent which housed the workers. Even though the home was larger, Carrie found it easier to care for her family's part of the house, as well as that of the workers.

It was finally quiet one warm, summer night, after a long day's work for William and Carrie. In the country, where there were no city noises, it was very peaceful. They had the windows open to allow the cool night air to circulate. In the background, an occasional howl of a coyote or the hoot of an owl could be heard. It was times like these life slowed to a bearable and almost peaceful pace — especially when the two were together.

Lying in bed with his wife cuddled up to him, William broke the silence. "I wish you didn't have to work so hard, Carrie." He and his mother-in-law had lost the battle over Carrie having more children several months ago, and now Carrie was very pregnant with their third child.

"I could say the same of you, my dear husband. All your men are at the dinner table by six o'clock, but you just keep on working until it's too dark to work anymore."

"But I'm not carrying a baby." There was a bit of an edge in William's voice.

"Are you upset that we are having another baby, Will?"

"Of course I'm not, Carrie. I love children. I love *our* children, especially, and I would like nothing more than to have a whole houseful of them. But each time you deliver a child, I risk losing you. That's a gamble I don't like to take. Carrie, I never want to be without you." He reached over to caress her face in the darkness and found it wet with tears. "I'm sorry, Carrie," he whispered, "I didn't mean to upset you."

"It's not that, Will. I have felt strongly that I am supposed to have these children. I have to have faith that I will be allowed to live in order to raise them. I love you, Will, and I am touched that you worry so about me, but please place your faith in the Lord and know, as I know, that all will be well."

William wrapped his arms around his wife and pulled her closer. "Sometimes I think you are the one who is teaching me about the Gospel, instead of the other way around." He kissed her cheek. "Let's hope this one is a girl so you won't feel the need to have any more children," he added.

"That's not going to stop me," Carrie said in disbelief. "Did you hear what I said? I am supposed to have several children — not three — several! I'll be finished when the Lord says I'm finished."

Freeing one of his arms, William threw it up in surrender. "I give up. You win. And I will even try to have the faith you have when I'm up to my elbows in your blood as you deliver this brood of children." His voice faltered, but the message was clear.

Carrie put a gentle hand on her husband's cheek, as if to calm him, then snuggled in closer. "We will be okay, Will. We will be okay." She kissed him and laid her head on his chest and drifted off to sleep.

William lay still with Carrie's head atop his chest, but sleep didn't come. Instead he prayed. He prayed for his wife, he prayed for his children, and mostly, he prayed for faith — faith to know what Carrie already knew — that they, Carrie and William, would, indeed, be okay.

As if prophesied, Carrie went into labor the next day. Carrie Brenna Rappleye was born on July 31, 1918.

Carrie experienced the same complications, but the doctor had been warned about them and seemed ready for the worst. Thankfully, Brenna was breathing and the hemorrhage dealt with quickly. William felt certain Carrie's faith was what continued to save her each time she threatened to bleed out. He felt so very grateful to be married to a woman of strength, a woman of courage, a woman of great faith.

Keeping busy on the ranch, William couldn't be of much assistance to Carrie during her long, exhausting days. Taking care of a newborn and two small boys was challenging, especially while preparing meals and cleaning up after a houseful of dirty men, but Carrie rose to the challenge. William was in awe of his wife.

When anyone, especially one of William's ranch hands, would dare complain about his lot in life, Carrie was quick to remind him that there was a war going on and good men were dying. They had no cause to complain. William chuckled listening to her set his men straight.

Thankfully, the war didn't affect William or Carrie directly. However, William's brother, Roy, was called on to serve his country. When the Great War, later to be known as World War I, ended, there was great rejoicing.

This was good news save for the diseases brought into the country as a result of the men returning home. The Spanish influenza killed people as fast as the war itself did. Every school and available building in Greybull became a hospital for those afflicted by the deadly illness.

It was nine o'clock in the evening when someone knocked at the door. "Who could that be so late at night," Carrie murmured.

William opened the door to his neighbor, Mr. Stephens, and his son.

"I'm sorry to call so late, Mr. Rappleye, but I was hoping to speak to your wife."

William narrowed his eyes as if questioning the man, then called Carrie to the door.

"Mrs. Rappleye, could you please cook for the thrashers? My wife just had a baby a couple of weeks ago and she's not up to it just yet. I know the thrashers are done with your property, but we really need our property attended to and the thrashers need to eat."

"Of course I will, Mr. Stephens. Please don't trouble yourself about it. Go home and take care of your wife," Carrie answered.

"Thank you, Mrs. Rappleye. This means a lot to our family."

With that, the neighbor and his son took their leave.

Carrie looked down at her own newborn baby and sighed. William took in the concern on her face and gently pulled little Brenna out of her arms. "You should have declined, love. You have a newborn of your own."

"I know, but somehow I think I've been blessed with strength to handle these things better than some."

"I would say better than most."

The next morning, the thrashers showed up for breakfast. The usual commotion that accompanied the men was missing.

"What's wrong with you men? Is my cooking so bad?" Carrie quipped, trying to lighten the mood.

"It's not that, ma'am," answered one of the thrashers. "It's just, the man we are to do the thrashing for, Mr. Stephens, and his son died during the night."

Carrie, clearly shaken by the news, nearly tripped, toppling a bowl she was carrying to the basin. "How could that be? They were here just before bedtime and they both seemed fine."

"The Spanish flu kills in a matter of hours. You're lucky you and your family aren't sick, since they were both here just before they died."

Forgetting the hungry thrashers for a few moments, Carrie instinctively checked each of her children, making sure they were all okay. Then she ducked into her bedroom where she said a prayer of thanks and a prayer for Mr. Stephen's widow and new baby.

By some miracle, the Rappleyes escaped the Spanish influenza and Carrie was grateful when Greybull, Wyoming had seen the last of it. Too many of her friends and acquaintances had fallen victim to its deadly grip.

Greybull, Wyoming
April 1919

Carrie didn't have much time to settle into a routine before she began experiencing signs she had become very familiar with. Signs of pregnancy. "Brenna's just now eight months old. I can't be expecting another child so soon," she said to her husband over a breakfast she could only look at.

"Are you certain? Could you just have a virus?" William placed his large hand over Carrie's cold, clammy hand, then up to her forehead.

"It's not just nausea I get, Will. There are many signs, and I have them all. Yes, I am quite certain."

"Then we will rejoice in expecting a new addition to the family. If the Lord thinks we can handle another mouth to feed, He will provide." William then pulled Carrie onto his lap and held her close, cherishing a moment without a tot on her, or his, knee.

Carrie melted into his embrace, grateful he had finally come to terms with her determination to follow her heart where their children were concerned. Grateful, too, for his faith.

This pregnancy was different than the others. Carrie was growing rapidly, making her petite five foot frame quite awkward. Near the end of third trimester, Carrie looked as big around as she did tall. It also became a challenge to keep up with a four-year-old, a two-year-old and a baby. But Carrie bore it well, and not only took care of her growing family, but also the men working on the ranch.

William did all he could to help Carrie out with the family, but he too was stretched thin.

It was a cold, blustery day in December when Carrie felt water trickling down her leg, and then the painful grip of labor took hold of her. She needed William. She knew he was milking cows and working on the ranch, but right now she needed him more. This baby was not going to wait.

Her nearest neighbor lived in the two bedroom house down the hill; the home that she and William once occupied. Weighing her options, she decided to take a chance on finding William herself. She doubted that if she descended the hill to summon a neighbor, she would be able to make it back to her own home in time to give birth.

"Foster, I need you to take care of Bill and Brenna while I go find your father," Carrie motioned to her now five-year-old son.

Foster was a very good boy, when he and Bill weren't getting into mischief. He loved his mother and would do whatever she asked. Narrowing his eyes, causing his face to look quite serious, he nodded his head. "Yes, Mama. I'll take care of them."

Carrie's labor pains seemed to increase with every few steps she took out into the wintery weather. She couldn't find William fast enough. Finally, a ranch hand came into view. "Eddie, I need to find William."

The pained look on Carrie's face made the severity of the situation clear. She had taken such good care of him and the other ranch hands working for William, Eddie seemed to jump at the chance to help her out. "Yes ma'am. I'll fetch him. You go back into the warm house and I'll send him right home straightaway."

"Thank you, Eddie. And after you find Will, could you please ride into town and alert the doctor that I am soon to deliver this baby?"

With a quick nod, Eddie was off and running.

It felt like an eternity before both William and the doctor made it to Carrie. She knew from experience that the baby would be making its way out soon — doctor or no doctor. She preferred to have the doctor.

When he finally arrived, the doctor took one look at Carrie and said, "It looks as if you were about to have this baby without me."

Three pushes and out came a beautiful boy. William was poised and ready, towels in hand, for the hemorrhage to begin. But instead of the familiar gush of blood, the next push brought another perfect baby boy. "Twins!" exclaimed the surprised doctor.

There was still a lot of bleeding, but not as much as with the others. William said a quiet prayer of thanks.

"Six pounds each. You carried two six pound babies to term. That's unheard of for a woman of your petite frame. Look at them. They are perfect!" the doctor said incredulously.

Both William and Carrie were in a bit of shock. Although Carrie was abnormally large this time around, neither had expected twins.

The babies were carefully wrapped in blankets and handed to their parents. With Carrie holding one, William holding the other, it didn't take long for the shock to turn into adoration.

"They're beautiful," Carrie exclaimed, looking from one to the other.

William nodded in agreement. "How shall we tell them apart? They are identical."

"I will need to give them a thorough examination, when you are ready," the doctor interrupted.

Clearly reluctant to relinquish his hold on the twin he was lovingly caressing, William gently handed the baby over. He watched as the doctor counted fingers and toes, then began feeling around for the essential organs. Concern began to tug at his face.

"What's wrong, Doc?" asked William, feeling a surge of panic beginning to rise.

The doctor motioned for William to come closer. "Feel his spine. There is a gap near the bottom of it — a disconnect, if you will."

William felt the soft spot the doctor was pointing at. "What does that mean? Will he be all right?"

The doctor shook his head. "Not without surgery. I need to check the other child. Chances are he'll have the same problem. Identical twins tend to share the same ailments at birth.

Sure enough, the other baby suffered from the same malady. Carrie and William, who were both elated to have two perfect baby boys just moments ago, were now disheartened at the news. Surgery on a newborn was risky.

My advice would be for you to allow me to operate on one twin, and then, if it is successful, I will operate on the second.

"What will happen if we don't operate, Doctor?" Carrie asked.

"They will live for a few weeks, maybe even months, but with the disconnect, the babies cannot grow and unfortunately they will die."

Carrie and William spoke privately to each other, deciding that the doctor's recommendation was most likely the wisest course of action.

"Before we do anything, Will, we need to give them a name and a blessing," Carrie said, a lump forming in her throat.

William agreed. "I'll ask Thales Smith to help me with that."

The names they bestowed upon the two precious babies were Cedric Edward and Kenneth Franklin, in honor of their babies' grandfathers.

Kenneth was selected to be the first to receive surgery, and he was quickly whisked off to the hospital in Greybull.

Carrie remained at home, still recovering from giving birth to twins and also caring for her four other children while William paced the waiting room floor of the hospital. Little Kenneth was one day old — old enough for his parents to fall in love with, but too young and fragile for a complicated surgery.

After several hours had passed, the doctor came out of the operating room. His face looked grim. William's eyes filled with tears as the doctor explained that during the operation, one of little Kenneth's kidneys was damaged. The baby was still alive, but wouldn't live for long.

Kenneth lived for two weeks, and then was laid to rest on December 30th in the family cemetery in Cowley.

Cedric fared slightly better, lasting five months before joining his brother.

"Are they still ours, Will?" a tearful Carrie asked, standing at the gravesite of her two infant sons buried next to their grandfathers.

Holding his precious wife close, he comforted her with his words. "Not only are they still ours, love, we will have another opportunity to raise them after this life. We have been sealed as a family forever. That means any children born to us, whether they live or die, will be ours — for eternity."

Once again the knowledge of temple blessings gave Carrie and William the strength to carry on. They had never felt more grateful for the Gospel and its promise of an eternity with their family — their greatest treasure.

Greybull, Wyoming
Summer 1923

William walked into the house carrying letters from the post office he had just visited. "Here's one for you, Carrie." He handed her a letter postmarked from Connecticut.

"It looks like it's from an attorney in Hartford. Why do you suppose I would get a letter from an attorney in Hartford, Connecticut?" She opened the letter and began to read. Tears began to burn in her eyes as she read the news.

"What is it, Carrie?" William, his mail forgotten, was to her side in seconds.

"It's my Uncle Arthur. He has died."

William had never met Carrie's Uncle Arthur, but knew of his fondness for Carrie. He understood Carrie's grief. Arthur was one of the few relatives on her birth mother's side of the family with whom she had really become well acquainted.

"I'm so sorry, Carrie. Why did news of his death come from an attorney?"

Carrie kept reading. Then, she pulled another piece of paper out of the envelope.

"He left me some money in his will." Her eyes grew big. "Can this be real?"

There it was in black and white, a check for the amount of $2,500.

"I don't know what to say. I can't believe he is gone." Her eyes were still riveted to the check. I only wish I had been able to see him recently. It's been ten years, at least," she counted in her head, "since we left Vermont. You would have liked him, Will." She handed the check over to her husband.

"Are you all right, Carrie?"

"Yes, I'm just a bit sad as well as completely overwhelmed at Uncle Arthur's generosity. This kind of money can buy a lot."

"He really loved you, Carrie."

"We need to invest this money wisely."

"I agree, love. We'll put some serious thought and prayer into making a decision like that.

Once William knew his wife was all right, he turned his attention to his own mail.

"What came in the mail for you?" Carrie asked William, as she picked up a crying baby, her newest, John. The couple had now resided in Greybull for several years and also added two more children to the family: Marcella, nearly two, and John, two months old. William had gone from foreman at the first ranch to foreman at yet another. Greybull was growing, but one thing was missing, a Mormon meetinghouse. There were a few members of the church in Greybull, but not enough, yet, to warrant the building of a meetinghouse. Therefore, the few Latter-day Saint families in Cowley met for Sacrament Meeting at one of their homes. There was no Sunday School, Priesthood Meeting, Relief Society or Primary.

"It's another letter from the Westfalls in Twin Falls, Idaho. They are still attempting to coax us to move there."

"Our children are growing up without Primary and Sunday School. Idaho has so many more members of the church. Maybe we should take the Westfall's advice and relocate," said Carrie.

After further discussion on the matter, along with fasting and prayer, the couple decided to move their family to Twin Falls, Idaho in the fall of 1924.

Twin Falls was a small town with one thing, besides a meetinghouse, the Rappleyes had been missing — Mormons. Twin Falls had no shortage of members of the Church of Jesus Christ of

Latter-day Saints. Now their children attended and made friends with other children with the same beliefs, and the void felt in Carrie's and William's lives by not being able to attend their meetings regularly, was filled.

First, they rented; then later, thanks to the inheritance from Uncle Arthur, purchased a house on Van Buren Street, just on the outskirts of town. What they didn't know was that they had moved right into the path of some serious illnesses which had been plaguing the city.

William was out looking for land he could rent or buy for a farm. By now, he knew that farming was to be his chosen occupation. It's what he did best and he enjoyed it. When he came home later that afternoon, his heart dropped. There was that sign he had learned to dread while on his mission,

"QUARANTINED"

on *his* front door. And of course, there was a police officer stationed in front so there would be no going in or out of the house.

"I've got to get in, sir," William pleaded with the officer. "My wife needs help. She has five children in there."

"Five *sick* children — with measles, no less," said the officer. "That's why they're quarantined.

"I was just with them this morning; I've no doubt been exposed. Please allow me to go be with them now."

"I'm sorry sir, I've got my orders."

"Do you at least have something I can write on to let my wife know where I'll be staying?"

The officer pulled out a notepad and pencil and handed them to William.

William knew very few people in Twin Falls, as they had only lived there for a short time, but he was certain the person who talked him and Carrie into moving to the area, Jim Westfall, would be willing to put him up for a while. He scratched a short note on the small piece of paper the officer had given him, then handed it back. "Please see that my wife gets that," he said. Then he turned and made his way to the Westfall's home.

Jim and Sarah Westfall had become great friends of the Rappleyes, first in Greybull and now in Twin Falls. William hoped they could make room in their home for him to stay until the quarantine was over or until he talked the officer into letting him back into his home. The Westfalls had six children of their own; William knew it would be asking a lot for them to put him up, but he had nowhere else to turn. "I should be used to begging for a bed after my mission experiences," he said to himself. "Somehow it never feels good to ask for charity."

The Westfalls were only too happy to house William for the duration of the quarantine. James even loaned him some clothing, since he literally had nothing other than the clothes on his back. Still, every day, William walked over to his home on Van Buren Street to check on his wife and children.

When the measles began to ease up, somehow smallpox reared its ugly head in the Rappleye residence. Carrie was fortunate enough to stay healthy for the first month, but, tired and run down, could not beat the smallpox. Foster, at only nine years of age, did his best to cook for the family and take care of all the sick, including his mother.

Finally, enough was enough for William. "You don't understand, officer; I have been exposed to smallpox before and remained healthy, and even if I get sick, it's worth the risk in order to take care of my family. They've been in there for a month and I don't intend for them to go another day without my help."

The doctor and officer eventually relented and William became one of the quarantined.

It was two full months in quarantine, and only two days before Christmas, when the quarantine sign on the Rappleye household came down. Carrie and William rushed to town to buy some gifts for the children.

Life began to show some signs of normalcy after all the sicknesses had passed. Carrie was so happy to be able to mingle with the Saints at regular meetings and was given a calling to work in the Primary organization for the children at church.

"I've never been to, nor worked in Primary," she said to the Bishop who issued the calling. "I truly know nothing about it."

"I think you will be a quick learner, Sister Rappleye. And you will enjoy working with the children, as well as the other Primary workers."

Carrie accepted the call and found she was delighted to be teaching children the basic principles of the Gospel — something she herself had missed out on in her early years.

A woman from the Stake Primary presidency visited their ward shortly after Carrie had accepted the calling. She chose to observe Carrie in action, having heard that she was a convert and had no exposure to Primary in the past. Perhaps she could give Carrie some pointers.

Feeling a little nervous, Carrie decided to just pretend the visitor wasn't there. She taught her lesson and had the children color, then cut some figures out that went along with the message.

The sister visiting from the Stake was clearly impressed and reported in glowing terms to the Stake Primary President how well Sister Rappleye knew Primary. Carrie was immediately called to work on the Stake Primary Board. This was the beginning of a long list of callings that Carrie served within the Primary organization. She would later work in the Mutual Improvement Association, as well as the Relief Society. But wherever she served, she felt honored to be able to be part of the Lord's work.

As for William, missionary work seemed to flow in his veins. He was called to serve as the President of the Stake missionaries and Stake Superintendent of the Mutual Improvement Association. And later, the Apostle Melvin J. Ballard visited the Twin Falls area. William was then privileged to have Elder Ballard lay his hands on his head and ordain him a Seventy. He then was chosen to serve as the President of the Seventies Quorum.

While Elder Ballard was with William, he told him he would soon be called to serve a mission. Carrie didn't like the sound of that at all. She knew many missionaries in Vermont who left families, some as large as hers and William's, to preach the gospel. She hated the thought of William leaving her, even for a short time. Her respect for those elders she had known who heeded the call and left their families on the Lord's errand rose immensely.

Another baby was born to William and Carrie in Twin Falls. Donna Laura came into the world on August 18th, 1927. Donna was their little princess, adored by parents and siblings alike. Carrie had now given birth to eight children, six of them living. All of them happy.

This truly was a season of contentment for William and Carrie. Their six children were thriving, both in school and in church. William and Carrie were thriving as well, making friends wherever they went.

The farm where William ended up working was an itinerant farm. This meant William did the farming, but didn't own the land, thus some of the proceeds from what the farm produced went to the landowner. It wasn't very near the house they owned on Van Buren Street, so William and Carrie opted to rent out their home and move closer to the farm in Wendell, Idaho.

The meetinghouse for the Mormons was not a convenient distance from Wendell, but the Rappleyes were just happy to have a meetinghouse at all and they happily attended all of their meetings.

Early one Sunday morning, William kissed his wife goodbye and drove the distance to the church for early morning Priesthood Meeting. When he pulled up to the building, four-year-old John's head popped up from the back of the truck. "What in the world are you doing in my truck, Son?" William asked, taking in his little one's dirty arms and legs from sitting in the back of his dad's truck.

"I wanted to go to Priesthood Meeting with you, Papa."

A smile tugged at William's lips. "Well, John, you're not exactly dressed for Priesthood Meeting. And you got a bit dirty sitting in the back of the truck. But being that it's too late for me to take you home, I guess we'll sneak into the washroom and clean you up." He lifted his mischievous son out of the truck and whisked him into the meetinghouse washroom. After cleaning John up and explaining that he would have to be very reverent in Priesthood Meeting, he kissed him on the head and took his hand and quietly walked into the chapel. Ignoring all of the questioning glances, William acted like it was the most natural thing in the world to bring his tiny son to Priesthood Meeting, as he scooted onto the pew.

Priesthood Meeting wasn't the only thing John was left out of. When things were slow on the farm, William would take time out to help build a tabernacle, which was under construction in Twin Falls. And when school was not in session, he took Foster and Bill along to help, as well. This structure would serve as a gathering place for special services, such as Stake and Area conferences. Once finished, it would be a beautiful, brick building.

William came in from working on the farm for his noonday meal one summer day, with Foster and Bill in tow.

Carrie, noting the concerned look on William's face, asked if something was wrong.

"It's the tractor. It has broken down again," William answered, clearly exasperated. "Sometimes I think farming was easier the old fashioned way with a horse and plow." Turning to his sons, he said, "Since we will have to wait for Mr. Dixon to come fix the tractor, how about we drive to Twin Falls and see about helping with construction of the tabernacle?"

Foster and Bill were always eager to drive to Twin Falls, and working on the tabernacle was a welcome break from working out in the hot fields. They nodded their agreement.

"Me too, Papa?" a hopeful John spoke up.

William hated to disappoint his little son, but taking a five-year-old to a construction site would be dangerous. "I'm afraid not, John. But in a few more years, you will be old enough to join us on all of our outings."

He walked around the table to where John was sitting with his lower lip jutting out in a pout, picked John up and began tickling him. This put John into a fit of laughter.

"How about we walk to the ice cream parlor for a treat while your dad and brothers are away?" Carrie said to John and the girls. William knew his wife had a soft spot for John, and this was her way to smooth things over for him.

A chorus of cheers rose up from the table. Suddenly, Foster and Bill didn't look so happy about working on the tabernacle, but went anyway.

Over the course of the day, ominous, black rainclouds filled the sky, and by the time William and his sons were back on the road to Wendell, rain fell in torrents.

William's truck was navigating the muddy roads pretty well until they were just a few blocks from their home. The mud had gotten so deep by then that when they hit a dip, they were nearly swallowed up by the murky soil. Try as he might, William could only get the wheels on the truck to spin, causing it to burrow further into the earth.

Foster and Bill were both out pushing the truck, but they weren't strong enough to make it budge.

"Foster, run on over to that house over there," William pointed to the house nearest to where they were stuck, "and ask if there is anyone there who would be willing to help us out."

Foster did as he was told and returned to his father with not only one, but two helpers — Mr. Kassen and his teenage son.

William asked the younger Kassen to run the motor so he could add his own strength to the task of pushing the truck out of the mud.

It took several tries, but eventually the truck was dislodged and the Rappleyes, after thanking the Kassens, were on their way once more.

Mr. Kassen wasn't a member of the church, nor did he associate with the Mormons. However, his wife was an inactive member. When the Kassens returned home after helping William dislodge his truck, he had quite the tale to share with his wife. He began by telling her how impressed he was with William. "I just met a man who never swears," he told her. "His truck was so stuck and, we kept thinking we could get it out, but it would slide back into the muddy ruts the wheels had created. Mr. Rappleye never said a swear word the whole time. He didn't even holler. I even asked his sons, when Mr. Rappleye was in the truck, if their dad ever loses his temper," he continued, "and do you know what they said?"

His wife shrugged, inviting him to go on.

"They said that if their dad ever gets mad, he curls his tongue between his teeth so he won't lose his temper, but he never ever says a swear word." Mr. Kassen was chuckling out loud.

His son joined in the conversation. "They said their uncles call their pa *Tongue-biter-billy-goat* because of the way he bites his tongue." Everyone laughed at that.

Mr. Kassen's son continued, "The younger Rappleye kid, Bill, was tellin' me 'bout how he once got into his father's tools — had 'em spread all over the shed — when his pa walked in. Bill was scared that his father would be furious, as he was bitin' his tongue real hard-like. But then he just calmly sat down and helped Bill clean everything up. You woulda whooped me if I got into *your* tools like that, wouldn't ya, Pa?" he said, looking at Mr. Kassen.

Mr. Kassen looked chagrinned, but didn't deny it.

"I really liked 'em, Pa. I hope we can get to know them better."

It turned out that William was called to be Mr. and Mrs. Kassen's home teacher, which meant he, along with a companion, was assigned to visit the family regularly to make sure everyone was doing all right. Mr. Kassen was quite opposed to the Mormons and never let a home teacher come.

William and his companion began their home teaching route, which they did once a month. William, being new to the area, began to walk up the driveway of the Kassens' home. His companion stopped him and said, "We don't ever go there. Mr. Kassen has a habit of shutting the door in the Mormons' faces."

William answered, "If he does that, it will be his fault, but if we don't even try to go in, it will be ours."

When Mr. Kassen saw who was at the door, he invited the two home teachers in. Mr. Kassen had grown to respect William a great deal. They kept the conversation light and friendly — nothing too deep was discussed. William just wanted Mr. Kassen to know he was a friend.

After three visits to the Kassen's home, Mr. Kassen began asking questions about the Gospel. William was only too happy to answer them, and it wasn't long after that Mr. Kassen was baptized.

The two, William and Mr. Kassen, became very close friends. Mr. Kassen often even referred to William as his brother.

Wendell, Idaho
1930

It was late spring, 1930. Carrie was asleep in bed when the cool breeze coming in through the open window became a little too cold and she instinctively reached for William to cuddle up to. He wasn't there. Shaking herself awake, Carrie looked around the room; then, not finding him, began a tour of the house. She noticed that the door to the back porch was open. It was dark, but when Carrie drew close enough to see outside, she found William sitting on the top step of the back porch. She started to call out to him but before she spoke, the words died on her lips. What is he doing? she wondered. His head was buried in his hands as if he were carrying the weight of the world. She opened the screen door quietly and tiptoed out and sat beside him.

Startled, William's head came up, meeting Carrie's questioning eyes. "I'm sorry, love, did I wake you?" he asked in a gentle voice.

"You didn't wake me, but I was a bit alarmed when I couldn't find you inside. Why are you out here, Will?"

"I had a lot to think about and I didn't want to disturb you. It seemed like a good place to think. You should go back inside where it's warm."

Carrie kept a steady gaze on him, trying to discern what had really brought William outside at two o'clock in the morning. He was generally a deep sleeper. "I've got my robe on. I'm not cold. Can I sit with you for a while?"

William nodded and pulled Carrie closer to keep her warm.

"Do you remember the first time we met? I had been sick and was wearing a robe," Carrie reminisced. "I was so embarrassed."

William chuckled. "I'll never forget it. That was the day I fell in love with you, Carrie. We have been so blessed ... I have been so blessed. I felt like the luckiest man in the world when you agreed to become my wife."

Carrie's eyes misted up. "We have both been blessed. We have six beautiful, healthy children, and most of all, we have each other ... forever."

William held her closer and turned his head so she couldn't see his face, but his voice broke when he said, "Yes, forever."

Carrie could tell something was wrong, but her husband kept most of his problems to himself, and she didn't think he'd appreciate it if she pushed him. "I hope you know I'm here for you and will do anything you need to help, if I can."

William held her back and looked into her eyes. "Let's just treasure every moment we have together. And don't you ever forget how much you mean to me. Truly, Carrie, I will love you throughout eternity."

Feeling a little bit nervous about what William wasn't telling her, Carrie asked, "Does this have something to do with Elder Ballard's prediction that you will be called on a mission soon?"

"Perhaps, something like that. But for now, sweetheart, we should try to get some sleep. Four o'clock comes early." He kissed her and held her for a few more moments, then stood up and helped Carrie to her feet.

For the next few days, Carrie saw a marked difference in her husband. He was still busy with the farming, but when he was home, he was at her beck and call. And sometimes he just seemed thoughtful — almost distant. Then one morning he woke with a nasty cold.

Carrie, concerned about him working when she knew he didn't feel well, begged him to let his ranch hands handle the day's work.

"It's just a little cold, Carrie. I'll be all right. There's too much to do this time of year to take time off."

"You probably caught it from sitting on the back porch in the middle of the night last week," she teased.

William stocked up on handkerchiefs, picked up his dinner pail, then headed out to the fields.

When he returned that evening, William looked terrible. He was pale and his cold had moved down to his chest. He began a coughing fit that worried Carrie. "I'm going to get a doctor, Will. You sound horrible." She put her hand on his forehead. "And you're burning up."

After examining him, the doctor was certain William had pneumonia. "Perhaps even double pneumonia," he said, pulling his stethoscope away from William's chest. "I'll come back with some medication. In the meantime, swab him with damp cloths and keep him comfortable."

Carrie stayed right by William's side, sending fifteen-year-old Foster on any errands that needed to be run. The conversation they'd had on the back porch echoed in her mind. She could never forget how he looked when she first caught sight of him — head in his hands, looking so troubled.

William came in and out of consciousness. His chest became so tight, he couldn't speak.

Brother Richins, the president of the Wendell Stake, of which they were members, happened to be in the area and stopped by for a visit. He didn't know of William's illness and was surprised to find him so incapacitated. He administered to him, and, directly after the blessing, William could speak again. They visited for a while, and William invited him to stay for the night. Brother Richins said he had an appointment in Hagerman that afternoon, but would stop by the next day.

After Brother Richins left, William turned to Carrie and said, "That will be too late, I won't be here."

A shiver ran down Carrie's spine. "What do you mean by that, Will?"

William hesitated for a moment before he looked up at Carrie and began to speak. "You know the night I couldn't sleep and you found me outside?"

"Of course, that was just over a week ago."

"The reason I couldn't sleep, Carrie, was because I had a dream ... no, it was more like a heavenly communication. I was told that either I or Brother Mower, who you know is my Stake missionary companion, would soon be called on a mission to the other side of the veil."

Carrie stiffened. Her heart began pounding wildly.

"Carrie, I didn't want to tell you this because the next part will put you in a hard place. You see, you are the one who has to decide which one of us it will be. You know the Mowers, Carrie. Please think about this. It is your decision."

Tears were pouring down Carrie's cheeks as she pulled William's hand into hers. "No, Will, I can't let you go. Please ... please don't leave me." Her words turned into wracking sobs.

William closed his eyes, clearly not knowing how to comfort her. "I don't wish to leave you, Carrie. Truly, I don't. But please try to think of Sister Mower."

Carrie composed herself, and did as William asked.

Sister Mower was a good person, but much more needy than Carrie. Carrie reflected back through her life and all of the hardships she had been called on to bear to this point. It was then that she realized she was being prepared for this very circumstance. She knew what she had to do. Still, it took everything she possessed to admit it to Will.

Pulling her chair back up to William's bedside, she took his hand, once again, and softly said, "I understand now what you are trying to tell me. I do not think that Sister Mower will be okay if she loses her husband. I won't either. But somehow I will adapt ... I always have." The tears began again. "Just promise to stay close, Will. I need to know you are always there and that you'll always be mine."

Tears now spilling down the sides of his face, William rasped out, "I will ever be yours, Carrie, for all eternity. And I promise to stay near you. It isn't going to be easy for you, but no other woman I know of has the strength, courage or faith that you have. I will always love you, Carrie."

Carrie wanted to respond, but the words just wouldn't work their way around the lump in her throat. She wanted to tell William that he was a wonderful husband and father; that his example to, and love for, others was unmatched and that she knew of no better person than he. She wished him to know how grateful she was, and ever would be, that he brought her the Gospel of Jesus Christ; hence, blessing both herself and their family. Most of all, she wanted to thank Will for making her his wife and eternal companion. She loved him.

Not able to choke out the words, Carrie looked into her husband's eyes. Their hearts connected and she knew he knew. The words did not need to be spoken.

William weakly lifted Carrie's hand to his mouth and kissed it. "I need to speak to the children, Carrie. Will you send them in one at a time?"

"Of course," she said, as fresh tears began.

William didn't want to alarm the children, but there were things he needed to tell them. First and foremost, he needed them to know how much he loved them.

Foster, the eldest, entered the room first.

Motioning for Foster to take a seat, William began, "Foster, should I not recover from this illness, you will become the man of the house. That is an unfair burden to be placed on your shoulders, but you are a strong young man. I know you will rise to the challenge, Son."

"No ... you have to get better; we are a team," Foster said, as he realized what his father was telling him. "We do the farming together. I don't want to do it without you." The tears began to fall.

William felt his heart breaking at his son's distress. "Foster, there are some things we can't control, and this is one of them. However, we can try to be prepared. That's why it is so important that you listen to me carefully, so you'll know what to do, should the need arise."

Foster just nodded. A numb expression began on his face.

William then explained everything Foster would need to do to bring in the summer's harvest. He was grateful for the many days he had spent farming with his two oldest sons. They would need help, but knew, in general, what needed to be done. He expressed his love to Foster and then, realizing his strength was waning, asked him to send in Bill.

And so it went until William had spoken to each of his six children, even two-year-old Donna Laura.

By the time he was finished, William was exhausted. He fell, nearly instantly, into a deep sleep.

Carrie kept a vigilant watch over her husband, only dozing in a chair placed next to the bed.

The doctor arrived the next morning and declared that William was getting better. A flicker of hope seized upon Carrie as she thought perhaps the Lord had reconsidered and would spare her husband. "Can I feed him now, then?"

"Yes, soft foods. Otherwise it will be too painful for him to swallow," the doctor answered.

Carrie went straight to work making up some custard. She also sent Foster to town to buy some ice cream.

Some of the sisters from the Relief Society heard William was sick and stopped by to see how they could help. When the time came for them to leave, Sister Peterson, who served as the Relief Society President, paused. "I feel like I should stay a while longer. You three go on home without me." The other sisters left and Sister Peterson remained with Carrie.

No sooner had the sisters gone than William went into spasms. It took both Carrie and Sister Peterson to hold him down.

"Mother, I've got the ice ..." Foster's voice trailed off as he took in the scene before him.

"Foster, I need you to get the doctor back here."

Foster stood as if stunned for a moment, a horrified look stamped on his face. Then he dropped the ice cream and ran out the door.

The doctor and Foster were back in record time. William had stopped convulsing and appeared to be sleeping. The doctor felt for a pulse. He found one, but it was weak. Shaking his head, he said, "There's nothing I can do for him at this point. I felt certain this morning that he was improving. I'm so sorry, Mrs. Rappleye."

Carrie sat motionless ... numb. Was the doctor really giving up? Was the Lord really taking her sweet husband away?

William grasped Carrie's hand, his eyes fluttered open to meet her intense gaze, only to close one final time.

"He's gone," Carrie whispered. She laid her head on his chest and wept.

Wendell, Idaho
June 1930

It was only fitting to hold the funeral in the Twin Falls Tabernacle. William helped build it, Foster and Bill helped as well, and they all donated money to the cause. Many people attended, as William had become a very well-respected man in the community. He would be missed.

Carrie watched as loved ones filed into the recreation hall, which they chose by default for the service, since the building was still under construction. It felt right to have it here, Carrie thought. Her children were somber. Even two-year-old Donna Laura seemed to understand the gravity of the situation.

When Brother and Sister Mower walked in, tears gathered in Carrie's already bloodshot eyes. She couldn't help but wonder why such a decision as who should live or die would rest on her shoulders. Then the realization dawned on her. *It was always going to be Will. I just had to be okay with it. God wanted me to understand and give my consent.*

Warmth filled her heart and she felt William's arms around her, just as he had promised; he was with her.

There were several talks given describing William — a man of honesty and integrity, a hard worker, a missionary, a worthy Latter-day Saint and to all who knew him, a very good friend. But what Carrie loved the most about the service was the music. It took her back to Vermont when the missionaries had gathered around the piano while she played for them to sing hymns of praise. Then, there was William's voice — so beautiful and sincere. He could quiet a noisy crowd and bring them to tears with his tenor, solo voice. Strains of his favorite songs echoed in Carrie's heart. It warmed her.

When the Wendell Ward choir finished the last verse of *O, My Father,* Carrie thought her heart would burst. The warm grip around her tightened. William never left her side. How could she go on without him?

Carrie stumbled out of bed in a panic. It was five o'clock already and she hadn't waked Foster up to set the irrigation water. By the time she reached the kitchen, the back door flung open. There was Foster. Suddenly he looked so much older than his fifteen years. Carrie swallowed a lump in her throat, realizing that, without any direction from his mother, Foster had gotten up at four o'clock in the morning on his own and set the water.

"We need to wake Bill up," Foster said. "It's time to milk the cows."

Carrie just nodded and turned to go roust Bill. Her heart swelled just knowing what a sacrifice her boys would make to attempt to keep the farm going — at least through this year's harvest.

They put all they had into the work. Carrie, Foster, Bill and even six-year-old John labored over the crops. William had taught his boys well. The Elder's Quorum pitched in when the time came to put up the hay, which helped a lot. Farming was hard work, but they pulled together and brought in the harvest. It was one of the finest crops the Rappleyes had raised. In fact, it was one of the finest harvests in Idaho. A newspaper article was written featuring the generous quantity and size of the vegetables harvested by the Rappleyes.

Despite their efforts, however, the owner of the farm, a very mean-spirited and greedy man, was not satisfied and demanded that Carrie and her six children leave the farm along with all of the wheat and potatoes they had harvested. He even insisted that Carrie pay $40.00 to take her own cow with her. Carrie turned to one of William's friends, George Ward, to aid her in talking some sense into the greedy man, but the landowner still did not budge. She was left with no recourse.

Thankfully, she and William had had the wisdom, or perhaps the inspiration, to purchase a home a few years back — their little Van Buren Street house on the outskirts of Twin Falls. On November first, Carrie moved her brood back into that home. There was no farm, which Carrie would miss, and she would now need to find a job to put food on the table, but there was also no landowner to harass her family.

The job market was not a good one in 1930. In fact, there was probably not a worse time to be looking for a job — especially if you were a woman. If there was a job to be found, it went to a man. After all, the men were providing for their families during this time of economic depression.

Carrie was worn down and feeling discouraged. and when influenza again came to town, she caught an especially bad strain. With her weakened immune system from being over-worked, the flu didn't plan on making its stay a short one.

On Thanksgiving Day, young Marcella began complaining of pains in her side. Carrie, thinking it was the same flu virus that she was ailing from, had Marcella stay in bed and rest. The searing pain only intensified until it was too much for young Marcella to bear. Carrie began to fear it was something more and sent Foster out to fetch the doctor.

The doctor gave his diagnosis. "Your daughter has appendicitis, Mrs. Rappleye. She needs to be admitted to the hospital and have her appendix removed. Hopefully it hasn't already ruptured."

Carrie, feverish and weak from the flu, somehow got her sick daughter to the hospital for the surgery. She wished she could stay in the hospital the whole time with Marcella, but she had five children depending on her at home. She settled for going to the hospital twice a day to check on Marcella.

When she'd arrive home, weary and still very sick herself, Sister Peterson, the same friend who had helped Carrie during William's passing, would greet her with a hot water bottle and a blanket. "You must lie down and rest, Carrie. How are you going to beat this virus if you aren't taking care of yourself?"

Carrie was very grateful for a good friend.

After several days of visiting and worrying about her daughter in the hospital, taking care of the five children at home, all while suffering from influenza herself, Carrie felt as if she were fighting a losing battle. She lay in bed thinking about happier times as she drifted off to sleep.

The sun was warm on her face as she stood out in the hayfield. The smell of warm hay always made Carrie smile, as it reminded her of William. The sky was azure blue that day and only a few fluffy clouds floated lazily through the sky.

"Carrie. Carrie."

"William? Is that you?"

"Yes, love, it is me."

Gradually William came into view, his handsome features made even more becoming by the aura around him, and the light in his eyes.

Carrie ran into William's embrace. "You are here! I've needed you so badly," Carrie sobbed out.

"I know, Carrie." William's voice was just above a whisper. I am always nearby.

She could see grief in his eyes. Was that grief for her? But she was so happy that he was here. Why was he sad?

"Why do you look troubled, William?"

"I am troubled to see the pain that leaving you and our children has caused. Carrie, I never wanted to go. You are very ill and still caring for so many."

"I will recover, as will Marcella. I can do this, Will. You taught me that I can."

"That, I have no doubt, Carrie, but you don't have to. If you desire it, you may stay with me."

Carrie ached to go with William — longed to follow him wherever he would take her, but her heart and her head seemed to be at odds with each other. For a few moments Carrie said nothing, just let William's presence absorb into her spirit. Then, tears filled her eyes as she looked into William's penetrating gaze. "I cannot go with you, Will. The children have suffered enough. Should I leave them, they will be orphaned. I know it will be hard ... it has already been harder than I ever thought possible, but I cannot join you until they are grown."

William's expression was a cross between disappointment and pride ... pride in his eternal companion, who would always choose the correct path, even when it was the most difficult. He wiped her tears away and held her close one last time. "I am with you, Carrie. As ever, I am yours."

Sweat saturated her pillow when Carrie awoke. "William?" she called out. Nobody responded. Trying hard to clear away the delirium, Carrie took a drink of water from the glass sitting on her nightstand. "William was here. He was with me and invited me to go with him," she said aloud. Her heart began to twist, feeling the loss of her husband all over again. "But I must stay." She reached for a handkerchief and scrubbed at her eyes. Carrie then felt warmth surge through her, as if William was acknowledging her declaration. "He's always with me."

The doctor showed up first thing in the morning. After checking her temperature, he looked up and smiled. "I'm happy to tell you that your fever broke during the night and your temperature is down. Things are hopefully looking up. I don't mind saying that after I checked in on you yesterday, I was a mite concerned that your children would become orphans. Your fever showed no signs of dropping and it has been two weeks. Most people with this strain of the flu are well after one week, at the most."

"*Most* people haven't lost a husband, nor are they traveling back and forth to the hospital twice a day to sit with a sick child," Sister Peterson, who was standing in the doorway of Carrie's bedroom, chimed in. "I'm relieved to hear that Carrie is doing better."

The doctor nodded his agreement. "And if I remember correctly, your daughter will be coming home from the hospital soon."

Carrie sat up and scanned the room for her robe. "That's right! She'll be coming home today if the surgeon clears her. I must get to the hospital right away."

"Slow down, Carrie. You're finally beginning to show signs of improvement; how about you let me pick Marcella up?" Sister Peterson suggested.

"Oh, no, I need to be there for her. She's been so ill."

Both the doctor and Sister Peterson just looked at each other as if their mutual friend was daft.

"And you've been home just lying around, letting the housekeeper do all of your work?" Sister Peterson half teased and half scolded.

"Well, I still want to pick Marcella up," Carrie said stubbornly.

Twin Falls, Idaho
Autumn 1930

"I'm sorry, ma'am, we have no job openings. Times are hard, you know."

"But there is a sign on your front door stating that you need a clerk. I can do the work." Carrie stood erect, nerves jangling, yet trying to remain calm. This was her fourth attempt, the fourth store, the fourth manager she was pleading with for a job.

"That job is for a man. You must agree that men, who are the providers for their families, are the ones in most need at this time, would you not?"

"What about *women* who are trying to provide for their family? Do they not deserve the same consideration?"

"Well, I don't know what you did to have a need to provide for your family, but I'm certain it is none of my affair." The manager's smug look said it all. "You should be home taking care of your children; that is, if you even have any." His eyes dropped to Carrie's tiny waistline.

Carrie, incensed by the man's callousness, wasn't sure how to react. "I have six children and a dead husband. If I don't provide for them, they will starve." With that, she turned on her heel and stomped out of the building, leaving the manager looking chagrinned.

Carrie was beginning to feel desperate. The stock market had crashed just over a year before, putting the economy into a tailspin. Carrie was aware of the erosion of the economy, as the farm produce she and William had so carefully grown yielded a much smaller amount of money than Carrie expected. But with losing William, moving the family, then, dealing with sickness all within the last seven months, Carrie hadn't realized the full impact "Black Monday," as it was being referred to, had wreaked upon on the country. Now, however, it was becoming abundantly clear.

Foster quit school and took any odd jobs he could find to help out. Carrie always told him and her other children that any honest work was honorable work. It became a family motto.

The other kids were in school, for now, except for three-year-old Donna Laura; she was still too young. Carrie arranged for a neighbor to care for her. This was difficult for Carrie to do. She loved her children more than anything, and trusting someone else to care for them went against everything Carrie believed. But she had no choice. She absolutely had to find a job.

Finally, the local JC Penney department store manager agreed to hire Carrie as a salesperson. She was elated to have work.

Winters in Idaho can be brutally cold, especially early in the morning. Carrie pulled on her boots, warmest coat, gloves, and hat to set off for work. JC Penney was in downtown Twin Falls. The Rappleyes lived on the outskirts of town. They only had William's old truck, which Carrie couldn't drive, not only because she didn't know how, but she didn't have a driver's license. Nor did she want one. Therefore, Carrie was forced to walk to work each day. The air was bitter cold on the days it didn't snow, but on the days it did snow, conditions were worse. Carrie had to leave extra early to trudge the three and a half miles to work through snow and mud, taking care to keep her skirt out of the muck lest she look unpresentable when she arrived. But she didn't shrink from the challenge; rather, she stiffened her spine, smiled and faced it head on.

Carrie became well-known at Penneys. Everyone who knew her liked her. She, in fact, attracted customers who came in just to see her. At first, Carrie's manager was pleased to see the increase in his customer count, but as time went on, he must have realized that many people were just window shopping and visiting with Carrie. "Mrs. Rappleye, your job here is to get the customers to make a purchase, not just look around," a perturbed Mr. Goodwin told Carrie, during one of her breaks.

"But Mr. Goodwin, with the economy the way it is, most people cannot afford to buy anything. Their sole entertainment, at times, is window shopping."

"I'll not have my store be anyone's source of entertainment, Mrs. Rappleye," he snarled. "If the customers are not here to buy something, you must ask them to leave."

"I will do no such thing, Mr. Goodwin. At some point, our economy is going to improve, and if I turn customers away during the bad times, do you really think they will return later?"

"It's not your job to think, Mrs. Rappleye; it's your job to make sales, and all I see you making, thus far, is friends! Kick them out, or you will be fired. There is a line of men waiting to take your job who will be willing to do just that."

Carrie wasn't about to be badgered into kicking customers out of the store just because they weren't making a purchase. That would be the vast majority of the customers, after all. Working downtown, she had become acquainted with other proprietors in the area during her off hours. One of them was Henry Van Engelen. He and his wife, Addie, owned the Van Engelen's department store. During her noon-day break, Carrie made her way over to Van Engelens, more commonly known as simply "Vans." She sought out Mr. Van Engelen in his back office. There, she explained what Mr. Goodwin, at JC Penney, had charged her with and asked for his advice.

"Well, Mrs. Rappleye, the way I see it, being fired from JC Penney is the best thing you can have on your resume. I've seen the way you talk to the customers; they adore you. You can have a job here starting tomorrow if you would like."

Carrie was thrilled. She marched back to Penneys, found the manager and told him that she refused to kick any customers out of the store — paying, or not paying.

"Then I'll have to let you go, Mrs. Rappleye," Mr. Goodwin said, shuffling some papers on his desk, acting nonchalant.

"If that's how you want it, I will collect my belongings and leave right away, Mr. Goodwin."

Stammering from the surprise at Carrie's reaction, Mr. Goodwin looked up from his mess of papers. "Well, of course you are going to wait for me to replace you before you leave, aren't you?"

"Mr. Goodwin, as you told me before, there's a line of willing workers just waiting to do your bidding. I'm certain one of them can take my place. I begin my new job tomorrow. Therefore, you'd best start calling on them right away. I will finish out the day."

At that she returned to the customers on the floor with a big, welcoming smile, happy that she would never have to turn any of them away just for looking and not buying.

Carrie enjoyed working at Van Engelens very much. The customers there seemed to gravitate to her friendly personality, just as they had at Penneys. The difference was, Mr. Van Engelen seemed to understand that having Carrie work in his store was a great asset, and while the customers weren't always making purchases at the present time, they would in the future.

Still the three dollars per day that Carrie brought home to her family was barely sufficient.

⁓

"Mama, Mama!" John, who was just entering junior high, came bursting through the door.

"What is it, John?"

"I figured out how I can help pay the bills."

John was Carrie's little sweetheart. She knew he was always looking for ways to help ease her burden. At six years of age, he had been too young to work when his father passed away. Now, however, he made a discovery that would save his mother a little bit of money.

A smile split Carrie's face as she looked at her young son. "And how is that, Son? What are you going to do to help with the bills?"

"You have to trust me, Mama. Just stop paying the water bill, and I promise I will take care of it."

Carrie's smile grew into suspicion as she realized that John was serious. "John, you have to tell me more than to just stop paying the bill. We could have our water turned off if the bill doesn't get paid."

"Please, Mama, just give me a chance to make it work. If it doesn't, you can start paying the water bill again."

Wanting so much to trust John with this responsibility that he was taking very seriously, Carrie decided she would put her faith in him and see what would come of it. The next time the water bill arrived, Carrie carefully placed it aside and watched a small miracle unfold.

Every day, after school was out, John would run home, get the largest broom his family owned and begin sweeping the streets.

Carrie observed, thinking he surely wouldn't last long doing such a thing. She was wrong. She realized John was determined and kept the streets in his neighborhood spotless. When the water bill came, the balance was zero. Noted on the invoice were the words, "Street Sweeper." Carrie just stared at the words in amazement. John really was helping her with the bills.

An overwhelming feeling of gratitude filled Carrie's heart. Circumstances were far from ideal, but with all three of her boys doing their best to add to the family's income, and her girls taking care of the household chores, things could have been so much worse. She recalled a paragraph in her Patriarchal Blessing which said, "Your table shall be spread with the good things of the earth and they, your children, shall never want for bread, for it shall be given unto them and their water shall be sure."

She began to think back. Had her children ever gone without food? The answer was no. They went without many of the luxuries of life, but they always had enough food to eat. They even had enough to share. Carrie thought of the many hobos who came through her neighborhood, especially during the lowest years of the depression. Carrie never turned one away. In fact, she wasn't sure how they did it, but hobos marked the homes of those who would share a meal with them for other beggars to find, thus making the Rappleye's home quite popular among the homeless.

No, Carrie wasn't poor. She felt very richly blessed, indeed.

CHAPTER FORTY-ONE

Twin Falls, Idaho
Spring 1933

Carrie clutched the letter from Salt Lake City, Utah. News from her mother was always welcome. Emily's time spent working in Logan had been short-lived. She soon after relocated to Salt Lake City. The distance between Twin Falls and Salt Lake City was not terribly far; however, Carrie and Emily rarely found themselves flush with traveling money, so visits were few and far between. Communicating through the United States Postal Service would have to suffice. Carrie was ever grateful to her father for teaching Emily to read and write all those years ago. How would we communicate now had he never taken the time and effort to do so? Carrie often wondered. She loved her father all the more for it.

> *Dear Carrie, I have good news, Clara and Simpson are going to be sealed in the new Mesa, Arizona Temple. I am so happy for them. Other than their brief visit last year when they were moving to Arizona, I haven't seen them, nor held their sweet little ones. It's been ever so long. I sorely miss them. But now they will be sealed together forever.*

The letter went on with news about Emily's day-to-day routine. It gladdened Carrie's heart to know her stepmother did what she loved — cooking — and was able to support herself doing so. She knew it was quite a blow when Aaron died, but Emily had picked up the pieces and was doing all right.

"I must write a letter to Clara," Carrie said to fifteen-year-old Brenna, who was reading over Carrie's shoulder. This is such good news!"

Carrie and Clara had remained close. They weren't sisters by blood, but their bond was every bit as tight as if they were. Clara had always been a strong-willed girl, but that characteristic brought her to Carrie, and Carrie was grateful. Clara was one of the people Carrie could confide in and with whom she shared her grief and happiness. She only wished Clara lived nearby so they could celebrate the good news together.

Raymond Romprey, who had grown up as Carrie's brother, always held a tender place in Carrie's heart, as well. Since birth, he'd had health issues that made learning difficult, yet she loved him very much. Whenever Carrie thought of Raymond, she was reminded of those little arms that reached out to William when William was Elder Rappleye. Just as so many others' were, Raymond's spirit was drawn to William's. "My little friend," Carrie whispered, remembering what William always called Raymond.

As a man, Raymond's mental deficiencies became too much for Emily to handle on top of her own health issues, and he was eventually placed in a home for the mentally disabled.

Carrie didn't like to think about her mother living alone and, for several years she invited, even urged, Emily to move to Twin Falls. But Emily seemed content to stay put. Carrie was doubtful things would change. Deep down, she knew Emily was where she wanted to be.

Carrie also kept in contact with William's family. Mother Rappleye, as Carrie referred to Laura, William's mother, had always been there to lend her support, either by her visits or through the mail.

William had five brothers and two sisters. Some of them still lived in Wyoming, while others had moved to various locations in the West. Roy, three years William's junior, had always been dear to both William and Carrie. While William was serving in Vermont on his mission, Roy was earning a living and would often send money to support his brother. Later, Roy served in the Navy in World War I — the Great War. Unfortunately, Roy passed away only two years after marrying his sweetheart. Pneumonia had claimed his life just as it had William's. Despite the distance between them, Carrie was grateful for her extended family.

Carrie kept up her correspondence with her extended family members as well as her busy life permitted; however, her own little family in Twin Falls constituted her highest priority.

In December of 1937, Emily Drew succumbed to her ailments. Carrie knew the day would come, but when she received the news that her mother had passed away, she still felt unprepared. "I should be grateful she lived as long as she did," Carrie said to Foster and Bill, who came home to offer Carrie support. "She had health problems for many years."

She packed up the kids and bought seven bus tickets to Salt Lake City, Utah for her mother's funeral services. Emily's body would then be shipped to Wyoming, where she would be laid to rest next to Aaron.

Carrie continued working at Van Engelens for many years. She was a hard worker and was well respected at the store. Mr. Van Engelen often commented that he was wise when he'd hired Carrie, for just as he had predicted, she drew customers in through her friendly and generous nature.

At times Carrie thought back to her father's store. She recalled very little about that time in her early life, but she remembered enough to know her father loved his store and mourned the loss of it for a time. "Maybe I take after my father," Carrie said to herself, as she realized that she truly did enjoy working with people in the retail industry.

Carrie's family continued growing into maturity. And while not everything went smoothly, Carrie wouldn't complain, as her children were proving to be hardworking, caring adults, who served the Lord without complaint. They were all developing testimonies of the Savior and his teachings, each at his or her own pace.

The season of peace for Carrie was shattered, however, as Adolf Hitler's greedy fingers reached into the United States of America and plucked her three sons from their homes. By the year 1942, Foster, twenty-eight, Bill, twenty-six and married, and John, eighteen, were all involved in some capacity in the war.

Carrie wasn't alone in her fear for her sons' safety. Still walking to and from her work at the store, she observed gold stars appearing in her neighbors' windows, signifying the loss of a family member. With each new star, fresh fear gripped Carrie's heart. She prayed fervently that her sons would be spared. She even visited William's grave often to talk to him about it. Carrie knew that only his physical remains were at the cemetery where he was laid to rest, but she felt like William's spirit often found her there when she needed him.

She recalled a time when young Donna wandered from the home of a neighbor who was supposedly tending her. Donna would have fallen into a pit, but her father's voice warned her to turn back. There were many other similar instances which left no question in Carrie's mind that, even though William wasn't on the earth physically, he was still with his family in spirit.

"I know you are still ever with me, William ... with us, your family," Carrie whispered as she knelt by William's grave. "If you have any power to do so, please watch over our sons and preserve their lives as they are fighting for our freedom. They are good boys, like their father. But this war is ugly and taking good men away from their families daily."

Carrie felt the familiar warmth spread through her that she experienced when William comforted her. She had no doubt he was with her. This gave her an abundant amount of strength and comfort.

"Have faith, love, have faith," she was sure she heard William respond.

Carrie resolved to carry on with faith as her guide. Knowing that God and William were watching over her boys, there wasn't much left for her to do now besides pray continually for their safe return.

Foggia, Italy
January 1944

It was January 1st, 1944. The weather had been gloomy for days, but today it was even worse than usual. Foster's 28th mission, as a radio operator on a B-17 bomber, proved to be more exciting than the routine missions, thus far. They were to fly from Foggia, Italy, where they were based, and bomb the harbor at Athens, Greece. Since the German forces were on the run, they didn't expect fighter opposition to be very great.

They flew down the east coast of Italy along the Adriatic Sea. When they reached the peninsula, commonly referred to as the heel of Italy, Foster looked out the window on the right and saw the Gulf of Taranto. On the left he saw the Strait of Otranto. He was impressed that the peninsula was so narrow that by flying down the middle, one could see clear across it. Leaving it behind, they were soon over the Ionian Sea to Greece's Peloponnesus Peninsula.

The sky became heavily overcast with almost zero visibility as they flew into the dark clouds. Out of nowhere came a deafening crack. Was it an explosion? Foster couldn't tell. The plane heaved and jolted as men screamed "We've been hit!"

Foster lost his balance, grasping at anything to regain it, but only found air. The plane convulsed as pieces of it broke away.

"We're going down!" another man yelled.

Foster had to think fast. The ground was rising quickly. The plane had been struck with something. It couldn't be anti-aircraft guns; they were still 100 miles from their target. Foster looked out the window. Number three engine was on fire. He turned and looked at the waist gunner, who was one of the ten crewmen aboard. The waist gunner was looking directly back at him. Neither said a word. The pressure in the plane was so great that it prevented the men from moving; it felt as if they were stuck to the floor. Foster uttered a prayer. "Lord, I'm supposed to live through this war, remember?"

His answer came in the way of a feeling of comfort and a clear mind. Foster understood, at that point, that his chance to survive was not lost.

At last the pressure eased. They were able to move. Foster and the waist gunner both scrambled for the door. Foster hollered above the noise, "You go first, I'll be right behind you." The waist gunner was taking too long. He had the door open, but for some reason, he wouldn't jump; it was as if he were frozen with a death grip to the frame of the door. Realizing the tail of the plane had been blown off, Foster left the waist gunner to exit through the door, while he dove head first through the hole in the back of the plane.

He had no sensation of falling; he just felt a terrific wind on his face. He pulled his ripcord; the chute opened and he swung into a sitting position under his parachute. It was a short ride before he felt a jolt. He was on the ground, his chute draped over a scrub cedar. Although he'd safely jumped out of the careening airplane, there was a problem – he'd landed in enemy-occupied territory on one of the Grecian islands.

As he cleared his head, shaken by what he'd just experienced, Foster began to look around at the wreckage — the remains of the plane, which landed nearby. There in the doorway of the plane stood the waist gunner. He was not alive, but somehow held his same position in the doorway of the plane. Foster was grateful that he hadn't waited before he took action and jumped through the hole which was once the tail.

Of the ten men on the B-17, only three survived. It was a miracle that any remained alive. Foster had a sprained ankle and a broken rib, but that was nothing. He was alive. Limping through the wreckage, it became clear that there had been a mid-air collision with at least one other plane. Foster thought how ironic it was that many men lost their lives because of an accidental collision with their allies.

Foster and the other two survivors weren't out of danger, however, having landed in enemy territory. As he and his comrades carefully moved along, praying they wouldn't be spotted, they came upon some peasants. Thankfully, the peasants were friendly and helped the men pick their way through the scrubs to a monastery. This was definitely an answer to prayer, as the nuns at the monastery nursed the wounded soldiers.

Getting them back to their base proved to be a monumental task that would take months to accomplish.

Carrie arrived home from a long day of working at Van Engelens to find Donna Laura setting the table for supper.

"What's wrong, Mother? You look like you've been crying."

"It's just this war. I passed the Hendersens' house on my way home from Vans, and I noticed that one of their blue stars is now gold. My heart aches for them, Donna. I don't know what I will do if that ever happens to us." Carrie glanced at her own front room window, where three blue stars signified three men fighting in the war from their household.

Donna bobbed her head in clear agreement, but stopped what she was doing and swallowed hard.

"I don't think anybody comes away unscathed from this horrible conflict thrust upon us." Carrie looked up to see why Donna stood motionless. She observed her as tears filled her eyes. Then she remembered that Donna was a good friend with the Hendersens' daughter, Camille. The gold star meant that one of Camille's two brothers died fighting for freedom. She rounded the table to give her daughter a hug.

"I hope we never have to find out how the Hendersens must feel right now." Donna picked up another plate to set on the table.

"I suppose the Lord will take any or all of my sons if He chooses, but if there is any way they can be spared, I have God's and your father's assurance that they will be.

"Do you think that it's too soon to call on Camille? I would like to be there for her." Donna swiped at her tears.

Thinking back to when William died, Carrie remembered the great comfort Sister Peterson was to her. "I think it would be nice for you to call on her. Take her some bread, too. I made some fresh loaves yesterday. If the Hendersens aren't receiving visitors, they will tell you and at least you will have tried." She gave her daughter another squeeze, then took the plate out of her hands. "I'll finish setting. You go pay your friend a visit."

Donna smiled at her mother, picked up the loaf of bread and headed out the front door.

Carrie heard the screen door shut, then, open again. "Did you forget something, Donna?"

Donna stood in the doorway with a glazed look, her face pale as a sheet.

Carrie, observing her daughter, rushed to her side, "What is ..."

Before she could finish the sentence, an officer and a chaplain came up the walk behind Donna. Donna began shaking her head, then, the words started softly at first until they reached a fever pitch, "No, no, no, no!"

Carrie gently pulled her daughter from the doorway. When she finally dared look into the officer's eyes, she saw sadness reflected back. Her heart hurt for them nearly as much as it hurt for her, as she anticipated what they were about to tell her.

Finally, the officer spoke. "Mrs. Rappleye, we are here to inform you that your son, Foster, was on a plane which we believe was shot down over Greece. He is missing in action and presumed dead. I am very sorry."

Carrie looked straight into the officer's eyes and without missing a beat replied, "He's not dead. He may be missing, but he's not dead."

"But, Mrs. Rapp—"

"He's not dead. Please let me know when you find him, because he's not dead."

The officer clearly didn't want to give Carrie any false hope and continued, "Even if he survived the plane crash, chances are he was caught and killed by the enemy. I just don't want you to get your hopes up, Mrs. Rappleye."

"Without hope, I cannot have faith. Without faith, I cannot go on. My son is not dead."

The officer finally gave up and bid the Rappleyes goodnight.

Donna sat on the sofa quietly crying. "Mama, do you really believe he's not dead, or are you just saying that to make yourself and me feel better?"

Carrie turned a determined look to her daughter, "I know he's not dead. Your father is telling me he is not dead. I would stake my life on it."

Word spread quickly about the soldiers who were missing in action. People treated Carrie differently. Some expressed their condolences for her dead son; some acted like she was fragile and treated her as if she might break and said nothing, just looked at her sympathetically; some said she was in denial because she refused to turn one of her blue stars to gold; and others just said she'd lost her mind. Carrie didn't care; she knew what she knew and no one was going to change her mind.

Days, weeks and even months went by. Carrie never doubted. Finally, after three full months, the same officer who had delivered the bad news in the first place was back, this time without the chaplain. He wore a much different expression. Carrie was cautious when she opened the door.

"Mrs. Rappleye, I am happy to inform you that your son, Foster, has been located and has been shipped to safety. You should be getting a letter from your son with full details of his experience. Please let me express how happy I am that you were right about this."

Carrie hugged the officer, which she knew probably wasn't appropriate, but she was so happy to finally have her son found. "Thank you, Officer. I never doubted that he would be found, but it sure took long enough to happen."

"Evidently, your son and two other survivors from the plane crash have been hiding out in a monastery in Greece. They were waiting for a night with no moon before they could ship out, otherwise the enemy would have seen them. Your son is very lucky."

Carrie had too many questions she needed answered. She decided to let the officer take his leave so she could sit down and write a letter to her son — her very much alive son.

Twin Falls, Idaho
1945

The war ended and all of the Rappleye boys survived. That was a miracle in Carrie's eyes. She thanked her Heavenly Father and she thanked William for keeping his promise and watching over them.

They all looked older, wiser and maybe even a little harder; Carrie couldn't really put her finger on the word, but she knew the war had changed their lives forever.

Bill and John remained in Twin Falls, at least for the time being, and Foster went back to Brigham Young University, which he was attending before the war interrupted his studies.

In the meantime, Marcella had joined Brenna and Bill in the married ranks of the family, and Donna appeared to be headed in the same direction.

Carrie smiled down upon a recent family picture of her adult children. They had turned out well despite the hardships the family had suffered.

Carrie was in a rush to go to work. The dress she put on when she arose at the break of dawn had a small hole growing in the skirt. Carrie was not rich, by any stretch of the imagination, but she was always proper and looked pulled together every day. A hole, even a very small one, would not do. She didn't have time to mend it; therefore, she reached for a different dress. The time she spent changing her clothes would cost her.

She made it to work on time, but out of breath and panting. She also felt a stabbing pain in her side.

"Are you okay, Carrie?" asked one of her friends and coworkers, Evelyn.

"I'm fine. I think I just rushed too quickly to get to work. That's all," Carrie answered.

"After your daughter, Donna Laura, gets married in November, you should really consider moving into an apartment closer to the store."

"I've been thinking of doing just that." Carrie barely got the words out before she doubled over in pain. "Maybe there is something wrong with me, Evelyn."

Evelyn grabbed Carrie by the shoulders and steered her to a chair. "I've never heard you complain about anything before, Carrie, and by the look on your face, I can tell you're in pain. I'm driving you to the hospital."

By now Carrie sat with her head down, trying her hardest to be strong through some terrible chest pains. She thought of arguing, but the pain intensified. Carrie nodded her head and let Evelyn and Mr. Van Engelen, who had emerged from the back office, help her out to Evelyn's car.

"Don't worry about the store, Carrie." Mr. Van Engelen opened the car door and practically lifted Carrie onto the front seat. "I'll call in some replacements for the day. You just get better."

It was no secret that Mr. Van Engelen valued Carrie. He told many people that she was one of the best workers he had ever had. She worked hard, attracted customers and she was a good person. Carrie had grown to feel more like a daughter than a mere employee. She loved and respected him and his wife.

As the car sped out of the parking lot, everything going on around Carrie became a blur. She couldn't think past the pain. Her chest was constricting, making it hard to breathe.

Thankfully, the hospital wasn't very far away. Nothing was far away in the small town of Twin Falls, Idaho.

Evelyn helped Carrie in. The nurse at the front desk took one look at Carrie's pained face and sprang into action. Pressing a button, she spoke into a microphone, summoning a doctor to come immediately.

The next thing Carrie knew, she was in a wheelchair being rolled to an examination room.

Evelyn paced and watched the clock. She, like so many others of Carrie's friends, loved and admired Carrie. To her, Carrie was a pillar of strength. Evelyn heard the stories of how Carrie had moved from a comfortable home in Vermont to a rugged, untamed territory in Wyoming before making her way to Idaho. Then, when she was finally somewhere civilized, her husband — the man Carrie loved more than life itself — died, leaving her with six children to rear by herself. Evelyn, somewhat younger and having a family of her own, couldn't help but admire Carrie's strength and determination. "I could never do what you have done, my friend," she mused, desperately hoping Carrie would be all right.

She also reflected on the many men who were interested in Carrie since becoming a widow. She had often wondered why Carrie didn't give any of them a chance. Carrie mentioned on more than one occasion that she was nervous about anyone trying to fill William's shoes — both for her and her children. They were big shoes to fill, to be sure. But Evelyn thought about how lonely it would be without a husband. Carrie went on outings now and then with men who asked her, but Evelyn only knew one that Carrie showed much interest in. Carrie called him the candy man because he sold candy. He had proposed marriage to Carrie, but after much thought and consideration, she turned him down.

Startled, Evelyn looked up as approaching footsteps pulled her out of her thoughts. It was the doctor. She tried to read the expression on his face; was Carrie okay?

"Mrs. ..."

"Gibbons. Evelyn Gibbons. I'm Carrie's ... Mrs. Rappleye's friend."

"Mrs. Gibbons, does Mrs. Rappleye have any family members nearby? Her condition is quite serious, and I think her family should be made aware."

Evelyn's face paled, "Yes, I can phone them. Can you tell me what's wrong?"

"Mrs. Rappleye has had a heart attack. It will be touch and go for a while. Her family should be here in the event that she doesn't pull through."

Evelyn felt faint. "I will call her daughter immediately."

<hr />

"Carrie. Carrie."

It was dark, like a tunnel. Carrie could hear his voice ... William's voice. She moved quickly toward it. "William, are you here?"

"I'm here, love," said William.

Finally it brightened and William came into view. Carrie's heart leapt with joy at seeing her dear husband. Tears pooled in her eyes as she closed the gap between them.

William hadn't changed. He was still the most handsome man Carrie had ever seen.

"Carrie, the children are grown now. Would you like to join me?" William looked earnestly into Carrie's crystal blue eyes.

Carrie wanted nothing more than to hold on to William and never let him go. Of course she wanted to join him. Still, she took some time to think about his question.

Finally she spoke. "William, I want to join you. My heart has always been with you — you know it has. But there is still something I must do. As a convert to the church, none of my family has received the temple blessings that are necessary to bind us together. Now that the children are raised, I feel that I must do the necessary work for them — my ancestors. I cannot come with you yet. Who else will do the work if I am gone?"

William smiled at Carrie, and she felt his love and admiration. It was as if he knew what her answer would be, but he needed her to realize why her work on Earth was not yet complete. "I understand, love. We will be together forever when your work is complete."

Carrie just nodded, unable to speak. She knew she was making the correct decision, but letting go of William, yet again, would be so hard.

"I am ever with you," she heard him say.

"Doctor!" the nurse who had been attending to Carrie called out.

The doctor rushed to answer the call. "What is it?"

"She's stirring. I think she may be waking up."

The doctor began checking Carrie's vitals for signs of life. Sure enough, her heart, which had been erratic just moments before, was now beating normally again.

"William?" Carrie said in a weak voice.

"Mrs. Rappleye, are you with us?"

"Where's William?"

The doctor wasn't certain who William was, but reassured Carrie that William would be nearby.

The fog began to clear. Carrie realized that she was in a hospital bed and that William was no longer with her. She felt a surge of disappointment, but then remembered clearly what she had told William she still needed to do.

"We thought we were going to lose you, Mrs. Rappleye. You're very lucky to be alive. You suffered a heart attack," said the doctor. "Your heart sounds strong now. Hopefully you are out of the woods. You'll need to stay here for a few more days, however, and then, you'll need to take care to not stress your heart further, lest this happens again."

By now, the family members who lived in town, Bill, Marcella, John and Donna, were all crowding into the hospital room, anxiety and concern written on their faces.

The disappointment at watching William leave her was replaced by gratitude for her children. God had spared her life again to complete her mission on Earth. Not only that, he had allowed William to be the one to gently remind her of what that mission was. She knew she could have joined William, but she also felt that his visits were more for her to realize what it was that she still needed to do. She said a silent prayer of thanks.

Twin Falls, Idaho
1947 — 1967

After Carrie recovered from her heart attack, she rented out her house on Van Buren Street and moved into an apartment in town. This made her commute to work considerably shorter. In addition, she earned some extra cash from the renters occupying her home. She could now save up until she had the funds to begin her genealogy.

As the years rolled by, her two remaining single sons, Foster and John, both found their eternal companions and were sealed to them in the temple. This brought so much happiness to Carrie. Now, all of her children were not only sealed to her and William; they were beginning their own eternal families.

Grandchildren were arriving in droves. This also added to Carrie's joy. If there was anything better than being a mother, it was being a grandmother.

By the attention they lavished on her, it was clear Carrie's grandchildren loved her as much as she loved them. It wasn't uncommon for a granddaughter to come over to Carrie's apartment before school to get her hair done. Carrie enjoyed doing little things like this which formed a bond between the two. Others would pop in at Van's unexpectedly to visit their grandma.

As for the grandchildren living in other states, Carrie — or Grandma Rappleye, to them — would occasionally take the long bus ride to visit them wherever they may be living. Grandma had a way of making each grandchild feel as though he or she were her favorite.

Carrie loved them all and felt well-loved in return.

True to her words to William, once Carrie could take time away from work and had the funds to do so, she began traveling by bus back to where her roots began. She traveled to Vermont, Connecticut and anywhere else she needed to go to collect names and data in order to complete her ancestors' temple work. To save money on these adventures, Carrie stayed at the YWCA.

Completing this genealogy work was no easy task, especially in a time when everything was handwritten and records had to be carefully looked up on microfiche. Often, Carrie needed to travel to where her ancestors were buried in order to get the correct names and dates. This was all necessary for her to trace her family line back as far as she could in order to be able to have them baptized, endowed and sealed together as a family in the temple. It was never an easy undertaking. In fact, it was quite daunting. Nothing in Carrie's life had been easy. She considered it a necessary work that had to be done. Carrie was, for the most part, alone in her efforts, but she continually felt gratitude from her family beyond the veil. This kept her doggedly pressing forward.

It was late at night. Carrie, especially tired from a full day of research, was in Montpelier, Vermont where several of her ancestors were buried. She found their graves. Now came the tedious work of recording names and dates on her pedigree charts. Making an error could cause problems in getting their work completed, so Carrie was careful to take her time doing this particular task.

She sat on the small bed at the YWCA with a book on her lap and the charts atop the book. Pen in hand, she carefully recorded her findings of the day. Her eyes drooped, but she forced them open, determined to stay alert until she completed her writing. Tomorrow, she would need to catch a bus to Massachusetts, so there wasn't time to waste.

There were voices in the room next to hers. That was puzzling; she had a private room. Carrie pulled herself out of bed, put on her robe and crept through the door to see who was doing the talking. After all, it was late.

Entering the room, Carrie realized it was daylight. She looked in the direction of the voices and quietly approached. Carrie didn't want to interrupt the conversation, but there was something about it that intrigued her ... it was the predominant voice. "It's William," she whispered.

Carrie needed to see him. She knew William's voice, now she needed to see him. Why is he here? she wondered. It was then that Carrie observed her surroundings. She was no longer at the YWCA. Things had somehow changed. This room — the room where she heard people speaking — is beautiful. There is a feeling of peace here.

Keeping a safe distance, Carrie listened to the voices. There were four people, three men and a woman. One of them was definitely William, and Carrie had to see him. Mustering her courage, she boldly walked into view. The four seemed undisturbed as they continued their conversation. It was as if Carrie were not there; she was merely an observer.

She took a seat and began to listen. The conversation seemed to be very important as the couple earnestly listened to what William was saying.

Memories flooded Carrie's mind. She was transported in time back to the year 1912 in Burlington, Vermont where she sat at the feet of the missionaries, being taught truths that would change her life forever, a blessing she would always be thankful for.

Suddenly, Carrie was hit with the realization of what was happening. She no longer worried about being seen as she pulled her chair close enough to hear the entire conversation. William and his companion were teaching these people the gospel — just as he had taught her so many years before. She listened as their names were mentioned. They were familiar, very familiar. She made a mental note.

Their conversation concluded. Just as it had happened when *she* heard the missionary discussions, the men stood and shook hands with the couple. Then William said something different, something she had never heard a missionary say. "Now that you have learned and accepted the Gospel of Jesus Christ, your necessary ordinances will be completed on Earth."

This gave Carrie chills. These poor people, she thought, have to wait for someone to find their names, then do their temple work. That could take years.

Before exiting the room, William looked at Carrie. Their eyes locked, and for a moment she felt his words echoing in her heart. "I am ever with you, Carrie. You are doing a great work." Then, he was gone.

Carrie's head jerked awake. "I was dreaming," she said aloud. "But it was so real. Those names. There was something about the names of the couple."

"Thomas Spooner and Grace Carver. I've done work for someone with the surname of Spooner." Carrie carefully thumbed through her pedigree charts, scanning the handwritten names and dates. "There it is. Samuel Spooner, of whom I am a direct descendant. But who is Thomas?"

She looked further down to see who Samuel's children were. "Aha! There he is — Thomas Spooner and his wife, Grace Carver."

Carrie felt warmth grow in her heart and her eyes began to mist. She had just witnessed something that she would never forget. William was teaching Carrie's ancestors the Gospel of Jesus Christ. Gratitude overcame her. Gratitude for William; gratitude for the gospel; and gratitude that she was part of this important work. Last of all, gratitude that God had granted her the time and resources to complete it.

Carrie put her work aside, knelt down on her knees and thanked her Father in Heaven for giving her a glimpse of the work she was a part of, a work she and her husband were doing together.

⁓

Snow had begun falling the week before and showed no signs of letting up yet. Marcella and her two teenaged daughters, Terry and Sherry, sat around the kitchen table sipping hot cocoa.

"If it's snowing this early, we're in for a mighty cold winter," Terry mused.

Marcella and Sherry agreed.

"I love the snow." Marcella added a couple of marshmallows to her cocoa.

The telephone rang, interrupting their conversation. Both girls jumped up, racing to be the first to answer it. Marcella smiled in amusement.

Sherry won. "Yes, my mother is here. I'll get her right away." Sherry had a habit of winding the coiled phone cord around her arm while she talked. It was an extra-long, extended phone cord that could reach any point within twenty-five feet of the base. Sherry fumbled with the cord, trying to get it unwound and to her mother. "It's about Grandma," she said, her face creased in concern.

"Hello," answered Marcella.

There was a pause while the voice on the end spoke.

"Yes, I am her daughter." Marcella's voice wavered.

Another pause. Sherry and Terry exchanged worried looks.

"Oh dear, where is she now?

More silent anticipation.

"I'll be right over." Marcella placed the phone on the receiver. "Grandma fell. She's down the street at the neighbor's house ... our old house. She went there to collect the rent and slipped on the icy steps. We need to get over there right away."

The trio threw on their coats and galoshes and hurried out the door.

When they entered their neighbor's house, Marcella found her mother sitting on the sofa. She gasped at the sight of her. "Mother, your face!"

"I'm sure it looks worse than it is, Marcella. I could have made it to your house; Mrs. Hayes was concerned is all."

Marcella thanked Mrs. Hayes, took her mother by the arm and began walking her out of the door and down the slippery steps.

Carrie faltered and clutched Marcella's arm a little tighter.

"Sherry, grab her other arm," Marcella instructed.

Sherry did as she was told, and together they were able to get Carrie back to Marcella's home.

"I think you need to see a doctor, Mother." Marcella closely examined Carrie's bruised face. "Is it just your face, or do you think you broke some bones?"

Carrie hesitated long enough that Marcella knew something wasn't right.

"I'm fine, Marcella. I just need help getting home," Carrie finally answered.

"Mother, you didn't even answer my question. I'm not taking you home. I'm taking you to see the doctor."

Carrie relented and the two prepared to leave to see the doctor. "Terry, you stay here just in case your father gets home while we're out. You can tell him where we are. Sherry, could you give me a hand with Grandma?"

Sherry nodded her head. "Anything to help Grandma."

Twin Falls, Idaho
January 1968

"You took quite a spill, Mrs. Rappleye." The doctor stated the obvious. "The question, my dear, is how hard did you hit your head?"

Lying on the examination table, Carrie thought her head might stop spinning, but the room continued to rotate around her.

"Mother, can you answer the doctor's question?" Marcella urged.

"Oh, I don't know. I took two steps up on those icy, concrete stairs that lead up to the front door, then I lost my footing, and next thing I know I am lying face down on the cement. I don't think I broke anything. I'm sure I'll be fine."

"You don't look fine, Grandma," Sherry chimed in.

"When did you get here, Terry?" Carrie asked, just noticing her granddaughter.

Marcella and Sherry looked at each other. Confusion creased their faces.

"Mother, Sherry is here, not Terry. And she has been with us the entire time. I'm worried about you. I think you should stay with us for a while."

"I would have to agree with your daughter, Mrs. Rappleye. Your injuries might be more severe than just the bruising on your face."

Carrie grimaced. She felt sheer exasperation with her circumstances and everyone involved – no matter how well meaning. She was fiercely independent. After all, she had raised six children mostly on her own, and then, once they were raised, she'd lived alone for several years. The last thing she wanted now was to be a burden on anyone.

"Just until you're feeling better." Marcella patted her mother's hand.

"Very well, but you will see that I'm fine. I just need to lie down for a spell."

Marcella and her husband, Darrell, kept a close eye on Carrie for the next few days. It was clear that she wasn't herself. She kept getting the kids mixed up, which she had never done before. And every time she attempted standing, the dizziness would overtake her and she would need to sit down.

Bill and his wife, Maureen, and their children also commented on Carrie's altered behavior. "I'm worried about her," Bill told Marcella.

"I am, too. But I'm not willing to put her in a care center. I'd rather keep her here with us so I can take care of her."

"How about we keep her at your house during the week, then Maureen and I will take her on the weekends?"

"That sounds like a good idea. Now if we can just talk Mother into it," Marcella said.

It wasn't as hard as Marcella thought it would be. Carrie was stubborn, but she was smart enough to know that if she couldn't stand up without her world tilting, she probably wasn't fit to take care of herself, at least for a while. She agreed to the plan, but made it quite clear that she intended to be back on her feet shortly.

Marcella knew it would be difficult for her mother to let others wait on her. Circumstances had always been reversed; her mother took care of everyone else. She hated being on the receiving end of service.

Over the ensuing months, Carrie's condition deteriorated. Marcella thought it seemed likely that her mother had suffered from a series of strokes. Carrie was going downhill quickly. The out-of-towners — Foster, Donna, Brenna, John and their families — all made their way to Grandma's bedside at some point during that time.

The youngest of Carrie's and William's grandchildren, Jan, Judy and Jeanie — all born within months of each other to Donna, John and Foster — were just five and six years of age, but even they knew something was not right with their dear grandmother.

~

"What's this for?" Young Jan picked up the little bell sitting on a table next to Grandma's bed.

Her mother took the bell from Jan and placed it back on the nightstand. "That's so Grandma can call for help if she needs to."

Carrie opened her mouth as if to say something and then just closed it again.

"You can't talk, Grandma?" Jan appeared horrified.

Carrie just gave her young granddaughter a sad sort of look.

"No, sweetheart, Grandma can't talk just now. That's why there is a bell for her to ring when she needs someone's help," Donna gently explained.

In the adjoining rooms, family members talked in hushed tones about Carrie's condition. For the jovial family they were, no one was laughing now. It was obvious Carrie was slipping away.

~

Carrie couldn't speak, but she could hear. Sometimes the things she heard made sense and she wanted to respond, but couldn't. Other times the words spoken to her meant nothing. During these times Carrie's mind would take her to different memories — times in her life once long forgotten became vivid. The memories of William, her loving, hardworking husband, who departed this life too soon in order to do important tasks in the next; the birth of each of her children, brought into this life at the risk of sacrificing her own; the two sons she and William buried at such a tender age. Then there was the pain in her heart of leaving her children in order to work so she could put food on the table. And then feeling the joy of completing temple ordinances for her ancestors long since deceased and unable to do it for themselves. These were just a few.

"For a small moment have I forsaken thee; but with great mercies will I gather thee. In a little wrath I hid my face from thee for a moment; but

with everlasting kindness will I have mercy on thee, saith the Lord thy Redeemer ... For the mountains shall depart, and the hills be removed; but my kindness shall not depart from thee; neither shall the covenant of my peace be removed, saith the Lord that hath mercy on thee."

This scripture from Isaiah:54 in the Old Testament had often spoken peace to Carrie's soul. It filled her heart and mind once again. Carrie knew, without a doubt, that through all of her trials, God had never forgotten her. He had always helped her find her way, as He would now.

Snow gently fell, blanketing the Idaho landscape on January 22, 1968. The sun hadn't yet risen, yet Carrie lay awake. It was early, but Carrie felt an urgency to ring the bell on her nightstand. She needed to see her daughter.

At the tinkling sound that Carrie's bell made, a very sleepy looking Marcella appeared at her mother's door.

"Mother, do you need something?"

Carrie smiled peacefully and motioned Marcella to her bedside.

Marcella knelt next to her mother and took her frail hand.

Looking directly into Marcella's eyes, she seemed to communicate something.

It was as if Marcella knew what she was saying. She was telling her goodbye. Tears filled Marcella's eyes as she expressed to her mother one last time how much she loved her. Marcella felt her mother squeeze her hand in response.

Carrie's eyes closed and William was standing before her. He reached out for Carrie. "It is time, love. You have finished your work valiantly." He pulled Carrie into his embrace. "The rest of the journey we will take together."

The peaceful happiness Carrie felt at hearing his words brought comfort to her soul. She let him gather her into his arms, and all the pain and suffering she had been experiencing melted away. "I am ready, William. Please take me with you. *I am ever yours.*"

284

William's joy was unmistakable by the sparkle in his eyes. He finally had his eternal companion by his side now — forever. "Carrie, there are some other people who have been awaiting your arrival," he said reverently.

As William gently turned Carrie so she could see beyond him, her joy became overwhelming. Aaron first stepped into view, followed by Carrie Foster, then Emily. Even though Carrie had never met her birth mother, she instantly knew her and their souls rejoiced. Such a glorious reunion it was. Each of her mothers carried a bundle. Carrie wept as she recognized her twin boys, gone long ago, but never forgotten.

Aaron, Carrie Foster and Emily each greeted their daughter; the happiness overflowed, then they parted. What Carrie saw next, she could have never imagined ... hundreds of people had gathered, all anxious to greet her.

Carrie looked at William with a question in her eyes. "Who are they?"

William looked down at his lovely wife with pride glowing in his eyes. "These are all of the people for whom you did family history and temple work. It is because of you they now have the same chance you and I do to live with loved ones forever."

There were no words to describe the feelings Carrie experienced. She thought back to the two other times William had offered to take her with him beyond the veil. Oh, how she had wished to do just that, yet she knew that her work on Earth was not complete. And now she understood the magnitude of just how important that work was; not only for her and William's own children and grandchildren, but also for all of these souls who could not do the necessary work for themselves.

"Now," Carrie smiled up at William, "our family can be together for all eternity."

*W*illiam and Carrie have a posterity reaching nearly one thousand. And it is rapidly growing. Those of us who are lucky enough to be numbered among the Rappleye ranks can never fully appreciate nor show our gratitude for the many sacrifices made in our behalf. We are truly blessed.

All of William's and Carrie's children are now with them beyond the veil. Their son, John, joined them a few months ago. They are likely having a glorious reunion. Ninety-four-year-old Avonell Rappleye, Foster's wife, is the last remaining member of their generation. She and John were excellent resources for this story. Please see resource page.

Carrie's thoughts during the final stages of her life were not recorded, thus making it impossible to know; nor do we understand what transpired on the other side of the veil. But through inspiration and spiritual promptings, I can say that I believe the ending (which, in the grand design, isn't the end at all), is as accurate as we mere humans can imagine.

*J*eanie Davis, wife, mother of four daughters and avid reader, has dabbled in writing throughout her life. She's written several songs (lyrics and music) as well as poems — several of which have been published. She studied Communications at Brigham Young University and Interior Decorating at Mesa Community College.

Now that her daughters are grown, she has decided to fill her empty nest with her own words and has discovered a love for writing stories, fiction and non. While battling Multiple Sclerosis for half of her life, she is happy knowing she can contribute to her corner of the world in some small way — even on the bad days. She is grateful for all the support and encouragement she receives from her family and friends.

Jeanie and her husband, Rick, live in Gilbert, Arizona, where, if she isn't busy spoiling her grandchildren, you will find her nose in a good book, or at her computer writing one of her own.

*E*xtensive research resulted in the following sources being used:

- William Edwin Rappleye's Missionary Journal (1911-1913)
- Carrie Drew Rappleye's Life History
- Foster Drew Rappleye's Life History
- William Morris Rappleye's Life History
- William Rappleye's Patriarchal Blessing
- Carrie Rappleye's Patriarchal Blessing
- Correspondence (letters, postcards, etc.) between William Rappleye and Carrie Rappleye
- Personal Accounts from John Rappleye (son of William & Carrie)
- Personal Accounts from Avonell Rappleye (daughter-in-law of William & Carrie)
- Personal Accounts from several Rappleye grandchildren
- FamilySearch.com

*T*hank you to the many people who contributed resources, time and input to help create this book — especially my family. I have been nudged from beyond the veil and provided with information I never knew existed. I've enjoyed every conversation and visit I was blessed to have with several cousins I have not seen for many years. And, thanks to modern technology, our connections will continue.

Also, thanks to those who took time to read, critique and edit this book. Anna Arnett, Avonell Rappleye, Cindy Williams, Joyce Horstmann and Madelyn Williams. Thanks for your expert eyes. And thank you, David Arnett, for heading up the production.

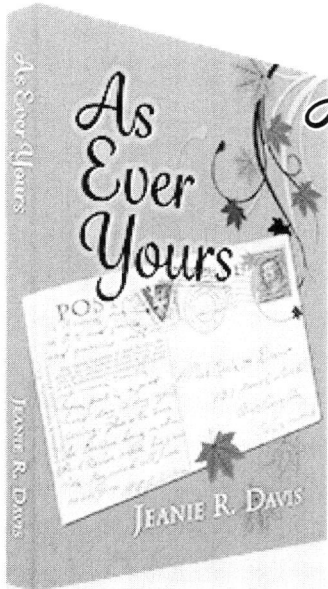

*A*s *Ever Yours* was produced, designed and formatted by DAVID ARNETT - dba PUNKINROLLER PUBLISHING SERVICES.

Colophon is a word derived from Latin and Greek meaning *summit* or *finishing touch* and has been used since early printing to give a few details of a publication. Here it is being used to proclaim the Adobe Creative Cloud software used to see this project to fruition...

    Adobe InDesign CC (2014)
    Adobe Photoshop CC (2014)
    Adobe Acrobat XI Pro

Fonts used inside and out include...

A770-Roman

    Adobe Caslon Pro
    ArialMT
    ccDooHickey
    ccJeffCampbell
    CharlemagneSTD
    Eduardian Script ITC
    GrafolitaScript-Medium
    MinionPro
    & *Squiggly*
    (   )

293